Little Rivers and waterway Tales

Little Rivers and Waterway Tales

A CAROLINIAN'S EASTERN STREAMS

Bland Simpson

Photography by ANN CARY SIMPSON

THE UNIVERSITY OF NORTH CAROLINA PRESS

Chapel Hill

This book was published with the assistance of the Blythe Family Fund of the University of North Carolina Press.

Designed by Richard Hendel
Set in Utopia and Johnston types
by Tseng Information Systems, Inc.
Manufactured in the United States of America

The paper in this book meets the guidelines for permanence
and durability of the Committee on Production Guidelines for
Book Longevity of the Council on Library Resources.

The University of North Carolina Press has been a member
of the Green Press Initiative since 2003.

Cover photograph by Ann Cary Simpson.

Library of Congress Cataloging-in-Publication Data
Simpson, Bland, author.
Little rivers and waterway tales : a Carolinian's eastern streams /
Bland Simpson ; photography by Ann Cary Simpson.
    pages cm
Includes index.
ISBN 978-1-4696-2493-8 (cloth : alk. paper) —
ISBN 978-1-4696-2494-5 (ebook)
1. Rivers—North Carolina—Description and travel. 2. Natural
history—North Carolina. 3. Rivers—North Carolina—Social
life and customs. I. Simpson, Ann Cary, illustrator. II. Title.
F262.A17S56 2015
910.916′930756—dc23   2015018712

For Jim Wann, Don Dixon,
and David Cecelski

With great appreciation to
Todd Miller, N.C. Coastal Federation;
Camilla Herlevich, N.C. Coastal Land Trust;
and Karen Willis Amspacher, Core Sound
Waterfowl Museum & Heritage Center

Down east the streams ran through flat land as dark as veins,

and the water looked too thick to stir.

— DORIS BETTS, *The River to Pickle Beach*

contents

Little Rivers and Waterway Tales

Little Rivers

Little rivers lace the terraced flats of the Carolina east, flowing slowly, most of them, past low bluffs and high, through swamp forests great and small to the big streams and sounds. They flow slowly, too, through the golden marshes of autumn, and on through them yet again in the bright green-up of spring, and through farmlands putting forth in summertime and fall, past snows of cotton and wealths of soybeans, flowering tobacco, and cucumber fields where deer graze thickly by the score by night, cornfields where the bear may sometimes appear for solitary sunset feasts. Above these narrow waters, ospreys throw their stick-built, roofless redoubts together, and bald eagles haunt the streamside jungles and hunt here and engage in amatory play with equal attention and relish.

All the eastern streams taken together form the patterns of our history, of our families, of the worlds the little rivers opened up for our forebears: all those turning basins, shipyards, sheds, and barns where so many boats of almost every imaginable design and description were crafted, lofted, laid up, launched, and the wharves they would head for and tie up to, and the spots where massive logs came out of the great, wide, wild forests and were rafted up and waterborne away to where mills would make wall studs, rafters and joists, and house siding and floorboards of them, and then send them on; the places where watermelons or May peas or corn, whatever grew and had to move and find its markets, came off of big fields and truck farms and small orchards alike, all out of the rich, loamy fecundity of eastern earth, down to landings many of whose names yet abide, and onto schooners and steamers bound for Carolina riverports and beyond.

Many of our little rivers are so close to the coast they have little fall and are just about as easy to float up as down, yet others, just a tad farther inland, know the full, real power of gradient, and of changeable nature, and of big rains of a night that may send torrents of new water down them like logs rushing down a flume, running a stream's level up six feet in twelve hours or not much more, fresh new water that cannot wait to get to the old, to the sounds, the salt, and the sea.

How well do I recall the bright cold January afternoon when Ann and I, just two weeks wed, put our jonboat into eastern waters for the first time together, onto the Pungo River just east of Belhaven beside the low bridge at Leechville, and were off and away upriver through the marshes under a proud blue winter sky, hundreds of buzzards kettling above us as if in some ancient dance, whether celebratory or penitential. And I well remember too sitting up into the night one other January, writing songs with Jim Wann, he with his mahogany Gibson blues guitar, at Hughes Motel and Marina, the old fisherman's spot right on the Shallotte River at Shallotte Point, within sight of inlet and sea. And late one June crossing with Hunter in the Whaler the broad Bay River shoal at its mouth at Maw Point, and, another time, sitting with Ann on that same river's long dock one steaming July morning up in Bayboro, after a whippoorwill in the road in broad daylight had stopped us in our tracks, and walking with her years later in the late-day mists of one gorgeous gray rainy May evening along the swamps of Camden's North River just to sing hosannas to the wild blue iris standing tall, roadside, flying their flags.

The lifelong object of our affection has been the water of our coast and coastal plain, and the people who love it, and love floating it, fishing it, hunting on it, studying its birds and plants, or for any other reason at all simply seeking out this world. My parents reared me in a home close to the Elizabeth City narrows, from which, going up, our big baylike Pasquotank River revealed its origins as a small swamp stream. Ann grew up in Sea Level, watching shrimp boats at night from her bedroom window, seeing their forest of lights and listening to their low-thrumming diesels as they worked the waters of Nelson's Bay just off Core Sound. We long ago lost count of how many explorations, launches, and revisits we have made in the water-loving Carolina lands that formed us both, and from *captivated* to *captured* by our ancestral lands has turned out to be a short, fortunate float indeed.

The little rivers have freely offered us far more than we can ever repay—offerings of joy and delight (songbirds back from the Tropics and the Equator flooding the swamps in spring, waterfowl honking and howling as they go about taking over shallows and fields in late fall), of honest tests of skill and strength, of new and unexpected awareness—welcoming us into their hidden, jungled narrows and windings, for whatever we would make of it all, the visual feast of all that green, the aural feast of all that birdsong,

Wild irises,
North River
swamp,
Camden
County,
May 2014

Indiantown Creek in the rain, headwaters of North River, flowing between Camden and Currituck Counties, May 2014

the smell of yellow jessamine as its cascades set lemon upon the air, the touch of cool dark water in summer and of its icy frigidity in winter, and, in estuary country, the good clear taste of salt.

We have sought to find many of those rills, prongs, branches, right where they have come to be called rivers, and, in seeking them out, to hear their voices, their tales, whether of glory or woe, of works well wrought or of loss unavoidable. We have set off together into the whole chain of eastern Carolina sound-country being, into as much as we could possibly get our arms around of this wide wild land, and onto a host of its loveliest and most intriguing little rivers and waterways, bringing back from them these glimpses, and these visions.

The Upper Pasquotank

Gaither's Lagoon

My first swamp was Gaither's Lagoon, just off the west side of the Pasquotank River in northeastern North Carolina, a mile or so downstream of Elizabeth City's striking, curving waterfront. The lagoon itself was a small, densely jungled cypress backwater, dappled in full noon sun, which flowed slowly under a small bridge we sometimes fished from and, once past it, right into the broad, baylike Pasquotank River.

The watery redoubt near the bridge has been all gussied up, now elegant lodgings called the Pond House, but the natural setting is still and all Gaither's Lagoon. As in most places way down east, even with all the cleared land and all the farming, wherever there is water, there is land right near it that is highly sympathetic to it: wet, water-loving land, with shallows sheeting up over it in wind and rain, advancing, retreating, tonguing up into woods, making swamps.

When Hurricane Hazel's powerhouse sidewinds and torrential rains swiped our corner of the world the day before my sixth birthday, October 15, 1954, water piled up and lay everywhere in Elizabeth City. Water filled the side ditches and ran the creeks out of their banks, and the long, thin, drooping branches of the willow trees caressed the flooding streets and yards. Less than a year later, when Hurricanes Connie, Diane, and Ione roared through the sound country in quick, late-summer succession, dropping nearly fifty inches of rain, water again stood everywhere and the Pasquotank spread out, and for a spell our homes seemed to be in the very river itself.

Though the hurricane rises were an acknowledged extra, water everywhere was what we always knew, and expected. Three of the four property lines around my family's West Williams Circle home were ditches, cut to help drain a huge cornfield out back, so that modest postwar houses could be built along the outer edge of a turn-of-the-twentieth-century horseracing track.

I do not recall, now, the name of the neighborhood boy who found the old forty-gallon washtub and brought it to the edge of a long lateral ditch into the Lagoon, before coming down the street and rousting me and engaging me in this enterprise, or how exactly we thought the tub, which the two of us eight-year-olds could barely squeeze into (we practiced how we would embark on dry land), could really be controlled, steered, or in any way made to come ahead on—we had neither paddles nor poles, only a small board or two. Still, on that bright Saturday morning we knew what we were about—we were going boating, heading down the lane of this ditch into the swamp, and we knew that once we reached Gaither's Lagoon, we could explore at will and leisure, licking honeysuckle when we got hungry, and the Pasquotank River itself could soon be ours. What we knew nothing of was *center of gravity*. We did not know what *top-heavy* was or meant, till we slid the tub into the dark swamp water and then, simultaneously, clambered and half-fell into it, and over it went and we were sloshed and soaked. No real shame in it—all of us who lived and played around the swamps and the river were used to getting shoes and socks and pants-legs wet. Yet a full-body, mucky immersion would require a hangdog explanation to an astonished mother, who would see in all this much more in the way of mess and danger than adventure and glory.

For a few minutes, though, before gravity did what it always does, my boyhood friend and I with our small craft at the ready were as bold as Captain Blood, as ready for the vinetangles and impenetrable thickets ahead of us as Ramar of the Jungle. We had a boat that would float us away from civilization, from nearby cornfields and flowerbeds; we had what we needed to get us into the heart of the swamp, and out of it, too, if we ever chose to leave.

First Sailing

Many sailors say the dark Pasquotank River at the Narrows was pretty much made for them. Protected waters, only a quarter mile wide just below the horseshoe bend, where it starts to open up . . . a light chop, if much of any, and yet still plenty of breeze blowing through.

How well I recall my first time before the mast, out under sail on the little river of my youth—one early autumn afternoon with the Weeks family, whose home was on Forbes Bay, right on the Pasquotank. We set out from there not even half an hour after school was out, Doctor—and Captain—Weeks figuring on two or three hours of it. When we were well out into Forbes Bay, Doctor Weeks cut the engine and he and his sons, my friends Harry and Frank, raised the mainsail and we were well under way, heading for the Camden County shoreline, the unranked cypress trees bordering that coast rusty and aglow, golden in the fall and all lit up by the western sun off to our left, slowly sinking over the watertown.

In a trice the sailboat dove, splashing across a wave and throwing spray back over the deck and the young crew, three of us boys, ten and under. Cold spray, and plenty of it—a shock to me, and I remember thinking, "Did he say *two hours*?" But then the excitement of being out in the altogether, this great, wide-open riverine world, of feeling as much *in* and *of* the river as *on* it, being under the vaulted blue, the power of all this took over, and taking spray off the bow every now and again became a badge of courage, and nothing to worry over.

Not for river boys.

We came about, we tacked back and forth from one side to the other, we laughed, we lost track of time, till the sun fell and plated the river toward town with burnished gold, and Doctor Weeks reckoned we had burned enough daylight and had best head in.

One evening many years later, I stood alone in the small ballroom on the upper floor of Chesson's Department Store, the April weekend when the building was being rededicated as Arts of the Albemarle. I was looking down Main Street, down the river where the good doctor had taken us sailing that day, remembering, and watching the thick spring fog at dusk obscuring all as it moved upriver toward town. In a waking dream, I believed I could see us in Doctor Weeks's craft, coursing the dark Pasquotank that faraway afternoon—and if I could see us, I could just as well make out many another boat, schooners up from the West Indies in colonial times, freight boats bound for the Dismal Swamp Canal, too, Confederate craft being chased by Union gunboats in 1862, steamers bound down and out for Nags Head.

Before the fog closed it all down and blanketed the harbor that late April twilight, I even dreamed I could see a fleet of mothboats out there, just racing away for all they were worth.

The *James Adams Floating Theatre* and the *Bonny Blue*

Imagine the almost alarmingly busy, noisy morning on the *James Adams Floating Theatre* in February 1914, after laying up all winter at the Water Street wharf and then playing a two-week, season-opening run in Elizabeth City, when the boatmen at last fired up the two 90-horsepower tugboats, *Elk* and *Trouper*, that would haul her forth for the spring and summer. She was a seven-hundred-seat theater built atop a flat-end lumber barge in Little Washington in 1913, 122 feet long, 34 feet abeam, yet drawing only 14 inches—perfect for the Carolina sound country's shallow waters.

From here she could storm the Albemarle, playing Hertford up the

Moth boats
racing on the
Pasquotank
River,
Elizabeth City,
September
2013

Perquimans River; Edenton on Edenton Bay; Colerain and Winton up the Chowan River's west bank and Murfreesboro up the Chowan's tributary, the Meherrin; Plymouth just inside the mouth of the Roanoke River; and Columbia on the Scuppernong. And then there was the Chesapeake Bay country to take on, though to get there from here, the *Floating Theatre* must be towed up the ever-narrowing Pasquotank River above her home port, around short reaches and tight bends. Turner's Cut, dug in the 1800s to give mariners a chance to avoid the tortuous "Moccasin Track," would sink her once, in November 1929, the main Dismal Swamp Canal itself a second time in 1937.

No wonder the popular novelist Edna Ferber came down South to meet the aquatic theatrical venue in Bath, North Carolina, and toured aboard her for four gypsy-souling days in April 1925. She found drama aplenty on the *Floating Theatre,* for the partying actors and actresses kept the tugboat crews awake half the night, and then, by day, the boatmen calling back and forth did not let the performers get much sleep.

In her short week on the *James Adams*, Ferber threw herself into the life of the troupe, helping out in the box office (thirty-five cents for the 8 P.M. show, fifteen cents additional for reserved seats, ten cents more for the hour-long vaudeville show—magic, ventriloquism, and such *after* the play) and taking notes on it all. She titled her backstage love story *Show Boat*, calling her craft the *Cotton Blossom*, and her 1926 hit novel inspired the 1927 hit musical by Kern and Hammerstein. Both works were set way out on the Mississippi River, yet whenever any voice anywhere lifts "Ol' Man River" and "Can't Help Loving Dat Man" in song, sound-country waters aplenty, among them those of the Pamlico River and the Pasquotank, too, flow through all those deeply bluesy, soulful lilts.

Going after that very era, just that stretch of time, the legendary boat designer-builder Merritt Walter crafted, launched, and ran *Bonny Blue*, his gorgeous, trimmed-out blue-and-white-just-as-nice-as-you-please sixty-seven-foot double-decker, plumb-stem passenger yacht. Between 2004 and 2007, he and his wife made weekend overnight trips from Deep Creek, Virginia, on the high side of the Dismal Swamp Canal's northern lock, down to Elizabeth City, where they and their passengers would lay up Saturday night, returning to the Virginia dockage on Sunday.

One bright, hot August day in 2005, Cary and I boarded her at Betsy Town's waterfront wharf and traveled upriver aboard *Bonny Blue*. I quickly got up on the top deck, as we passed the old Weatherly Candy Company (now Tidewater Liquidators) and as the slowly rising flat-arms of the bascule bridge angled up to let the yacht with its blue-striped stack pass beneath. Northward we plied, stirring ospreys and great blue herons into flight, the dark river waters, sheeted in miniature duckweed and pollen, opening to *Bonny Blue*'s bow and yielding up a curving swirl of dark and green-gold wake as we wound along.

Not long before we entered the south end of Turner's Cut, a straight shot to and from the wider upper Pasquotank and the southern end of the Dismal Swamp Canal, we rounded a bend and saw a bearded boatman in a rustic kayak with an outrigger to port coming at us, a man who might have floated out of two or three centuries past. Captain Walter slowed for him, then turned to me, saying:

"I reckon you pretty much know this river by heart."

"Cap'n," I said, "this is the first time in my life I've ever been on this stretch."

Merritt Walter, sandy-haired, deeply genial as most watermen are, smiled broadly at that. I knew the river quite well back at town, and on downriver toward the Albemarle Sound—but today the captain was really showing me something, and now he knew it. Now and again, green-headed dragonflies came aboard without asking, and as we got into the Cut we would see mallards and wood ducks.

"Say," he said after a while, "do you happen to know Brad Gunn?"

The man he asked me about had been a popular restaurateur in Chapel Hill back in the 1970s, but then got gone, as we say. Around the year 2000 or so I heard he had become the harbormaster at Manteo. Change of career; change of venue. Now that Captain Walter brought him up, I recalled an evening in Manteo just a couple years earlier, sitting at the copper-plated bar of 1587, looking out on Dough's Creek and Shallowbag Bay beyond, finishing up a steak and a pint of amber ale and asking the bartender at last if he knew where I might find Harbormaster Gunn. "Sure," said the barkeep. "He's sitting right beside you, and has been for the last twenty minutes."

"Yes, sir, Cap'n," I said in the here and now. "I do know Brad Gunn, saw him in Manteo not too long ago."

"Well, that's one of my boats," said Merritt Walter, "that he has. Or had."

"The *Downeast Rover*?"

"That's it—two-masted topsail schooner."

"He's still got it, far as I know," I said. "He told me to come visit anytime when I was in Manteo, but said that he couldn't hear worth a damn when he was below, told me not to stand there on the dock hollering but to rap on the hull a few times and he'd appear."

"Brad bought it, brought it up to Manteo from Wrightsville Beach," said Merritt Walter, grinning as he gazed up the Cut. "As pretty a boat as I ever made."

One should note that Captain Walter did not say *prettiest boat*—that would have been akin to choosing among children, never good posture or policy. What he had said about the *Downeast Rover* could quite easily have been laid to the craft we were on, plying northward. Many who saw her in person, or who even gazed upon her image, might well agree that as pretty a boat as ever floated the Pasquotank, and tied up at a Betsy Town wharf, bore this name:

Bonny Blue.

Miss Martha and the Appomattox

Miss Martha, a twenty-five-foot Albin Fisherman, came slowly dieseling out of a cut on the Pasquotank's west side just above town a ways, Captain Bill Welton at the helm, his eighty-two-year-old friend Enno Reckendorf and I standing on deck nearby. It was Enno, a long-since-naturalized

American citizen from Holland, who had named the boat—after one of its Belhaven former co-owners and also after the Chapel Hill doctor's wife (Martha Tippett) who had long ago cosponsored his immigration.

Fifty or sixty yards out, the fit, aged skipper gave me the wheel, and I spotted a huge blue heron lift up off a cypress limb on the far shore at just the moment I took it. This was a sea trial—I was looking for a small ca-bined craft and still am—and so I headed downriver for about a mile, then upriver, well past the cut, cruising lazily around the trees and tangles of Goat Island, before bringing her back in to Bill's covered dock.

Not even a year later, while I was checking into a local hotel, the coy, young, imaginative clerk would advise me that there was nothing whatso-ever to do in Elizabeth City.

"What about the river?" I would ask her. "And the waterfront bistros?"

"No," she replied, "none of that for us Bible students—there's nothing any fun for us to do except go out to Goat Island and *wrestle goats*."

And when I then remembered aloud for her my circumnavigation of Goat Island with Bill and Enno, my coming fairly close in on it in Bill's Albin, and our seeing no goats whatsoever, she replied: "Ah, that's just it—you were there in the *afternoon*. You have to go out at night, usually about midnight, if you want to see them. I grew up on a goat farm," she continued, "and I thought I *knew* goats. But I'd never seen anything com-pared to those huge, wild billy goats out on Goat Island!"

Summer days and lighthearted lore, all this, yet one recalls other cruisers who have not had it so easy, or lazy, here on the upper river.

Confederates fleeing General Burnside's all-out assault on eastern Carolina in the winter of 1862 steamed right by here, the CSN *Appomattox* trying to outrun the Federal force that had just taken Elizabeth City. She might have done it, too, had she been just a shade less beamy—she was two inches too wide for the Dismal Swamp Canal, so the Rebels, rather than have her fall into Federal hands, burned and sank her in the upper-most Pasquotank River.

And there she lay, till the Mud Puppies, the skillful, fearless divers long in the service of eastern North Carolina's underwater archaeology, came looking for her. Over ten years they went through a number of other finds in this same stretch of river before team leader Phillip Madre laid his hands on the propeller of a new, promising candidate in August 2007. They dove on it for two years, going down in pitch-dark water, "going at it blind" in Joseph Conrad's words, maritime spelunking about these burnt remains in the river depths, till they found and brought to the surface an artifact with a sailor's name inscribed, the name of a man who (the old rolls showed) had served on the *Appomattox* on her final mission.

What a wondrous matter, that a ship, wrought, launched, and floated hither and yon by very many hands, might then lie sunken, unattended, and unknown beneath several fathoms of lightless swamp and river water for nearly a century and a half, and then, found at long last, might be identified not by transom title or bow nameplate or proud burgee, but only by faint scratchings, one southern sailor's name etched on the handle of a mere silver spoon:

J Skerritt

The Moths

On a partly cloudy Saturday in September 2013, the stars of the mothboat world gathered in the backyard of a Pasquotank Riverside home and engaged each other in a collection of short sailboat races—the annual Classic Mothboat National Championship. Fulsome cumulus clouds rose over the river, cooled the sunny day, then darkened up as a piece of a front moved in, while locusts lustier than peacocks sang in the trees.

A captain named Joel Van Sant had designed and built the first mothboat—an eleven-foot sailboat with a slightly humped hull, though designs vary widely—in Elizabeth City back in 1929, as his sailboat *Siesta* was being rebuilt at a local yard. The diminutive moth proved to be an extraordinarily popular craft, and Beans Weatherly, a longtime Betsy Towner and sailor piloting a pontoon boat around the periphery of this day's races, remembered as many as eighty of them at the starting line in 1945 and '46.

Today there were thirteen.

As they jockeyed for position for the next race, Beans, a big man at absolute ease behind the wheel, reminisced: "In the old days, Elizabeth City had mothboats named for all seven of the Seven Dwarfs. I sailed *Dopey*—that boat loved choppy water, but on flat water, I couldn't beat *anybody*!" He spoke very warmly of New Jersey's Peggy Kammerman, a champion who had died at eighty-seven only three weeks earlier and who had, at the age of eleven, won the Girls World Moth Championship and then gone on to win eight World Championships. "She was from Atlantic City," Beans said. "Had a boat named the *Southern Cross*— used to sail here. Won every women's championship there ever was. She was *really* good!"

Recovering a swamped moth, Pasquotank River, September 2013

The air horn sounded out over the river, a quarter mile wide here just below the U.S. 158 bridge and the Water Street wharf downtown, and the thirteen little boats bounded forward. Number 48, the blue-hulled *Try-Umph*, which skipper Joe Bousquet built in Norfolk in 1997, had won the second race and now took the lead in the third.

As the small craft bobbed, tacked, and wove their ways along the course, Beans steered the pontoon boat toward where they would be after another turn or two. Number 118, he said, was built in Denmark, adding that there were sailors here today from all over, including Annapolis, Philadelphia, Charleston, and Bowie, Maryland. "Number 55, that's an old boat, pre-1952—he's a first-class skipper—Randall Swann, a dynamic racer, I'll tell you that!"

"How about you, Beans?" I said.

"Well, I don't race anymore," he laughed. "But I do help out with sailing classes here for the eight- to fourteen-year-olds—they don't even know water's wet!"

Classic moth boat champion Joe Bousquet, September 2013

Some say these little craft got the name because they skipped and skittered over the water like moths. Some say that all it took to sail them in light air was the puff of a moth's wings. What makes a moth a moth? Dimensions! Eleven feet length overall, maximum beam sixty inches, minimum hull weight of seventy-five pounds, sail area of seventy-two square feet. The Classic Moth Boat Association cared not whether the hull was skiff or scow, dinghy or pram, and the Elizabeth City race leader Erky Gregory put it most succinctly:

"The craft has to fit into an eleven-by-five-foot box!"

Erky, a compact older man who had been involved in starting mothboat racing back up in the 1980s (American interest had fallen off, he said, after the Australians "took over" in the 1950s, adding hydrofoils and "changing the game"), owned a Dorr Willey design. Willey had once run a boatyard by the Pasquotank River bridge and built classic Van Sant–style moth-boats—mahogany bow, rounded foredeck—and one of them now sat on display in the waterfront Museum of the Albemarle.

"Dorr Willey was quite a builder," Beans Weatherly said.

As Erky and I stood on the riverside grass and talked, a man walked by, said hello, and ambled on out to the far end of the viewing dock. His

Upper Pasquotank, above Shipyard Landing, October 2013

T-shirt read: 1996 Albemarle Challenge Cup Regatta. A young mother with three children strolled into the yard to give her family a look. Erky was clearly pleased with the way the day's races were going, and with the way the mothboat was going as well. One found it impossible to watch the little racing fleet, now close in to the near shore, now over the river by Machelhe Island, and not be a partisan of the craft, so thoroughly enchanting was the scene.

"There used to be lots of challenges, people raising the challenge flag," Erky said, smiling. "I said we could have challenges, but the fee for one was going to be $250.

"Since then, we haven't had a one!"

Upriver Birthday

When I asked around in late September, local people told me no, they knew of no one who rented boats in Elizabeth City. Had we not run into this before, back when John Foley and I tried to rent a canoe or skiff with

Duckweed,
Upper
Pasquotank

which to go back into the Great Dismal Swamp in the fall of 1972? Had nothing changed in forty years? At last I found a helping hand precisely where first my father and I used to find ourselves a skiff, the Causeway Marina. John Brothers there made me a real nice deal for the day on a big jonboat, a Polarkraft with a 75-horsepower E-tec engine, and Ann and I climbed aboard on a gray Saturday afternoon, Columbus Day, her birthday, and headed upriver.

A crane with a huge bucket was digging away on the east side of the Narrows, for new bridgeworks right next to the old span. Gone were the oyster-shucking sheds and the great sawmills of yesteryear, the wharves where steamboats and schooners filled to the rails with watermelons, or May peas, once called; gone, too, the old 1920s manufactory on Machelhe Island where seaplanes once got knocked together. We plied slowly on, made the bends and the reach past the hospital, then past Sawyer's Plantation, where two centuries ago the planter Enoch Sawyer had the young slave boatman Moses Grandy run his ferry flat back and forth across the river, and where the politician George Wood had lived in my youth, a pecan grove now full of homes. And through the railroad bridge near the canal that led back up to Lamb's Marina, mists and light rain greeting us as we moved steadily upriver.

We came around a bend and into the long, broad reach of Shipyard Landing, a lovely, lakelike, stately stretch of the Pasquotank, light green duckweed coating the surface of the old stream and making it hard to read as I searched for logs and flotsam to steer clear of. This had been a roomy place to put a schooner, or a skiff, over and into service, back in that old maritime day. Around the point ahead came a runabout with a platform, a couple of hunters now bound downriver. We waved and passed them, turned west at the point, and ran shorter reaches and bends for several more miles up the way—the Pasquotank ran narrowly through an unbroken swamp forest, without housing or clearing (excepting only one small cottage and dock) the whole rest of the way up to Turner's Cut.

By the time we reached the divergence of the upper Pasquotank's Moccasin Track (off to the left, or southwest) and Turner's Cut (the four-mile canal leading straight on up to the South Mills locks), the rain had picked up quite a bit. I guided the jonboat just a little ways up into the old river and we studied, and turned around near, a pair of wood duck boxes standing aslant in the shallows. This remote, upper river territory had decades ago been the haunt of the infamous lifelong moonshiner Alvin Sawyer, who kept getting busted and then coming out of stir swearing he would go straight this time, but somehow never could. Old habits die hard: just a few years ago, a sixty-one-year-old South Mills man, noted for having purchased twenty-one thousand pounds of sugar over a two-year period, was caught operating a still on the long island right before us, formed by the Moccasin Track on the west and Turner's Cut on the east. For his illicity, he would give up a small coupe, a Ford pickup, two boats, and two and a half years of his life in a federal pen.

No one except Ann and me was out here in the October rain right now, making white liquor or doing anything else, either. A few moments later, and only a quarter mile or so back downstream, we came out of the real rain, then poked along no more hurriedly than parishioners after church, looking at red autumn leaves and downed trees and woodpecker-dug trunks, both of us deep into it all.

Later, below the Shipyard reach, I took Goat Island slowly on its western side, relishing that tale about the furtive doings out here, desperate diversions of twenty-year-olds disallowed from drinking and dancing in the bistros, that the hotel clerk had spun for David Cecelski and me months earlier. Bible-college students rassling outsized billy goats at midnight, indeed.

The rain caught back up with us as we drifted at a barge's pace along my old town's waterfront, waving at a black woman fishing at the riverside park and she at us, right where the *Bonny Blue* used to dock, then on over to an empty boathouse near the Charles Creek bridge. Ann and I wandered fondly along the western shore, remembering the mothboat regatta we had beheld on these very waters only three Saturdays earlier.

If anyone were ever wanting for the loveliness of a little river defined, here it was: a dark stream drifting down out of a great swamp, an antique port town set like a dream at the river's last narrows, an estuarine bay aborning right there where we floated, one man, one woman, one boat full of romance and the knowingness of a wondrous place from over a lifetime, and this vivid warm gray autumn afternoon just as the cypress eternal were once again beginning to turn gold.

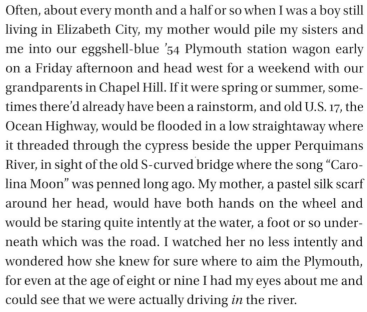

2

Cashie River Days

Often, about every month and a half or so when I was a boy still living in Elizabeth City, my mother would pile my sisters and me into our eggshell-blue '54 Plymouth station wagon early on a Friday afternoon and head west for a weekend with our grandparents in Chapel Hill. If it were spring or summer, sometimes there'd already have been a rainstorm, and old U.S. 17, the Ocean Highway, would be flooded in a low straightaway where it threaded through the cypress beside the upper Perquimans River, in sight of the old S-curved bridge where the song "Carolina Moon" was penned long ago. My mother, a pastel silk scarf around her head, would have both hands on the wheel and would be staring quite intently at the water, a foot or so underneath which was the road. I watched her no less intently and wondered how she knew for sure where to aim the Plymouth, for even at the age of eight or nine I had my eyes about me and could see that we were actually driving *in* the river.

Yet somehow we never plunged fully *into* it, always making our watery way to the bridge and then beyond. Soon we wandered on through Edenton, and I recall always gaping at the aged churches and wrought iron everywhere, impressed by the oldness of the place (this was long before I ever heard the word "antiquity"). And then a few minutes later we were away, over the big water where the broad Chowan River feeds the Albemarle Sound. The little river cottages on the far side coming into view and then focus as we approached them always pleased and thrilled me.

In another twenty minutes or so we would slow to cross the small, humble concrete WPA bridge over the dark Cashie River—a stand of cypress and lily-pad lagoon upstream of the bridge, a boathouse and broadening river below—and turn left. There at that corner, where now sits a convenience store, lay one of the wonders of my youth: a big log yard, hardwoods mainly, with the sawlogs all willy-nilly and akimbo as if they had been dropped from on high and lay all splayed out from one another just as they hit when they fell. This log yard, hard by the gorgeous black Cashie, featured a water-spraying system with perforated pipes all about, putting a fine mist into the air and keeping the logs always wet—nothing here was going to go up in smoke before it ever hit the saw blades! The logs out in the open and the adjacent tin-roofed mill took up about an acre and a half, maybe two, an eyeful to a boy: there was something so artful about that mess of logs forever bathed in their own rain. The only times I ever saw the rain stop was when a freeze stilled the spray and left the muddle of logs glazed with white icing.

In January 1989, Ann and I were out all over northeastern North Carolina on our honeymoon, jonboating hither and yon on cold sunny afternoons. We watched buzzards spiraling on up into the wild blue yonder above the upper Pungo River marshes, followed nutria on a mat of reeds floating in the upper Alligator north of Kilkenny Landing, and spooked huge great blue herons on a gunmetal-gray morning up Spanish-mossy Pembroke Creek on Edenton's west side. Not the way of it for all souls, perhaps, yet we thought it very good sport indeed, and we were very sporting about it, right down to the tying off of the metal boat atop the Subaru station wagon, usually at dusk, with yellow plastic rope that stiffened in the deep cold as we half-hitched our way to glory.

Our last outing of that trip was on the Cashie River, well down the lazy river from the Windsor bridge, and, though the afternoon was getting on, we still wanted to chance it and take a look at one more waterway before heading west to our upstate home. Down a sandy lane to the muddy, un-improved old landing we drove, and at its end I had just enough room to turn the car around. There was no ramp, just the river's shallows to put the boat in, and clearly no one, outside of a few duck hunters perhaps, had put in here for months. In a few minutes we were rigged and away upstream, where the river would narrow some and we would come up on oxbows and cutoffs, wiggles and waggles with great gums and cypress and oaks overarching. Ann wore a white-and-gray knitted headdress we had found for her in Iceland, and I had on my father's old tan hunting hat. We were warm enough, and the winding stream beneath the cold slate-gray sky was all ours and ours alone.

The resurrection fern, an air plant everywhere above us, just lay up there on the bigger branches getting whatever it wanted from breeze and bark, able to turn brown and play dead but, with the slightest moisture, able to green right up again. Everywhere this January day, on the cypress, the oaks and gum trees, the small feathery fronds were most of the green in sight, beyond the occasional holly and the jonboat's olive drab. There was something almost infatuating about a plant that vivid and colorful growing about and above us in the dimming winter woods, something that said *Watch me* and *Follow me* and *Spring will come soon*, the same promise one sees in a farm field after fall harvest when its winter cover, its wheat or rye, is coming up and asserting itself as all around the year is dying. In the here and now of the wintry Cashie, this fern seemed for us not only an omen of springs yet to come but almost a promise, too, of a long and happy life. So ubiquitous was the resurrection fern on the Cashie that one might've kept following colony after colony of it up and down these waters through the swamp woods as if it were all leading to revelation.

Yet ferns, however sensitive, are not sentient. A fellow in a jonboat one January long ago might be faulted, and justly so, for seeing such a promise in all that green simply because he wanted, or needed, it there. Such a fellow might just be forgiven for it, too.

Next time Ann and I were on this river, we were more miles downstream of Windsor, in the very early spring of 1993, with our nine-month-old daughter, Cary. After a shrimp and oyster feast (Cary partook, with vigor) at the glorious Sunny Side Oyster Bar in Williamston the night before, we had driven down to the tiny village of Sans Souci and met David Early, the Cashie River ferryman, and spent a few amiable hours with him and the few locals who wandered by to cross the river at this bend, and another man who just came down to keep Early company while he repaired a small wooden boat, its shellac shining in the morning sun. The craft Early ran, dawn to dusk, was one of only three small, cable river ferries still in operation in North Carolina—the Elwell Ferry crosses the Cape Fear River in Bladen County, and Parker's Ferry the Meherrin River in Hertford County. The Sans Souci quay down to this ferry was pretty fair and improved on the Cashie's west side, but on the east side it was just a swamp lane, flooded that particular day. We watched an osprey fish a pound net not far away, as blue herons scrawked and moved in and out of the mossy cypress, and we talked in the most relaxed fashion of bears and bass fishing and which side of the river Sans Souci was really on.

Some years later I took a turn much farther down the river, on the very lowest reach of the Cashie. In June 2002, Jake Mills and I came down Conaby Creek near Plymouth to the Roanoke River in his fourteen-foot Whaler, then fell with the river down to Albemarle Sound. We boated back up Eastmost River, past its bright, green-golden freshwater marshes, and then threaded our way around the "tourist hole"—a sixty-nine-foot whirlpool where the Middle River distributes part of its flow into the Eastmost, spinning into the depths as it does. We were in the braided, three-rivers area, which at least one old nineteenth-century nautical chart calls "the Mouths of Roanoke."

All that separates the Middle from the Cashie down here is a long narrow line of trees in the water, the now drowned head of Wood Island, and then that island itself, only a couple thousand feet long and several hundred feet wide at its widest. The last mile or so down to the mouth, the Middle and Cashie waters flow side by side, yet retain their color differentiation—the dark Cashie flows on the west side of the wide stream, the Middle's muddiness on the east—till they turn the corner between Cashoke Creek and Goodmans Island and together spill on out into Bachelor Bay and the sound.

Anyone casting a gaze hereabouts in these low precincts is very much looking at land going away, the Carolina coast reforming. Even old natives well versed in hurricanes, nor'easters, and floods may still find it strange to consider the days to come when a collapsed Outer Banks would leave Albemarle Sound a long estuarine bay, not unlike Mobile Bay, and when these islands, whatever is left undrowned of them where the various mouths of Roanoke come down and disgorge, would be left looking easterly past the north and south shores of the Albemarle and on out to sea, where the next lands to be encountered would be Bermuda and Africa.

In a canoe we rented from Roanoke River Partners, from a landing very near where my favorite old log yard had been, Ann and I set out and paddled upstream beneath the small tawny bridge I have been crossing all my life. Here the channel of the Cashie was nice and narrow, and the river skirted the backyards of homes or just wandered off darkly into cypress and gum swamp. Small white flowers were abloom here and there, and we floated on up along the east side of town as far as a park, turned into a small canal, tied up, and strolled lazily up the path beside it for a spell.

All this had been aflood with Hurricane Floyd's waters in the fall of 1999 and would be flooded again by the agency of Tropical Storm Nicole in the fall of 2010. Everyone in Bertie who lived through the disastrous high waters of Floyd was flabbergasted when the Cashie came out of her banks and rushed down King Street, filling it the second time, everyone knowing they had been hit by the five-hundred-year flood twice in eleven years. Windsor insurance man Joe Cherry laid it down sharply: "We've been through hurricanes, tornadoes and everything, but there's nothing like a flood. Nothing, really."

Our day, though, Saturday, October 14, 2006, was simply sublime, sunny and warm in the low sixties, a perfect time of day, month, and year to

Asters

be afloat and afield in the Carolina east—else there is no such thing. On the inviting dark water we paddled back downstream, back under the old U.S. 17 bridge, where swallows nested, and drifted back past our starting point, past what had been half a dozen wharves only seventy or eighty years earlier.

Though Windsor was only fifteen air miles from the Sound, the Cashie River wound twenty-five serpentine miles before it reached the Albemarle. In an 1896 report to Congress, the army engineers termed the Cashie "one of the tortuous fresh-water affluents of Albemarle Sound," adding that "lumber tows generally make use of the main stem of the Cashie, while nearly all other craft go through the Thoroughfare and thence down the Roanoke." There was river traffic galore back then: the fifty-eight-ton steamer *Bettie* ran back and forth daily between Windsor and Plymouth, carrying the U.S. mail. The Pettit Line steamers *Lucy* and *C. W. Pettit* made a trip or two a week between Windsor and Norfolk. Johnson's Mill was said to ship between 15 and 20 million board feet of lumber a year, and the engineers' report enumerated other Cashie exports that went out by river for the twelve months preceding: 1,250 bales of cotton, 17,650 bags of peanuts, 1,275 bags of black-eyed peas, and 10,000 railroad ties.

By the 1920s, the Cashie River Line ran a pair of sixty-five-foot gas-powered boats of seven-and-a-half-foot draft up and down the river, calling at these Windsor wharves and a dozen others the line leased between Windsor and the Thoroughfare, connecting the Cashie and the Roanoke. When the Corps of Engineers sent its eighty-four-foot district boat *Paquippe* up here on a mid-1920s inspection tour, the craft managed to turn itself around here at the head of navigation "without difficulty," and the district engineer observed: "With the exception of a narrow-gauge railroad in very poor condition, and some improved highways, the locality is entirely dependent upon water transportation."

Ann and I certainly were entirely dependent on it at the moment. We paddled a half-mile reach west and then another half-mile reach south, the river a hundred yards or more wide by now, yet still nice and protected. After meandering and messing about lazily among the logs laid into the river's edge, we called it an afternoon and pulled for the landing.

That night, we suited up and made our way to Hope Plantation, Governor (1808–10) David Stone's grand, restored Georgian home several miles outside Windsor. We looked about that high old pile a bit and then found friends and a table in the big Hope Ball tent out back. Presently a six-piece show band cranked up and shag dancers from eighteen to sixty-eight took to a parquet dance floor laid out on the lawn and step-kick-one-two-three'ed for the rest of the night, except for a moment of brief pause and polite applause when the band stepped back and let Lynda Bird Robb, older of President Johnson's two daughters, bring greetings to the crowd. Then the band fired up again, and so did the salamander heaters here and there around the tent. The temperature had dropped at least twenty degrees from its daytime high, and suddenly winter seemed very much at hand, and good-looking women in spaghetti straps and strapless party dresses, in green and maroon sequins and sleek black formfits, moved in desirously on the heaters in abject chills.

Nor were Ann and I immune to the evening's proud, convincing cold. We kept close to each other, knowing together and with no need to speak what a gift that balmy day had been, what an involving and invigorating time we had had just a few hours earlier on the Cashie. How bleakly bitter one would likely find the same stream just now, its surface bathed in bone-white moonlight, though the resurrection ferns rampant in the wet lowland forests, awaiting an even deeper cold and, ere long, ice sheets and shelves in the riverine swamps, in the chill of this night and through each cooling autumn day yet to come, would be right at home, enduring and green, never better.

3

scuppernong

Branning Days

The serenity of the Scuppernong River boardwalk, planking three-quarters of a mile long leading through a cypress swamp and right along the shore at Columbia, is all but undisputed and unchallenged. Only a motorboat's low thrum, or the bridge traffic's *swoosh* at low speed, might catch a stroller's ear from time to time, yet more likely the pileated woodpecker's cry would create more sound and stir.

A little over a century ago, though, the sonic scene in this same place was rather different—the old Spruill mill had been joined by a newer one with the name of Branning on it, and, lo, the mill blades turned and whined and split the sky.

One John Wellington Branning and his brother Clarence had come to Edenton from Pennsylvania in the spring of 1888, quickly setting up shop and acquiring timberlands. They were like Pennsylvania Snopeses, in a way, already in the *Town* and *Mansion* phase—they got themselves a big Greek Revival home in Edenton, they incorporated, they brought in more siblings to join them in building and developing the Branning Manufacturing Company, they changed the longtime name of Jacocks Landing on the Cashie River to Wellington (about twelve miles below Windsor), and they ran a train line, named in part for themselves, to move timber: the Wellington & Powellsville Railroad. To solidify their transit purview on the Cashie, they took over the Windsor and Edenton Boat Line as well.

In tackling the timbering of the vast forests of the Carolina east, J. W. Branning and his kin were two decades behind another gaggle of Pennsylvania sawyers, the Roper family, who had earlier migrated south and were operating out of Norfolk, Virginia. The Brannings went straight to school on the Ropers, finding lands and spots for river mills that the Ropers had not gotten to yet, and following the Roper model, right down to the specializing in kiln-dried North Carolina pine.

When the *Raleigh News and Observer* celebrated Edenton as the "Gem of the Bay" in August 1896, J. W. Branning's likeness ran closest to the headline, above the Chowan County Courthouse, the Cupola House, and the sitting mayor of Edenton. By the next May, Branning *was* Edenton's new sitting mayor. The Brannings built their Columbia mill and kiln in the late 1890s, and by 1899 they had shot an eight-mile rail spur into the big timber of eastern Tyrrell. All things Branning seemed to be going rather well.

Till just after lunch on March 9, 1900, when the dry kiln and 260,000 board feet of lumber burned. T. J. Rivenbark, a former—and discharged— Branning lumber inspector, was suspected of arson.

Till later that year, along about eight or nine on the evening of December 18, 1900, Branning employee W. S. Leary was working the hog, a two-belted machine that ran at sixteen hundred revolutions per minute, grinding slabs, running dangerously at night, making up lost time from when the millworks were down. His brother, a coworker, told him to go fix a broken belt on one side of the cylinder, while it was still in motion. The brother lost sight of Leary in the blinding spray of sawdust, and Leary, caught up in the belt, was killed.

Till the hard-charging J. W. Branning himself died at fifty-four in March 1901.

The deceased chief was succeeded at the Branning helm by his lumber-and-railroading lieutenant H. T. Corwin Jr., who forged on. At Branning Manufacturing's insistence, Norfolk & Southern ran a main rail line from Mackeys Ferry over to Columbia in 1908.

By now the booming town of Columbia and county of Tyrrell found themselves just rough enough to need a new jail, and the man who came to town to build it, in the fall of 1909, turned out to be my grandfather, Julius Andrews Page of Onslow County, just twenty-three at the time. One afternoon, on or about the Ides of November, young Columbian Mary Evelyn Spruill walked into the nearly finished brick jail on the arm of her cousin Nat Meekins, and there she met the young builder.

Six weeks later, the two were married in her mother's parlor, in the two-story, gingerbreaded Spruill house around the corner at Broad and Bridge, and for fifty-seven years they carried their lives through together in Wilmington, in Washington, D.C., and in Chapel Hill, where J. A. Page would direct the building of the Bell Tower, the Library, Kenan Stadium, and much else.

Branning Manufacturing, economic engine of the lower Scuppernong River, would not last as long as the Pages. H. T. Corwin Jr. would lead the firm till 1917. A. T. Baker, Corwin's successor, would die at forty-nine, young, just like the firm's namesake.

When the state's brand-new, nearly two-hundred-yard-long steel, timber, and concrete highway bridge over the Scuppernong River opened on Tuesday, September 7, 1926, featuring a manually operated pivot draw to let boats through, this great outside-world connection was feted by a parade, a barbecue, and dancing on the riverbanks. Yet the bridge's celebrants could not know that Branning Manufacturing had just about run its course in Tyrrell County, and the railroad that served the lower Scuppernong would not outlast the lumber mill by much.

No lumber-mill whistle has sounded out here for most of a century, and no train has called at Columbia since 1948.

Yet the wild territories of Tyrrell's pocosins and the Scuppernong River abide, and the long boardwalk where the mill once was offers a quiet way, once again tying town and stream and swamp together.

Estelle Randall Comes to Rest

Ephraim S. Randall of Canandaigua, New York, showed up in Washington, D.C., just after the Civil War as a boy seeking fame and fortune, and there he found them both. Early on, his command was a downtown billiard saloon, yet he had visions well beyond this fixed vessel, extending to the Potomac River. By the early 1880s he was operating the *Mary Washington*—as *Captain* Randall now—and he added to his fleet the *Samuel J. Pentz* and the *John W. Thompson*, which he rebuilt and rechristened, naming her for his son, *Harry Randall*. The Randall line dealt with passengers, freight, and mail, and specialized in the summer excursionist trade from the capital to destinations down the Potomac.

In 1897, Captain Randall commissioned the building of a new double-decked steamer (112 feet length overall; 25 feet beam; 6 feet draft; 211 tons), by William E. Woodall's yard in Baltimore, her machinery by Campbell & Zell. *Estelle Randall* was not launched on Monday, December 13, 1897, the date initially chosen and announced, and one when a sizable crowd had gathered under blue skies. At the last moment Captain Randall postponed the launch by a day, because, he said, he was too superstitious about the number thirteen and did not want her put overboard on that date. (One of his boats, which had thirteen crew members and for which he had paid on the thirteenth of the month, was lost off the Delaware Capes, and he said this misfortune had given him a superstition he could not shake.)

So on Tuesday, December 14, during a downpour, Miss Estelle Randall stood at the bow in storm apparel and broke a bottle of champagne on the boat, christening and naming it for herself. At her launch, reported the *Baltimore Sun*,

"The *Randall* took the water like a swan."

She was grand, and the *Washington Post* celebrated her postlaunch arrival on the Potomac River: beyond her freight space, she had a fifty-foot saloon with windows all around, "highly polished" hardwood walls, a ceiling "finished in white and gold." The *Post* cited her "large open decks forward and aft of the saloon," said she had "ample room for six hundred passengers during the summer excursion season," and wrote that overall *Estelle Randall* was "a very handsome little craft." During the summer seasons she would run popular day trips from her wharf at the foot of Seventh Street downriver to Chapel Point.

Yet, as with many a ship, *Estelle Randall*'s course was not without incident. On September 3, 1899, with Harry Randall at the helm, the *Estelle Randall* collided with the steamer *Kent* on the Potomac well downriver of Washington, at the mouth of Port Tobacco Creek—Captain Randall, the son, had his licensed lifted for a couple of weeks.

And several years later, one of her crew—William Crowley, a black fireman—fell overboard in Washington harbor and drowned on July 14, 1906. "He hit me and ran off amidships and dove into the water, and I thought he had swum ashore," was Harry Randall's story. Other men reported that Captain Harry was coming to beat Crowley for cursing him and that Crowley leapt off the *Estelle Randall* to escape the captain's wrath. A grand jury indicted Harry Randall in Crowley's death, but the Steamboat-Inspection Service found none of the *Estelle Randall*'s crew or command at the time responsible, and Harry Randall went free.

A year after the death of Captain Ephraim Randall in 1908, the *Estelle Randall* was sold to North Carolina's Farmers & Merchants Line, which had plans for her to cruise the Albemarle Sound as a grand passenger, freight, and mail boat, and to call at all her riverports.

And this is what she was all about when she entered Bull's Bay in January 1910 and made her way up the Scuppernong River and docked at the Columbia wharf. Yet during the night of January 17–18, *Estelle Randall* caught fire and burned and sank at the dock, where she still lies at the bottom of the river, though not quite all of her: North Carolina's Underwater Archaeology Unit, in league with the experienced, talented Mud Puppies divers, in the late 1980s and early 1990s explored the wreck, and in November 1992 brought up her machinery, including her vertical, direct-acting compound steam

Steamboat
Estelle
Randall

engine, her air and water pumps, a Westinghouse generator housing, and her very rudder, whose last task it had been to guide *Estelle Randall* into what would be her final maritime position.

Estelle Randall's fifteen crew members were all aboard when the fire broke out, and all made it ashore to safety. Yet in the dark and noise and confusion, not knowing that no one was still aboard, the black cook William Exley ran back on deck to see whom he might help, and, his Good Samaritanism notwithstanding, he alone perished with his ship that fateful winter's night.

Estelle Randall has not moved in over a hundred years.

The Ballad of Mister Schlez

One day along about 1916 or 1917, perhaps earlier, a few townspeople gathered at the foot of Main Street in Columbia, along the wharf and waters of the Scuppernong River, to watch the latest pilgrim approach this place. A man on a raft, paddling, his ramshackle conveyance moving crudely and as much side to side as forward, came slowly toward them. He waved when they hailed him, but said little or nothing. The people could not yet know that he had fled Germany, stowed away on a ship bound for New York, then jumped ship in the Verrazano Narrows to keep from being deported, swam ashore, and headed south. When he reached the Scuppernong wharf, they threw a line to him, as he had none aboard to throw them. In fact, he had nothing whatsoever except the raft with its tented tarp and the clothes on his back.

He was named Johann Fredrick Schlez, and he did not have a dime.

How he had come to the Scuppernong, and from where—how he had crossed the Albemarle Sound on these few planks—who and what he was, or what he now intended . . . none of this could he answer or explain in what little English he had at his command. He was a short man, a penniless, hungry man, soaked and ragged, that much was clear, and the people of Columbia fed him and clothed him and one of the Branning mill operators took an interest in him, enough so to hire him to sit with a kerosene lantern and guard the place, be its night watchman, and stay on in a mill shack.

He went by Fred, and he was a steady worker. Any man who could have crossed that broad sound on nothing more than a batch of scraps and slabs had to have had some steadiness about him. He worked at the mill right along for a spell and saved his pay, and they were not surprised about that. He was handy and artful: for Saint Andrews Episcopal Church, he carved a Gothic Revival altar rail, the very one that stands there to this day, and they were not surprised about that, either. He took up surveying, walking and working in the woods for the mill, till one landowner disputed his lines and stabbed him in the back, giving him a pronounced limp for the rest of his life. Schlez pressed no charges, and that surprised them some.

Yet what surprised them most was when Fred Schlez opened a moviehouse.

That was on Elm Street, a side lane off Main, in a two-story wooden building with a lazily sloping roof and a gabled front. He would surprise them, all right. He would show them. His moviehouse's very first feature, as it happened, was 1919's *Granddaddy Longlegs*, starring Mary Pickford. And he went on from there—he showed them Chaplin's Tramp and Keaton's engineer chasing his train, the Gish sisters as *Orphans in the Storm*, and in time had his town singing along with Roy Rogers and his cowboy comrades. Such as these flickered by on a screen down front, and for a few minutes each week, fishermen and timbermen and farmers, millworkers and shopkeepers, husbands and wives and boys and girls forgot they were sitting on planks balanced between nail kegs and shipping boxes, forgot where and sometimes even who they were as the flickering projector danced other worlds before their eyes.

Fred Schlez did that, all that, for Columbia and for the people of Tyrrell County and the Scuppernong: he brought them magic.

Pocosin Arts

On the east side of the old brick commercial building at the corner of Main and Water Streets in Columbia, at the top of a wooden stairway decorated with pots of ferns and pansies, just inside the door to the pottery and painting and sculpting studio, one not so long ago would have found hanging there on the interior wall an enormous woven bedspread, a big lacy coverlet, really. So intricate was it, with its globes and radii, it seemed to be something from another world, a challenging code made by beings or even machines all but impossible to imagine.

Yet nothing so far-fetched was involved at all. Its creator was Mrs. G. N. Hurdle, a Bridge Street neighbor of my cousin Virginia Yerby, and the artifact itself was a yo-yo quilt made from feed sacks.

Feather Phillips, the art-teacher founder and longtime director of the small, high-concept studio and gallery called Pocosin Arts, had acquired and hung Ms. Hurdle's work, and she led Ann and me up the stairs to see it back in the 1990s, and it was a touching thing indeed to see, and handle, this old labor of love. As Feather, a Pennsylvanian émigré to Carolina, found and displayed such gorgeous, former commonplaces such as this one, as utilitarian as it was artful, and others that, though homely—

like the walking sticks fashioned from gum saplings spiral-designed by climbing vines—nonetheless touched the heart, she was also challenging her community, and the whole pocosin region of the Albemarle and Pamlico peninsula, to bring forth its domestic arts, to put them together above (and, later, next to) an old appliance store and to see this colorful social collage of dolls and jugs and bedspreads as emblems of spirit and pride. She was trying, and in the long run succeeding, to get a small river town whose mill had closed down generations ago, whose train tracks had been taken up in 1948, events beyond the memory of most, to wake up *to itself* and to love anew its many handiworks, and, of course, the hands and hearts that lay behind them.

My Spruill kin had first come into this country just downriver of here, into what they called "Heart's Delight." Spruills nearly two centuries later had moved into Columbia from Alligator to the east and built the first two-story brick building in town. Paul Spruill, my great-uncle, was a handcrafter who would have loved what was now transpiring upstairs in the Pocosin Arts studio. He once carved and fashioned for me a small wooden wheelbarrow and painted it a bright forest green, a delight he presented to me when I was but five years old. Just as twenty years before that he had made for my mother the model of a two-masted lumber schooner, like so many he had seen on the Scuppernong and the Little Alligator, naming it and painting *Betty* upon her stern, a small ship that would one day come to be docked atop my piano so many miles from this river.

Another craftswoman, my great-great-aunt Buena Vista Spruill McLees (named after her father's ship *Buena Vista*) had spent hundreds of hours with scissors and threads and made a vaunted tapestry out of her times, an eight-by-eight creation now in the Columbia museum just up the street from Pocosin Arts, in the old movie theater Mister Schlez had built (the Columbia, his second) in 1930. Her name—*B. V. McLees*—she had stitched in gold on a black panel, adjacent to which *1888* lay in gold on pink satin. Aunt Buenie's work was a crazy quilt with tiny panels (of red, black, gold, and brown) of all sorts of geometric shapes, and icons upon the panels of all manner of things: a star, a leaf, a kite tail, a piece of wheat, daisies, a pelican, a cross, and a straw-hatted boy with a fishing pole.

It was more than important that Pocosin Arts be within sight and a few steps of the river—it was essential, for the river that we still fish in and float on drains no small part of the great pocosins to the town's south. The Scuppernong, the slow-moving, dark yet shining stream, flowed by below the gallery, then around a pair of bends, opening into Bull's Bay and the Albemarle—and the river was why any of this, any of us, were here, the river as always in some good measure giving meaning to us all.

Crab pots, Willy Phillips' Full Circle Crab Company, May 2014

Spruill's Bridge

At high noon one hot June day, David Cecelski and I put the canoe in at the Spruill's Bridge landing on the Scuppernong, just east of Creswell, and paddled downstream. The river being only forty or fifty feet wide for some miles, we knew we would not want for shade.

Our starting point, a generally quiet spot whose peace was occasionally violated by the acute, banging noise of metal on metal as pickups, dump trucks, and grain trucks clanged over the bridge, had been the high point of trade on the river for all of the nineteenth century and a fair bit of the twentieth. Our landing's parking lot lay on the old site of the steamer *I. D. Coleman*'s warehouse, and directly across the river once sat the warehouse of the steamer *Mary E. Roberts*. These first few yards of Scuppernong waters (on the river's south side just below the bridge) we traversed had served as the turning basin for schooners, scows, flatboats of any sort come upriver to deliver goods to the vast nineteenth-century Somerset and Pettigrew plantations and to pick up cotton or wheat, or corn shelled by a water-powered mill, loaded and lightered down the long, straight, slave-dug canals from these farms.

Not quite a year afterward, Ann and I would come back to Spruill's Bridge on a warm Friday afternoon, the second of May. The Scuppernong then ran high, and the ramp was flooded. Spring flowers bloomed:

Old turning basin, just below Spruill's Bridge, Scuppernong River east of Creswell, May 2014

white clover, the five-petaled pink sorel, blue-eyed grass, buttercups. The old turning basin lay placid as a pond, and one might stand at the ramp and imagine the maneuvering of a big two-master—deckhands and men ashore handling lines as the current backed a boat downstream, and then other men at the bridge, or in rowboats pulling on bowlines to get the bow southward into the basin, the river flow now helping with this slow, purposeful spin that would get a schooner aimed back toward sound and sea again.

Downstream, somewhere near the second bend, beneath David's and my canoe lay whatever was left of the boards and bones of a Columbia-built schooner, the long-abandoned and sunk *Lawrence*, forty-seven tons, sixty-six feet long, with a twenty-foot beam and four-foot draft. This old craft, listed as having been removed from the river on August 26, 1885, by the Army Corps of Engineers, had in fact only been (on further word from the Corps, in its 1886 report) raised and floated long enough for all interested parties to judge her "old, rotten and almost worthless," whereupon she was then "moved a short distance and allowed to sink where she would be out of the way." Not much of an obituary for a ship that had served the Scuppernong for over thirty years before being left to go to pieces, but there it was.

Not even ten minutes below Spruill's Bridge, we spooked a big white-tailed bird, which flew downriver, and I yelled "Eagle!" But David's skepticism—based on the bird's low-to-the-water flight, not unlike a heron's—made me doubt my call. We spooked it a second time, yet got no better a look. Another hundred yards or so, and we raised it a third time, and in this instance the bird flew sideways and upward, and we saw its bright head:

A bald eagle.

We flushed many a wood duck, and watched them both singly and in pairs as they noisily flapped and skittered along the river's surface before gaining a little altitude and taking up new positions on ahead of us. Kingfishers flew past and away, too hot, or too hungry, to sound their standard, chattering cries. Lively dragonflies flitted everywhere, some blue, some green, pairs chasing each other, now and again a large pappy dragonfly noisily popping the dark water.

The prize of the day, though, came to us not far from where the Thirty-Foot Canal hits the river, at the bottom of an old oxbow out of sight and off to the south. Two eagles high above the river flew out of and soared in avian play around an enormous pine tree, a thick tangle of grapevine sleeving it for much of the way up its trunk, quite a sight and one just right for a river named after the sweet sport of the muscadine:

Scuppernong.

No spectacle comes without its modest counterpoint, and today's lay on a branch I dodged as we sought shade along the riverside most of the way to the mouths of the Somerset and Bee Tree Canals, moments after David had spied a muskrat trying to hide from us behind a stump. Our small wonder was a tiny, two-inch squirrel tree frog, frightened by our presence into a most solemn stance, trying to mimic a leaf, as still as an emerald on a shelf, and no less lovely.

4

Little Alligator and Milltail Creek

Spruill Kin

Once, my cousin Virginia Yerby and my mother were busy performing one of their childhood's forbidden feats: the two small girls were climbing around on the vines atop the grape arbor at their grandmother's home, the old Spruill place in Columbia. *What if Little Grandmother comes out and catches us?* my mother wondered. Which is exactly what happened, whereupon Virginia said, "Be still and she won't hear us. She won't know we're up here." Little Grandmother approached the arbor, thinking the girls were under it, and, not finding them, leaned back, looked up, and saw them at once, frozen, huddled among the scuppernongs.

"I may be *deaf*," she shouted up at them, "but I'm not *blind*! You girls get down right this minute, and we'll just *see about this*!"

Another time, when Virginia was still just a little girl of about five, the Yerbys caught the ferry at Fort Landing, fourteen miles east of Columbia, within sight of where the Little Alligator River (sometimes called "the creek") joins the Alligator River and both of them flow into Albemarle Sound. Virginia's family ferried across the big Alligator River to mainland Dare County, on their way to the seabeach of the Outer Banks. Tom, her father, went into the little store at the East Lake landing, and Virginia got out of the car and followed him inside. All her short life she had heard about the illicit whiskey making that went on over here in the East Lake precincts, and she had picked up a sense of its intrigue and even some of its lingo, and she was anxious to show that she was in on something. So she entered the store, let the screen door slam behind her, put her hands on her hips, and announced proudly and profoundly to the storekeeper and all attendant parties, in her loudest school-yard voice:

"Hey, y'all—I want me some *moonshine.*"

It was cousin Virginia, slight and merry and purposefully focused, who took me back out to Fort Landing at the end of the Soundside Road, where the old settlers' fort from the Tuscarora War once was, its pilings now out in the water, the land having subsided so and the water levels having risen. She drove us out there on a warm April afternoon back in 1993, to meet and eat hard crabs with the Phillipses, Willy and Feather, he the owner-operator of Full Circle Crab Company and she of the then-new Pocosin Arts in town.

Because of these three folks, to whom I owe so much, I have gone back many's the time to meet the ghosts and phantoms of our Spruill family past in these eastern Tyrrell lowlands, long remembered and spoken of by my family up in the Carolina hill country.

Virginia showed me where, or rather about where, Colonel Hezekiah Spruill and his wife Rhoda lay buried way out in the piney woods south of Soundside Road. And Willy has told me where all the graves of some very young Spruill children are to that road's north, their small stones all but lost among the briars and the brambly jungle. I have often thought of these long-departed souls, the young and the old alike, as I have opened the family Bible and stared at their names, read them aloud to honor and just simply remember them, wondering what they went through, wanted, felt, and believed. Of Joseph Ashby Spruill (who, after moving his family into Columbia in 1886 from way out yonder in Alligator, became a merchant and a state senator) I had little doubt, for he had signed the late-nineteenth-century Bible's inserted "Temperance Pledge" with real purpose and a very specific awareness of the Last Supper and the passing of the wine. Beneath his name were the clear and defiant words:

"As far as Christ and no farther."

To Alligator

My mother often admitted that, when she was in grade school in the 1920s, she was always so embarrassed on the first day of class, when the teacher bade the students to tell the class where their parents were born, and she had to say: "My father was born in Tar Landing, my mother in *Alligator.*"

On the morning of May 11, 1884, my maternal grandmother—Mary Evelyn Spruill—had indeed come into this world in Alligator, North Carolina, which was far more a swampy township than anything resembling a town, in eastern Tyrrell County. This was the wet, water-loving land between the Albemarle Sound and the Little Alligator River, where her direct ancestors had been making their stand for over a century, from before the

Revolution till after the Civil War, their distant forebears having come into the Tyrrell country a century even earlier than that.

That first group, Doctor Godfrey Spruill and his wife Joanna, had made their ways from Renfrewshire in west Scotland over to Virginia, then due south down from Virginia in the 1690s, crossing the wide sound into this south Albemarle country when it had no name in their language. They called their new territory Heart's Delight, their bayside home the Round-about, and they named the river that made their bay the Scuppernong. For this they borrowed the Algonkians' Askuponong (Where the Sweet Bay and Swamp Laurel Grow), a word spoken plainly and plainly spoken here for thousands of years before European or African or Asian ears ever heard it.

My great-great-aunt, the quilter Buena Vista Spruill McLees, was born in Alligator in February 1850. As her father, Benjamin Spruill, had just acquired the 188-ton, 94-foot brigantine *Buena Vista* (built in Beaufort County, North Carolina, the year before), he and his wife Nancy Midyette had proudly named their new girl baby after the craft. With the Spruills' Homestead Plantation on the Little Alligator River producing thousands of bushels of corn a year and Benjamin's shingle factory clipping out 350,000 cypress shingles a year in 1850, Spruill needed a substantial ship—and his new daughter might as well carry that ship's name on out into the world.

Yet, as she was nicknamed and known across the family as Aunt Buenie, few beyond kin, alas, knew the maritime provenance of her given name.

Though my grandmother's immediate family moved into town, back toward the original ancestral toehold, when she was just a small child, the family always recalled and told and retold tales of Fort Landing, of their home in Alligator, and of Free and Easy, which, though held by the Spruill family only for a brief span (1873 till the 1880s), was the place-name that seemed to them to go best with tales of that lost agrarian time. It was from Alligator that my great-grandfather, Joseph Ashby Spruill (1842–1904), had departed to go upstate and attend school at the military academy in Hillsboro, coming back home from there, still a boy of sixteen or seventeen, when Civil War clouds gathered; and it was from Free and Easy that Joseph Ashby years later set out to court and marry Evelyn Moore, my great-grandmother-to-be, from the family of new Maryland émigrés just across the Soundside Road.

Free and Easy was broken up among the many (nearly a dozen) Spruill children soon after both elder Spruills died, Benjamin in 1880 and Nancy Midyette in 1881, and most all of them then moved back across Tyrrell County from the Little Alligator to the Scuppernong, one little river to the other.

Yet they behind left the Free and Easy name, which lives on the land to this day.

And they left behind all those graves: Benjamin's and Nancy's plots of last repose hard by the Soundside Road; all those Spruill children's graves that lay about in a swampy willow jungle not far from Fort Landing; and those of the original patriarch and matriarch of this whole eastern Tyrrell crowd, Rhoda and Hezekiah (he the Revolutionary War colonel who raised a regiment for General Washington)—their long-lost tombstones way south of Soundside Road, at the old Spruill family cemetery, once for reasons unknown called "the Hosey burying ground."

Colonel Hezekiah was not only a stout patriot and, later, a member of the North Carolina House of Commons. Taken at his very last words, he was also a great fatalist, for the quatrain he ordered inscribed on his graveslab read:

My loving friends, as you pass by,
As you are now, so once was I.
As I am now, so you must be.
Prepare, my friends, to follow me.

My Camden cousin Nancy Meekins Ferebee, fond of poring over just such lore with me, told me of the couplet that my great-aunt Catherine had lodged in retort to Colonel Hezekiah's family-famous last declaration and imperative invitation:

Before I follow, I must know
Exactly where you intend to go.

Plying the Little Alligator

In the early fall of 2013, Ann and I were back at Fort Landing, staying at what Willy Phillips called "the Eco-tel": a tent inside one of the two elevated grain bins, thirty feet in diameter, that Willy and Feather were about to call home, after living since the late 1980s in a small yet commodious green trailer in the yard below. By day we stepped out of a subgale thirty-mile-an-hour wind and into the stillness of one of the bins, marveling at the *swoosh* and *hum* of the stiff breeze as it rolled around the surface curves.

By night, the wind having died down now, Ann and Feather and I sat out late on the high open deck, listening to the light lapping of the cove's waters in the willows and toasting the faraway lights of the Outer Banks, watching them twinkle out as the evening came fully into its shank.

North shore, Little Alligator River, September 2013

Next morning, we four had grits and fried flounder on the deck, then set out in midday under a cloudless, sunny blue sky in Willy's thirty-foot shadboat *Heart* to wander the Little Alligator River, just around Rock Point from the Fort Landing cove, and wonder over it too.

At South Shore Landing, mouth of the Little Alligator, lay a community cemetery with fifty graves, though no settlement had been there for a long time. A little ways up, still on the south side of the river, lay an enormous barge belonging to Kay Grayson, "the bear lady," who from her trailer back in the woods well away from the river fed dog food to, and in that way *kept*, a cohort of ten to fifteen bears. She had inherited this huge, wild land, which she named "Bearsong," from her boyfriend, said to have been a big-time Washington lawyer, and lived on it in something approaching a state of nature, until her remains were found in late January 2015 two hundred yards from her home, dragged there, thought the county sheriff, by the very bears she had long loved and tended. She had for some time many years ago lived on the barge, but the Coast Guard in the end ran her off it, though allowing the barge itself, by then settled into the Little Alligator's absolute mud, to stay on.

By now the huge metal craft has become something of a monument, but to what? An unusual wildlife advocate's desire for solitude and a home on the river? An eccentric's last stand? Or to something simpler, perhaps: a soul as lonesome as the old, deserted barge itself? Another mile or more west along the south shore, a marker closely resembling a granite gravestone stood in the shallows of Ludford Landing (once known as Millers Landing), another testament to rising tides and their mockery of the works of man. This significant rock, solid if wet, had once staked out a huge piece of territory for the fabulously acquisitive and proprietary Collins family of Lake Phelps and Somerset Plantation renown, and in making that claim it referred to the landing's earlier name, its chiseled legend, partially obscured by deep green moss and stark white barnacles, a grand territorial declaration undergoing a slow inundation, stating:

Millers Landing
J Collins
Patent
60 000 acres
1796

Over the way, straight across the river from this old marker, was Buzzard Point, the upper end of the long Deep Cove. As the diesel engine of *Heart* clattered on smoothly, Willy spoke over the motor tones of what he had learned about the Spruills and their shipping operations here.

"There are ballast stones all along the riverbottom here," he said. "The Spruill landing was *big*, maybe a hundred to a hundred and fifty feet long."

"How did they get out to it from the farm?" I asked.

Thick, low cypress riverswamp comprised the north shore, all it now was, the Little Alligator waters sheeting off and disappearing into the wet woods. No lane coming down to the shore through the morass. No bluff whatsoever for a ship to cozy up to.

"They had a platform," Willy said. "Built out, decked out from the end of the fields over the swamp to the wharf, so wagons could roll out there to the ships."

"But that's—"

"An eighth of a mile or so," he said, nodding, and we both just stared from *Heart* across the water and into the seemingly endless cypress swamp, imagining the almost incredible riverine stage the Spruills and their bondsmen had hammered out and laid into being here in order to

Collins Patent Marker, historic Millers Landing, now Ludford Landing, across from Buzzard Point, Little Alligator River, September 2013

make their world work, before he pronounced what the both of us in true awe were thinking:

"Pretty amazing."

Milltail Creek and Buffalo City

Across the big Alligator River and about five miles south-southeast of the Fort Landing cove was the put-in at Buffalo City in mainland Dare County. Just a roadside canal a couple miles south of U.S. 64, one followed its lead into a narrower canal, the entrance to the dense swamp forest that a century ago was the busy domain of the Dare Lumber Company. That firm cut cypress and juniper timber out of these swamps, brought the logs on railcars out to the waters of Milltail Creek and to the big wharf there at Buffalo City, where Milltail Creek was lakelike, loaded them onto barges and floated them several miles out to Alligator River—thence nearly forty miles north across Albemarle Sound and up the Pasquotank River to its mill in Elizabeth City, an enormous tawny brick affair with sluices, slides, and saws. I remember the old Dare Lumber mill from my childhood, a looming ruin, an icon of the old days on the Pasquotank River shore on the north side of town, huge, vacant and quiet then, no sawblades whining or screaming out, yet still holding on to us with the powerful grip of a ghost.

Hundreds of workers once lived in the company town of Buffalo City, in shacks and buildings set on sawdust fill. Entertainment occasionally floated in, also on barges, a floating saloon and dance hall. Everything that moved did so on and over water. Ben Basnight, a fisherman and boatman born in a cabin on Second Creek in eastern Tyrrell during the Year of the Big Freeze, 1895, when the Albemarle froze over, first courted his sweetheart Ella Ambrose, whom he later married, at the Buffalo City soirees. He recalled "one or more dances during the winter months at the Red Onion Hotel each week," and said: "It might have been at one of those dances that I got my eyes on a young girl in a blue serge sailor suit. And when dancing she would brush her hand across her dress, and when she would jibe it would crack like a jib sheet."

Bland Simpson, Willy Phillips, and Feather Phillips aboard the shadboat Heart, Little Alligator River, September 2013

Ella and Ben dated for years while Basnight saved up enough money to marry ("near 400 dollars"). During the second week of December 1928, now-Captain Basnight of the North River Line's steamer *Jones*, a sixty-five-foot freighter, stopped by East Lake on the way back from Fairfield and picked up his fiancée and brought her over to Elizabeth City to get married and live. "We went downtown and bought about 200.00 dollars' worth of stuff including 2 plates 2 cup and saucers 2 each knives—forks—spoons. Come home and set it all up and had ham and eggs for breakfast."

When the logwoods played out and Dare Lumber Company gave up in the 1920s, Buffalo City soon became a ghost town, and nothing now remains of it except the name and the memory and one noble structure: the pilings and the trestling frame that once supported the wharf, and from which so many logs, so many millions of board feet, were loaded off railcars and onto outbound barges, all of this lying under the waters of Milltail Creek at the edge of the swamp woods, rarely to be seen, and then only when a nor'easter has blown the waters well west into other swamps, those in the Roanoke and Cashie riverbottoms, lowering the Alligator River and its tributaries by several feet.

After the big timber was all felled, a well-trained labor force reconstituted itself and then turned its attention to pouring out a different prod-

*Tug **Pamlico** leaving **Buffalo City** with log barge **Dare Devil**, Milltail Creek, early twentieth century*

uct: white liquor, purveyed, with coloring, as East Lake Rye, or, if the buyer preferred a few juniper berries in his or her clear elixir, as East Lake Gin. Made in these swamps during Prohibition on an industrial scale, with workers going to work by steam whistle, the liquor floated up to Elizabeth City, then got run by car and truck up the Canalbank through the Great Dismal Swamp, to Hampton Roads and its thirsty sailors, what was left of it sent on up the Bay.

Over the years, I have boated and roamed the Buffalo City wilds many times with Carolina students in the spring; with my daughter Cary and my wife Ann too on one of those April mornings; and with my old friend Jake Mills and my son Hunter in the Whaler one June afternoon in 1999, after we three had struggled for much of an hour out on the big Alligator River to find the obscure mouth of Milltail Creek, all but curtained off from the world, guarding the deep secret of Milltail's loveliness. By canoe or kayak from the Buffalo City landing, the entry ditch led east right on in to Sawyer Lake, where one glided through freshwater marshes glowing a golden green in the spring, and where gorgeous patches of dark juniper graced its wooded banks and four-and-a-half-foot alligators sunned themselves on angled pines fallen over into the lake's edge. For years in the 2000s, an extra-large individual alligator carried the nickname "Mister Big"—some folks said he was ten or twelve feet, while others held that he had grown to sixteen feet at least. Either way, locals paid legendary respect to Mister Big.

Back out on broad Milltail Creek, near the Buffalo City landing early one spring afternoon, several of us in kayaks got our rare glimpse of the ancient trestle, the top three feet of it, which a three-day gale had indeed left uncovered, if only for a few hours. The old wharf remnant lies so abidingly concealed that Willy Phillips, who has lived at Fort Landing nearly thirty years now and who knows the Alligator River swamp country like few others, told me later that same day that he had never once laid eyes on it—for it was almost always beneath the dark water, submerged, like memory.

5

out on Ocracoke

Sandbar

On Ocracoke, our state's much-beloved sandbar twenty-seven miles out in the Atlantic, no rivers run to the sea. Only a few slender watercourses fall, or, really, meander or slide, out of marshes, little woods and sand plains and hills into Pamlico Sound. An incantation of the names of these creeks, following an old map from northeast to southwest, lays the place out in the mind's eye: Cockrel, Shingle, North Bitterswash, South Bitterswash, Knoll, Knoll House, Try Yard, Old Hammock, Island, Sand Hole, Cockle, and Old Slough. Running from ferry to ferry, the island's single highway crosses only half of them, and their names currently read: Try Yard, Parkers, Quokes Point, Molasses, Old Hammock, and Island.

Cockle Creek in the village of Ocracoke is by far the largest and best known, though to most by another name: it was dredged out by the Corps of Engineers in 1931, again by the U.S. Navy a decade later, and since then the rounded harbor has been called Silver Lake, as long as almost anyone can remember. Native Ocracokers, O'cockers, to a man and woman still call it simply "the Creek," and the cut leading out of it into Pamlico Sound "the Ditch."

My father, who claimed Nags Head as his true home when he went off from Elizabeth City to college in Chapel Hill, early on told me tales of Ocracoke and its harbor and its old chalk-white lighthouse, of the free-ranging ponies and cattle and sheep, and the sport fishing and the navy and the war. I remember going with him on the ferry across Oregon Inlet and roaming Hatteras Island, stopping in at the Buxton post office long enough for him to politick with the postmistress there, a boy my young single-ciphered age running in and asking to use the "flushbucket," and I remember not long after that crossing over from Hatteras to Ocracoke and seeing then-quiet Silver

Lake and its ghost-white fishing boats. If it seemed like the edge of the world, well, it was, and so be it.

My comrade Bobby Schwentker, my cousin Steve Lamborn, and I drove down there from Kitty Hawk in my family's '64 V-8 Ford Country Squire the very first summer I could drive, and had ourselves big cheeseburger lunches at the Island Inn, within easy sight of small wharves where fishermen, then as now, landed some of the freshest and best seafood in the world. Bill Parsons flew me out there in a Cessna 172 for my twenty-fifth birthday, and we landed at the seaside airstrip after cruising low up Core Banks and over old Portsmouth Village, tied down and walked the scant mile into town for another lunch at the Island Inn, and this time we fed on the fruits of the sea, faring a good deal better than I had years earlier.

So many other times on Ocracoke come to mind. Ann and I have stayed in the village in the only motel open at New Year's, when all restaurants were locked and under wraps, dining on pimiento cheese and crackers and sardines from the Community Store laid out on a newspaper on the bedspread; at the Pony Island in July (drinking beer on the stoop late into the night with our old friend Scott Bradley, now a longtime island resident, though this was back when he was new enough to the island that most folks simply called him "the bike guy"); staying with Don and Marti Jones Dixon at the cottage straight over Silver Lake from the fishhouse and boating over nightly in the jonboat to buy fish and shop at the Community Grocery back in '02; and, two years before that, Cary and I as happy guests out at Donald and Merle Davis's Swamp Turtle cottage the first time Cary and I went birdbanding with the adventurous, veteran bandleaders John Weske and Micou Browne.

Almost everyone in the Carolina province wants to go there, to see Ocracoke from the ferry deck as the island town rises out of the inland sea like a place of dream and myth, to touch it and breathe it in, our only villaged island that still must be floated or flown to, if one would be there at all.

Once there, none wish to leave.

Our Shangri-La, some have called it, and none would gainsay that. Hotelier and dance-hall, roller-rink, and movie-theater impresario Stanley Wahab once promoted Ocracoke as "the Bermuda of the United States." Yet no less valid is the judgment of an Ocracoke native, a woman in her seventies who went up in an aircraft for the first time ever and came back from the flight and told a neighbor: "Lived here all my life and never knew till now that we were just living on a toothpick in the middle of a bathtub."

Whose Idea Was This?

At 5 P.M. sharp, as always, the ferry gave a single blast of its deep horn, echoing all over the lake and through the forested, low-lying village of Ocracoke. The big craft pulled away from the slip, turned and started for the Sound and the mainland. Before the ferry even got into the Ditch, though, my phone was ringing, my wonderful friend and fellow author, North Carolina Center for the Advancement of Teaching Fellow and Crews Inn owner Alton Ballance, calling with this report:

On their way down the two-mile Ramp 72 road, a graded clay lane leading from the east side of Ocracoke village out to the seabeach, Alton et al. (in his four-wheel-drive pickup he had fellow statriots Bob Anthony, D. G. Martin, and Michael Parker with him) had fallen in behind a late-model car that was, as were they, bound for the dunes. When both vehicles reached the breach in the primary dune, where the lane became all sand and led, unimproved, out onto the beach itself, Alton's crowd was alarmed to see the car ahead of them passing the parking area and charging forth right on out onto the beach, exclaiming:

"Oh, no!"

"Why, that fool!"

"Can't believe he's—"

Alton followed the car, which was aiming straight for the Atlantic Ocean—it might have made it into the surf, too, but for bogging down and sinking into the sand only thirty yards or so out onto the beach, if that. Its driver jumped out, waving his arms in frustration and ire, and Alton pulled up behind him and all hands piled out of his truck, urging the man—who turned out to be coming straight from the very North Carolina seminar that had just concluded for the day, with my *car-stuck-in-sand-on-beach* song a key part of the conclusion—back into the car to power and steer it while Alton's quartet rocked it out of its sandmire and got it going.

And so with main strength the four Good Samaritans pushed and shoved and got the man (he was a senior school administrator from western North Carolina) turned around and moving again, whereupon he hightailed it back to the Ramp 72 road and, chagrined and embarrassed, headed back on into town.

All this before my ferry had even reached and cleared the Silver Lake cut!

A couple of days later, back in Chapel Hill, I saw Bob Anthony in Wilson Library, his professional home as longtime curator of the North Carolina Collection, and he was still shaking his head and laughing about the incident, as was I.

"My song was a cautionary tale about beach driving," I said. "*Not* a suggestion to engage in it!"

"I know, I know," Bob laughed. "He just did not know what he was up to. But, of course, why would he? He was from the mountains."

"I reckon," I said. "But I still can't believe that fellow went directly from my song and stories on this very topic, right out onto the seabeach, and sank his car in the sand."

"Oh! That's just it," Bob said.

"What?"

"It wasn't *his* car. It was a *state car*."

Trekking with Dixon

A grayish day early in a recent November, the brilliant, versatile, and renowned musician Don Dixon and I drove east to Swan Quarter in southern Hyde County, picked up our tickets out at the state ferry dock for the four o'clock out to Ocracoke, and, with plenty of time till we embarked, went back into the little fishing hamlet to a roadside vendor's, a little travel-trailer kitchen on an old gas-station lot, and got some lunch—a softshell crab sandwich. Then we turned down Landing Road, driving toward the waters of Swanquarter Bay, passing all manner and size of fishing boats and machine shops to serve them, and parked by a small, tilted dock and a half-sunk skiff and enjoyed the miles-of-marsh view and a car-hood lunch in paradise.

Three hours later, we would roll off the ferry after a slow, smooth crossing of Pamlico Sound about six-thirty and find our billets at Alton Ballance's Crews Inn on the Ocracoke Back Road shortly afterward. Turned out we were the only folks there, besides the young couple who were innkeeping that winter: others had canceled bookings after Hurricane Sandy wiped out—just the weekend before—the S-curves, the traditionally storm-beset, oft sliced-and-diced section of N.C. 12 above Rodanthe on Hatteras Island to the north. Don and I set up piano and bass in the Crews Inn dining room and played coastal melodies well into the night, alternately reminiscing with our old friend, the wry, jolly Scott Bradley, and warming up for the next evening's show at the Hatteras Civic Center.

James Barrie Gaskill, longtime waterman and conservationist of Ocracoke and Beaufort, had advised me to get "the Las Vegas story" from Rex O'Neal if I happened to see him, and when Rex walked up, smiling, to shake hands after the show on Saturday night, I asked him about it and he laughed and laid it right out:

There were several of them, born and bred O'cockers, Rex and James Barrie among them, heading out to Las Vegas some years back to observe the wildlife there and have a big time. Before they set out, though, they realized that it was unlikely Vegas would be able to meet their needs and standards when it came time for salty oysters—and that if they were going to have any, and keep their equilibrium right, they would have to bring their own oysters along with them. And so they did. And being O'cockers in a hurry to catch the ferry to the mainland to go and catch the plane to Vegas, they quickly grabbed and packed several Styrofoam coolers full of oysters and taped them up for the trip with duct tape.

When they landed at McCarran International Airport in Las Vegas, they made their eager, hungry ways to the baggage claim, where they—and all the other folks who had flown in with them—watched astonished as, in and among the suitcases and duffels and infant car seats, one Styrofoam cooler after the next came out onto the conveyor belt cracked and spilling good, salty, Pamlico oysters every whichaway and the oysters knocking and spreading all about, as if they were scurrying away on their own, and the O'cockers diving through the crowd, all hands on deck, grabbing at their goods, stuffing their pockets, collecting their precious cargo, their Carolina bivalves, however and as best they could.

"That," said Rex O'Neal with a wide, soundside smile, "was one great trip!"

Next morning, Don and I drifted out British Cemetery Road, past the little piece of England where four British seamen from the HMS *Bedfordshire's* torpedoing and sinking in May 1942 have long since slept, and on out to Scott Bradley's home on Pamlico Shore Road to pay him a morning call. As he had recently taken in a piece of his first-story deck, making a sunroom of it and putting a circular staircase up to a new high deck above, he wanted to show us his great, wide-open, broadcloth view of Pamlico Sound, glory of glories, the inland sea, the biggest part and portion of our vaunted estuary, the Albemarle Lagoon.

We were almost directly above where the U.S. Navy had built its base during World War II, and from Scott's top deck we took in Bigfoot Slough, the ferry channel, and Bigfoot Island, where we have banded terns, and we could see just about everything in the eastern world from Portsmouth Island off to the south (where lay Beacon Island, Shell Castle, North Rock, and, on out, Royal Shoal) to way around toward Hatteras Inlet to the north (past Howard Reef and Clark Reef, Terrapin Shoal and Legged Lump). This was a fitting (and I dare say *fitten*) perch and prospect for the genial elder leftist who now found himself mainstreamed, chairing as he now did both the Ocracoke Water Association and the Ocracoke Foundation, which sought to keep the Ocracoke community both sustainable and sane, and which had brought us to town to sing for its Community Square Redevelopment Project. Less than a year later, the Ocracoke Foundation would succeed in purchasing the Community Square, its grocery and its docks, securing the town's center for the people.

This November Sunday morning, whitecaps cottoned the sound, a stout nor'east wind bearing down, and we three stayed aloft for only a very few minutes. A mite brisk, it was, and the early-afternoon ferry would soon be boarding.

"Right nice, Scott," I said just before we went below.

"Thank you," he said. "Come back when you can stay longer—anytime. My attractive blond neighbor says this deck's the best place in Ocracoke to sunbathe naked."

"And?" said Don.

"Well," Scott answered, sheepish now. "That *is* what she said. Haven't seen her up here yet, though."

The ferry ride back over to Swan Quarter was nothing like the easy ride out. Our course was west-northwest for most of the twenty-seven miles, and our starboard was taking a twenty-five- to thirty-knot northeast wind abeam. The ferryboat was both wallowing in troughs and banging behind the cresting waves—Don and I stood at the bow just behind the chains and wallowed and banged with the boat—better than any ride *ever* at the State Fair, we agreed.

"There is *some talking* going on up there," Don said, repeatedly glancing up at the men on the ferry's bridge. "They're working the phones and the radios, all right."

Presently, the boat came around southerly and went with the drift of the surf, maintaining this far-easier course till the captain got his craft inside the mouth of the Pamlico River, where the waters eased up on him and flattened out a bit. Only then did he turn northward for the ferry slip at Swan Quarter. When Don and I moved inside, someone called for a song, and after he fetched a small keyboard from the van, we happily obliged, for the occasion singing our bravado hurricane chorus, with the tinny ringing of Don's toy piano keeping time and sounding out every boatman's stoutest hope:

"Ain't gon blow me away, ain't gon blow me away!"

Working Watermen and Their Oysters

It was raining like hell in Beaufort one morning several days after Christmas 2012, and like hell it kept up all the way while we were driving U.S. 70 between the brimful ditches and canals of Down East Carteret County, heading for the Cedar Island ferry slip. The highway seemed only the barest of interruptions in this watery world. Though the rain lightened—just a tad—as we coursed alongside the vast Open Grounds Farm west of Sea Level, the way grew ever foggier, and as we rose over the Thoroughfare on the high flyover Gaskill Bridge and dropped down into the 11,000-acre Cedar Island Marshes, we saw only a mass of fog perhaps fifty yards ahead of us, and nothing else but gray road and canal waters. Even though we both knew well right where we were on the face of eastern Carolina earth, we still felt lost and even afloat in this misty morass.

Yet just a short while after the ferry (one of the two new models, with high cowling covering the cars) departed Cedar Island for Ocracoke, there came a bold fairing off, first from the east, presaged by bright, golden breaks in the clouds, then a brilliant sunny midday across the Pamlico, and to our surprise we soon found ourselves laughing with friends outside on the top deck. So the skies would stay, holding just so till we reached Big Foot Slough and moved into the hairpin channel first south, then north to the cut into Silver Lake, the Ocracoke harbor.

Ann and I found our rooms at the old Island Inn and then blithely strolled outside to walk our small dog.

One rarely knows what god or goddess one has offended, only that one has put a foot wrong with the deities. As we stepped onto Lighthouse Road, the weather recast itself in a trice, and suddenly fine rain now blew sideways, mistclouds roiling out of the cedar-bemused sideyards of the little shingled cottages. Any idea of standing outside and laughing now seemed ridiculous, and we turned on our heels at the small, chalk-white masonry Ocracoke Light and headed back to the inn, the poor, dishrag-damp little dog shaking herself to no avail.

"I don't know if they're going to move too many oysters on a day like *this*," I said to Ann as we got back in out of the weather, bone-chilled.

Just like a couple hundred other folks, we were out there on the edge of the world to eat oysters and chowder served up by the Ocracoke Working Watermen's Association at the last fishhouse on Ocracoke Island, which the watermen now owned. When South Point Seafood on Silver Lake went on the block in the spring of 2006, and the end of three centuries of true maritime culture out here was within sight, Ocracoke's three dozen fishermen and their legion of inspired allies went to work to save the fishhouse and within two and a half years had put together enough capital, including a $407,000 grant from the state's Golden Leaf Foundation, to do just that.

Their victory was a shot heard round the sounds and across the state, and beyond. And a powerful shot it was. Ocracoke's message was simply this: not *every* working waterfront was destined, if not doomed, to shut down and be reborn as exclusive condominiums walling the people off from their own public trust waters—*this* was what it looked like when the traditional arts and grassroots activism bucked the trend, and triumphed.

As to the weather, I turned out to be dead wrong about the fate of this day, and was quite happy to be.

A second fairing-off laid sun on the waters and on the droves of oyster eaters who descended on the fishhouse that afternoon, many of them armed with their own oyster knives, and partook of the dream that had come true. Tall Hardy Plyler, the leader of the fishhouse pack, welcomed all comers with vigor and boisterous camaraderie. The air was redolent of sound-country fish chowder and endless bushels of oysters, poured steaming hot out into huge mounds on picnic tables, and the rate of production was equaled by the rate of absorption.

"How on earth," Ann asked, when we were a mere eighty or a hundred oysters into the fray, "did we not bring our knives?" We had six or seven of them back in Beaufort.

"It was a singular lapse of judgment," I said, confessing while cracking open yet another one with a borrowed knife. "Mea culpa."

The next December, when Outer Bankers with cameras were chasing a rare snowy owl up and down the dunes, the record would clearly show that we returned very well armed indeed for the grand, year-end watermen's oyster roast on Silver Lake.

Mirabile dictu.

To Ocracoke

Last fall, Ann and I stayed for a spell in a small, cedar-shingled cottage on Mary Anns Pond, a covelet on the top side of Ocracoke village, looking out north toward Big Foot Slough and Howard's Reef three miles distant. Over time we saw Pamlico Sound in most of its humors. In a lakelike flat calm, we kayaked dreamily down the shore to the jungle of Springer's Point. One morning at breakfast on the porch, we marveled as a heavy thirty-second rain shower breezed by from the south and headed out quickly, a couple of minutes later a rainbow appearing over the Sound. When it blew twenty from the north, I could see through the binoculars five-foot waves coming in from their twenty-mile fetch and breaking over the reef, those powerful winds also slamming whitecaps straight into the bulkhead out front, blasting spray over the sea oats and salting the porch screens with a lens of haze.

Sleek, fishy cormorants lived on the eastern sand bald of Big Foot Island by the thousands, going to work early of a morning and returning in dark, endless, low-to-the-water streams late in the afternoon and covering that bald. Vastly outnumbered, brown pelicans lived in among the cormorants, sometimes rafting up with them halfway between Mary Anns Pond and the island, sometimes closer in. Once, an enormous flock of both birds flew right by the pond's docks so noisily that I heard them from the kitchen and ran out to watch the spectacle.

Mornings, we wrote and read steadily, happily, in the cottage ("Knotty pine makes for a pretty cozy living room," said daughter Cary), then ventured out into the grand autumn. Everywhere shiny green pennywort grew, some small as pence, some big as doubloons, and goldenrod and white and lavender asters, and, too, red-and-yellow gaillardia, here called Joe Bell flowers for the wandering Washingtonian watch repairman who wound up on Ocracoke a century ago and who spread these flowers like charms all over the island. The village was a slow-moving spot where traffic stopped for free-roving bands of mallards, and where the general darkness allowed visions of the Milky Way on clear nights right in town.

One bright October day, Scott boated us down Teach's Hole Channel and across Ocracoke Inlet to Portsmouth Island, where, back in the scrub, he kept a four-wheel Honda mule—through cedars and mosquitoes he drove us, past a long pond full of blue herons, then out onto the seabeach

*Sandy lane
to Quawk
Hammock,
October 2014*

and way down the strand, where we stopped (Scott serving up a cheerful champagne-and-lemonade concoction: "Oh man, it's *the* summer drink of Ocracoke") and strode and swam and climbed the dunes to see and survey the great wide open, ghost crabs bearing witness to it all.

Other days we drove up Ocracoke Island, to walk Scrag Cedar Road through the dunes and short, scrubby woods back to the sound. Or the Hammock Hills Trail, past orange-and-black monarch butterflies crowding the goldenrod, through the piney woods, the big forested dunes ("Ocracoke high country," Scott called it), along a soundside marsh and back around to Island Creek, where we saw a falcon stoop and dive at wood ducks too quick for him. Or the lane that led through the Six Mile Hammock woods and marsh on out to Quawk Hammock, long-ago haunt of the legendary cantankerous fisherman Old Quawk (or Quoke or Quork

Offering of feathers, beach at Springer's Point, December 2013

or Quark), who, when a bad storm was brewing and no one else would venture forth, took his boat out fishing alone, cursing God and the elements all the while, never to return. Some people caught out there when the famed San Ciriaco hurricane of 1899 blew fiercely through sheltered themselves with nothing more than a piece of a sail.

Several village fishermen now kept their skiffs ready to go on a creek at this secluded spot, and, back in town one morning, one of them told us a spectral tale:

"We saw a ghost up there, one morning in March, couple years ago, two of us waiting for the fog to clear and as it did a little, we saw about 250 yards out a man poling a skiff, wearing a sou'wester—we both saw him— the woman who fishes with me, she thinks it was a ghost, but I don't believe in that kind of thing. No dingbatter is gonna be way up there, though, so I don't know who, or *what*, it was. But we saw it, and he was definitely *pushing* that boat, no engine on it. There is one guy who gets out sometimes up that way, but I'm kind of afraid to ask him. Afraid to hear what he might say!"

Though the big Halloween weekend gale scarcely lessened on All Soul's Day, we still went out in it to search for a spirit of our own. Ann and cousin Sal and brother Tad and his wife Linda and I all walked the Jim Stephenson Trail, which meandered through the scrub and marsh and live-oak

Skiffs in marshes of Lower Parkers Creek, November 2014

wonders of Springer's Point, site of the old eighteenth-century Pilot Town, where the Springers of South Creek once settled and left a haunted house that no longer stands. Jim was Sal's late husband; had he lived, the great conservationist, who worked tirelessly for clean waters across our realm, would just be turning sixty-three. As we strode the trail in Jim's honor and memory, we also passed the graves of Virginia foundry magnate Sam Jones and his beloved horse Ikey D.—Jones once owned Springer's Point, and he had built the many-gabled Castle on the eastern side of Silver Lake with low-pitched stairs so that Ikey D. could live indoors, like family, and easily climb them.

Days later, afloat one afternoon on Parkers Creek, we paddled upstream under the N.C. 12 bridge, only to discover and disturb several cormorants lazily fishing the headwater shallows. Two of them flew right smack-dab past us, wingtips flapping the water, but a third, hungrier than his fellows, fished on without hesitation or cessation. We drifted downstream, past a lovely white Down East skiff with a rubber glove set upon the throttle, waving, and spent an hour or so around the creek's mouth. The cedar-green hammocks perched on the sound shore and in the marshes, and we ourselves went floating slowly alongside the needlerush, nothing but duck

Mushrooms in the sandhills, November 2014

blinds dotting the mighty waters beyond us for miles, the natural and the human seeming to touch each other out here in this glorious emptiness in a fine, graceful way.

Our last evening, during the hour before sunset, Scott got us up the island, and on a secret sandhills path we went snaking along ridges, between enormous myrtles and cedars, past a range of short dark mushrooms, over smoky-green moss, noting a faded red net float that served as a marker for one turn, past a big pear-pad cactus, and ultimately down to a small, spiritually impressive live-oak forest hidden near the soundside, the oaks growing hydralike, strangely interwoven, beautifully wild. From the high ridgetops, as we walked back, we watched the all-around sundown sky burning, all sand, forest, sound, and sea first glowing, then darkening and slowly vanishing before our eyes.

A huge, waning gibbous moon rose over the Oyster Creek marshes that night, and, at Hatteras Inlet beach the next morn, sunlight went bouncing aslant off the little tidal ponds. When we stopped to say farewell at the fishhouse, where Hardy Plyler and Morty Gaskill were overseeing the icing and packing of a fortune of flounder, we left by the grace of God and the working watermen with five pounds of greentail shrimp on ice, one big pompano, and four star-butters to boot.

The ferryboat soon pulled out of the creek, through the ditch, and up

Spreading live oak, Soundside Maritime Forest, November 2014

the channel through Big Foot Slough, and the cormorants and pelicans we had watched so closely for so long now paid us little mind as we went gliding by, the village and its aquamarine water tower and chalk-white lighthouse dropping away, hammocks and hills to the north fading too, as if our dream of many years had been nothing more than that, as if we had never seen any of it, nor been so deep within it for a time.

And yet we were, and would be again before the very year was out.

6

An Occurrence at Bear Creek Ford

When Bryan Grimes, the imposing Pitt County planter and former major general in the Army of Northern Virginia, one of the heroes of Robert E. Lee's Confederate command, awoke and arose that Saturday, August 14, 1880, he bade his wife Charlotte stay in bed—their two-month-old baby had kept her awake during the night. She dressed, even so, and came downstairs—he had finished his breakfast, and now she was having hers, and he asked her if she needed anything from town. He was bound from Grimesland, the family's Tar River plantation, nine miles into Washington, to attend the Beaufort County Democratic Convention in session there today.

Grimes, bearded and with a high forehead, dark hair over his ears, walked out to the top buggy, let all their children except the baby clamber aboard with him, held the littlest in his lap, and took the reins of the two gray horses in hand and drove to the Grimesland gate. There the children had to disembark, and they stood and waved as the buggy passed through the gate and moved east and disappeared, the clopping of the horses' hooves receding, muffled, rhythmic, till muted at last.

Miss Lou Gilliam, the governess, stood at the window watching it all, and she remarked to Charlotte: "I never saw anyone like General Grimes—he is so indulgent of his children."

At about six that evening, General Grimes and young Bryan Satterthwaite, fourteen years old, met at Bridgeman's store in Washington and climbed into the buggy, and when the general snapped the reins, the two grays pulled forward and headed back out into the country. The long, early evening light came at them as they slowly crossed the drawbridge (once owned and run for tolls by the general) over the river, where the Tar River yields its name and becomes the Pamlico, the sun bathing the river in gold off to their right and reddening the brick of the big old gable-roofed Havens and Fowle warehouses on the river-banks falling away behind them. They came up out of the long swamp, passed through the village of Chocowinity, and turned west. The general meant to leave the boy at his uncle's place—that was Colonel Stickney, Grimes's cousin—and be back at home with Charlotte and the children before darkness fell.

Presently the horses drew the buggy down toward Bear Creek, into a summer gloaming, the swamp full of water and the creek running high at the ford. Grimes shook the reins, the pair of grays lunging up out of Bear Creek and starting to climb the west bank, the swamp jungle right up close to the narrow lane on both sides.

And then the woods erupted with fire and smoke, a single shotgun blast cracking the swamp's silence like a cannon.

Full dark and the general was not back yet, but he would be soon. Charlotte Grimes sat in the relative cool of the parlor—the evening heat outside nowhere near breaking—and soon heard the horses pulling the buggy up the Grimesland lane from the gate and coming at a canter, then stopping sharply.

Well, he is home now, she thought, and she felt the heavy footsteps on Grimesland's front porch as much as heard them. *Why so many?* And then she heard the voice, not Bryan's but Colonel Stickney's:

"Mrs. Grimes! Charlotte!"

And so she walked to the front door and opened it and in a second saw Bryan's buggy and the pair of grays out beyond the men and saw their horses and then the colonel's ashen face, and before he even spoke her heart fell.

"Charlotte," Colonel Stickney leaned toward to her. "General Grimes is dead, there in the buggy. Someone shot him at Bear Creek—he was already gone when the boy got to my place."

Dead? Dead—dead.

"We brought the general to you as fast as we could."

The boy?

"Son?"

Bryan Satterthwaite stepped around from behind his uncle and stood and waited while the woman before him wept, thinking as a youth would that the weeping would end in some prescribed time but feeling too for the first time as a young man that he was in the presence of *forever*, something he had never before known of and now could never forget, that there was such a thing in this world as tears without end and he was seeing and hearing only the first welling up of them. He knew to wait, till his uncle gripped his shoulder, then eased his grip and said again:

"Son."

And now it was the boy's turn, and if he had ever before spoken so fast, he did not know when. He told everything, the swollen creek, the gunfire from the woods, the general calling out *"What are you doing there?"* to whomever it was that had lain in wait, and then saying to the boy, *"Bryan, I am shot"* and young Bryan asking *"Are you hurt badly?"* and General Grimes answering *"Yes, it will kill me"* just before he slumped and slid down onto the buggy's floor. Bryan Satterthwaite had gotten the reins in hand, driven the buggy up the hill from Bear Creek to the Carrow place, where not Carrow but Lucas Bates came out and helped Bryan get the general's legs back into the buggy so they could keep going, though Bates was sick and could not come along with him, and the boy had to drive on alone in the failing light, another two miles to his uncle's.

"And then we came on to Grimesland, ma'am."

That was all he had to tell, and the boy stopped there.

For a moment no one spoke. The cicadas sang, the tree frogs with them, and in the presence of this night choir the woman who had begun the day with her living man beside her wept and leaned against Colonel Stickney and took his arm and stepped forward toward the buggy.

"Don't tell the children just now."

Someone had already left on horseback for town, to fetch the nearest doctor there was. Nothing to be done for him now; nothing to be done for anything now but wait. Word was already out across the plantation, and some of the tenants had come around front, white and black commingled, not on the porch but just before it, respectful, curious, some standing in the outer dark, some in the faint light coming through the windows.

It would be past midnight before the doctor from town could come over the river and get out to Grimesland. He would enter the old home and study the corpse and see where a single shot had enter the general's upper left arm and passed through it into his side, and the doctor knew at once what had happened, a severing of the left subclavian artery, with massive internal bleeding and virtually immediate death. If he had known any pain, the doctor would assure Charlotte Grimes, he had not known it long.

They would bury the general in the graveyard at Grimesland on Monday, two days hence, his old warhorse Warren bearing his army saddle and gray coat from the war as he came plodding along behind the hearse. But before that, at first light Sunday morning, Colonel Stickney and whoever else he could gather would get down to Bear Creek and set about seeing just who had done this.

Just who it was that had ambushed and killed General Bryan Grimes.

At dawn Sunday morning, this quartet of men went with Colonel Stickney as he drove his buggy to Bear Creek: J. M. Carrow, Lucas Bates, Kit Bright, and Captain J. J. Laughinghouse, a neighbor and friend and ally of General Grimes, and a Ku Klux Klansman as well. They backed the buggy down to the ford and positioned it just above the creekwaters, which had receded five or six feet from the previous evening's higher water, and then went into the thick woods just off to the buggy's left, and took a look.

A few branches had been broken off to make for a clear shot. The assailant, it appeared to these men, had been standing in a foot of water just behind, or beside, an enormous cypress tree, a mere twelve or thirteen feet from the road, which was only twelve to fifteen feet wide by Stickney's calculations. Studying and following what he called "a direct line to the road," he went to its far side and found holes in a tree there, and with his knife dug out a ball of buckshot that would undoubtedly match the ten or twelve balls Bryan Satterthwaite would find in the ribs of General Grimes's buggy top.

Major General
Bryan Grimes,
CSA

Colonel Stickney's search party strode upstream through the swamp to the place where it made sense to them the shooter would come up out of the water—but the ground there was covered with pinestraw, and they could make no tracks. At a branch farther on, though, they found plain tracks—made by a round-toed, broad-heeled shoe, a size 6 or 7, said the colonel . . . "fan-footed, toes turned out," said Laughinghouse—and those tracks led away to the southwest. Bates and Carrow and Laughinghouse all agreed: they knew but one man in this part of the country who walked that way, a man in his early twenties who lived with his father in a small settlement southwest of where they stood, over at the head of Grimes's millpond.

That man's name was William Parker.

William Parker went to church at Black Jack that Sunday, and, later that same day, John Mayo saw him at the Paramore brothers' store at Nelson's Crossroads, about a mile from where Parker lived and not far from Grimesland. In the few hours since Colonel Stickney's group had searched the woods, talk had flown around the countryside that Parker was already suspected and might be implicated in the murder of General Grimes. At the store, Mayo asked him bluntly:

"Why did you kill General Grimes?"

Parker was twenty-two years old, a blue-eyed, dark-haired man who stood five-seven, weighing about 165 pounds. He was thin-lipped, and he worked his square jaw on a chaw of tobacco, answering cryptically:

"He had lived long enough."

And then Parker posed a question of his own: "Was he shot with a gun or with a pistol?" Parker told Mayo he had heard it both ways at church earlier that day.

Soon, after being arrested and questioned and released, William Parker had words with each of the two men, John W. Blount and A. C. Saunders, who kept a store at Chocowinity, across the river from Washington. Blount had been away the weekend of Grimes's killing and did not see Parker until the Thursday afterward, August 19.

"I'm glad to see you out of jail," Blount told him, and Parker replied, "Yes sir, I did not stay in long."

They walked into the store together, and Parker asked Blount if he could attest that Parker had been at the store on the day General Grimes was shot.

"No," said Blount, who had been in Morehead City seventy-five miles away at that time. Later Thursday evening, over the river in Washington, Parker again made this same request of Blount, and again he was refused.

"Well," said Parker, "if I can't prove it by you, I can by your partner, Saunders."

What Parker did not say was that Saunders had already, two days earlier, turned Parker down in his request for an alibi.

Blount said the store's ledger-books would tell if William Parker had been there, and he went back to the store and checked.

Nothing. Not a thing about Parker having been there at any time on Saturday, August 14. Blount could not, and would not, corroborate Parker's having been at his store.

A week or so later, Parker asked A. C. Saunders a second time if he would attest to Parker's being at the Chocowinity store when General Grimes was killed, and the store's second owner refused him a second time.

William Parker had now tried each of the storekeepers twice. Come what may, neither man was willing to lie for him.

Another time at Paramore's store, Parker came in from a squirrel hunt, talking up his shotgun, saying in the hearing of all that this was the gun that had shot one Johnstone Mills. Neither of the Paramores was there to hear this, though—a *Tarboro Southerner* article five days after Grimes's murder, implying their possible involvement in "the bloody deed," prompted their flight from the area and disappearance before the next day was done.

After a drink inside the store, J. T. Smith caught Parker at the door on the way out and said, "You say this is the gun that shot Johnstone Mills, and I suppose the gun that killed General Grimes?"

Parker only winked and tapped Smith on the shoulder, and the two men walked around out back of Paramore's and stood hidden by lumber stacked there. Parker asked Smith to repeat what he had said out front, which he did.

"This," Parker then allowed, "is the gun that killed General Grimes."

"Who handled it?" Smith asked.

"That's enough for you to know," replied Parker.

"Who?" Smith insisted.

But William Parker said no more.

Parker did not need to speak further—he seemed to have said quite enough already. And there was the matter of that splayed-out, "fan-footed" track leading away from the scene of the assassination, witnessed by Colonel Stickney and his posse the morning after the shooting.

A detective and former Washington policeman named Fowler spoke to the black man Dick Chapman, who had been turpentining in the woods near Bear Creek with William Parker on the day General Grimes was ambushed. Chapman sang a song of Parker's leaving that work and going off after Grimes, with such detail and conviction that Fowler had Chapman locked up in Washington for safekeeping on Sunday, September 19, 1880.

On Monday, September 20, 1880, William Parker was arrested on suspicion and held, too, in the Washington jail, where his lawyer James Shepherd came to visit him alone. Also, according to Dick Chapman, who was in a nearby cell, lawyer Shepherd told Chapman to speak no more of what he knew. By the time a grand jury indicted Parker, on December 4, 1880, for the murder of General Bryan Grimes, Chapman—who seemed to have known so much about the events of August 14 at Bear Creek—no longer figured as a witness in the case.

The state went ahead and tried Parker immediately in Washington, in Beaufort County, but one juror fell out ill from nervous prostration, and the case quickly ended in mistrial. Then they changed the venue and moved the whole affair twenty-odd miles north to Williamston in Martin County, and tried Parker again the next June.

The prosecution's witnesses trooped through, told what they knew, what they had heard. Parker sat and listened and chewed tobacco, and whispered often with lawyer Shepherd, who wanted the case seen as that of a lowly woodland laborer unjustly set upon and unfairly accused for the killing of a wealthy planter. Of the twelve men in the jury box, Shepherd did not want to see a single clean shirt among them.

Young Bryan Satterthwaite took the stand and testified that he thought he made out someone in the brush that August evening, and thought it had been Parker, though he also said, "It was light enough to see a man a little ways but not light enough to distinguish one." Could he really have identified a figure in the dusky roadside jungle after the gun roared at them? General Grimes, sitting to young Bryan's left, had been between Bryan and the woods from which the shot had come, blocking his view, and Parker's lawyers swarmed over the boy—how could he have seen anything to the buggy's left? What had he meant by that remark? Bryan had barely been able to control the frightened horses, which galloped up to Carrow's home near the top of the hill before the boy could rein them in.

Bryan Satterthwaite had no comeback to the tack of Parker's attorneys, and they wore him out.

No one alive had, in fact, seen Parker standing in the brush. No one had seen him fire the gun.

Still, the prosecution had a ring of circumstance to close around Parker, though, and close it did.

Storekeeper Blount testified that Parker told him he had "taken dinner with Sam Dixon," and after dinner had gone with Dixon and stayed with Dixon all night "the day General Grimes was killed." Yet Dr. J. A. Arthur, a Main Street, Washington, merchant said he "saw Sam Dixon several times in town on the day of the murder—between five and six p. m. saw him in front of my store," drunk, and "lying on a goods box, with the reins of his horse in his hand."

Richard Mills said he had seen Parker's dog, a yellow half-fice with ears that stuck straight up and a "short thick body," near Bear Creek on the evening of the murder.

Edward Smallwood had seen Parker at Blount's store on the second

Monday after Grimes's murder—"I noticed the fact that he wore shoes two sizes too large for him."

John Keel, in the Washington jail for the theft of a pair of pants and $1.30, was still doing time when Parker was arrested on suspicion the previous fall and thrown into the same cell with Keel. "Parker talked freely to me," said Keel, repeating what he alleged Parker had told his cellmate: "'I drank too much on the day at Paramore's store and talked too much to Smith.'" He blamed Smith for getting him locked up. According to Keel, Parker admitted that he had fired his gun on August 14, reloaded it with buckshot, and left Dick Chapman—with whom he was working in the woods, chipping turpentine boxes—and went down to Bear Creek, where he "broke out a place as wide as two hands and waited for General Grimes to pass along." He knew the Grimes buggy and shot at him, then waited ten or fifteen minutes and walked home. When he attended church on the next day, he acted as if he knew nothing about the killing of General Grimes.

So testified John Keel, convicted thief, under oath.

On Saturday, June 18, fourth day of the trial, Walter S. Dickinson testified that he went into the Washington jail on the prodding of Grimes's friend Captain Laughinghouse—"He told me I might get something out of Parker." Dickinson said that Parker asked him if people thought he would be hanged, and that Parker mused, "If I confess, wouldn't that play hell with the witnesses?" He added that if he did confess, it would hang storekeeper Howell Paramore. Parker could not stop, according to Dickinson: he said he would confess it was Howell Paramore who had put him up to killing General Grimes, advising Parker that if he did not perform this murder, Paramore would turn on him and do him in. Further, Paramore—Dickinson testified Parker had told him—had left money to pay for Parker's trial.

Incriminating evidence, or simple hearsay?

Dickinson was the state's last witness.

Judge Gilmer called a recess, after which defense cocounsel James Edward Moore stood and stated flatly that the state had failed to make a case against William Parker and then said:

"The prisoner will introduce no evidence."

The defense rested, and those in the Williamston courtroom were shocked.

Court would stand adjourned till Monday, when closing arguments were made and the case sent to the jury. On Tuesday, June 21, the jury stayed out from 2 P.M. until 7 P.M., then filed in and, to the clerk of court's query, responded:

"Not guilty."

Again the crowd was astonished, only Parker's friends nodding and speaking in approval—the judge ordered the sheriff to arrest anyone making further noise. Parker sat quietly, as he had for the whole of the six-day trial, chewing tobacco, his stolid demeanor unchanging. The popular eastern Carolina Judge Gilmer glared at the twelve good men and true, but his ire changed nothing.

The Martin County jury had let William Parker walk.

Many said, of course, that Parker had just gotten away with murder. Talk was that to keep General Grimes from testifying in a criminal matter, a house-burning and well-poisoning case stemming from Grimes's bitter boundary-line dispute with the storekeeping Paramore brothers, Parker had been paid by them to silence Grimes. Talk was that for a hundred dollars and a saddle horse and a new suit of clothes, Parker had ambushed the Confederate hero. In time, incredibly, he even came to say it of himself, boasting when he was in his cups of killing the general, and so his loose tongue got him both the brief attention of his fellow inebriates and a long-standing notoriety among the citizenry beyond the barrooms.

Neither of the Paramores, Howell or W. B., could add to, or gainsay, the word of William Parker. For Howell had lain down in a South Carolina hotel room in May of 1881, taken a straight razor, and slit his own throat. W. B., while staging a robbery in faraway Baltimore in 1884, had gotten himself killed.

Where did—where *would*—such a man as Parker go for years on end, to lay low, thinking things might blow over, that dust might settle, that somehow people who loved the general—this man in full who everyone knew had by God guarded Lee's very retreat from Gettysburg, who had fought at Seven Pines and Chancellorsville and in the Valley Campaign and had seven horses shot out from under him, and who would have taken his regiment and galloped away from Appomattox to go south and join Joe Johnston in Carolina against Sherman, if to do so under a flag of surrender would not have disgraced General Lee—that somehow people would forget and leave off with their suspicions, that they would somehow have a change of heart about Parker, this man who had been heard uttering callously, dismissively, of Grimes:

"He had lived long enough."

Strong feelings among the people over the loss of such a man, a southern war hero, were like iron, and so they lasted, and gave no quarter.

Now came the *Beta*, homeport New Bern, a seventy-seven-foot, forty-ton steamboat built in Washington the year before, plying up the Pamlico

River toward the Tar very early on the morning of Tuesday, March 13, 1888, about 3 A.M. As it passed Castle Island and slowed and cruised on up to the bridge, the pilot blew his whistle, signaling the bridge tender to open the draw.

But as the tender tried to do so, the draw lodged and would not swing clear.

When the bridge tender investigated, he found something heavy blocking the bridge, hanging from one of the draw's crosstimbers and keeping the draw from cranking open in the middle of the night.

This dead weight was the body of a man.

William Parker, stolen out of custody in the Washington jail (where he lay, arrested on a charge of drunk and disorderly conduct only the afternoon before, after he had stood on a nearby street corner bragging to a crowd that he was the man who had killed General Bryan Grimes and been found not guilty of it and could not be tried again for the same crime) only an hour earlier by a group of at least a half a dozen masked men, the old black jailer unable to stop them in the dark from wrenching the lock off the cell that held Parker or even to identify any of them (though Captain Joseph John Laughinghouse would later be said to have been among the men who told the jailer on pain of death to remember none of this, and none of them either), was now hanging dead from the river bridge, lynched at the hands of persons who would be forever unknown, unsought, unchallenged, uncharged.

When the rope was cut and Parker's body, noose tight around its neck, fell to the deck of the *Beta*, the steamboat crew found a placard pinned to the chest of his corpse, bearing this clear and present legend:

"Justice at Last."

7

Contentnea Creek

Tuscarora War

At the edge of a two-lane blacktop in Greene County now stands a tall, bright silver, polished-steel arch, a very recent addition to the lane and the farm fields, a commemorative much of whose legend is inscribed in Tuscarora, for it was they who suffered a final and tragic loss at their fort—Neoheroka, or Nooherooka—that once stood beside Fort Run, a branch of Contentnea Creek nearby. No one who lives here between Stantonsburg and Snow Hill now reads or speaks Tuscarora, nor has anyone done so for three centuries, as the fall of Fort Nooherooka in March 1713 not only marked the end of the Tuscarora War, but also meant the end of these people in this land.

The fearless eighteenth-century adventurer John Lawson, back from his daring, freewheeling 1701 arc of exploring the Carolinas from the mouth of Santee River to the future gold country near present-day Charlotte and then over to Pamlico River, gained a common-law bride in Hannah Smith, a planter's daughter, and then lived peacefully and in a state of natural love with Hannah among the Tuscarora Indians of eastern North Carolina.

For a time.

Whatever they thought of the little grid he had laid upon the tiny peninsula in Bath Creek, creating Bath, North Carolina's first town, in 1705, the Tuscarora apparently did not begrudge him much, for John and Hannah next moved a little to the south and settled on a piece of another peninsula, on a creek now called Lawson's Creek near the confluence of the Trent and Neuse Rivers, where the Tuscarora had a village named Chattoka.

No idler he, Lawson spent his non-hunting-and-gathering time composing an account of the amazing trek he had undertaken within days of his arrival in the New World, his significant, expressive, even exuberant observations on flora, fauna,

Tuscarora Memorial, near the site of Fort Neoheroka on Fort Run off Contentnea Creek, N.C. 58 between Snow Hill and Stantonsburg, December 2014

and native humanity and language here in Carolina, such as he found it. He would take himself and his manuscript back to London, the city he had not seen in nearly a decade, and publish it as *A New Voyage to Carolina* in 1709, promptly and successfully using his popular tome as a prospectus for colonization.

In 1710, Lawson and his new, monied partner, the Swiss baron Christoph von Graffenried, ferried hundreds of Palatine refugees from London to Chesapeake Bay, then brought them (those who had survived the voyage) overland south across the Carolina swamp country and pine barrens to their new home at Chattoka, which, honoring the underwriter of this venture, they promptly renamed:

New Berne.

During this fall and winter, the Tuscarora came to see Lawson no longer as an explorer or, like them, a man of the wilderness. They now viewed him as a land developer.

They now viewed him as a mortal threat.

Perhaps, when Lawson and the baron boated up the Neuse River in the early fall of 1711, they really were in search of wild grapes, Lawson's pitch to von Graffenried to get him to make that trip. Scuppernong, our native grape, would have been in near riot in September, and the leaders of the newest and biggest town in Carolina might have had a boatload of them, just for the shaking of a few riverside vines. Perhaps Lawson sought another site for another settlement. Whatever his motivations, whatever they thought they were going toward, Lawson could not have known how severe his miscalculations were, or what they were really leading him into.

First off, the Tuscarora captured Lawson's scouts, a pair of African Americans going along the south bank of the Neuse in advance of Lawson and the baron, ostensibly to set up camps for them along the upstream way. Then sixty Indians swarmed upon Lawson's party afloat, and caught them too, and carried them to one of their towns along a main Neuse River tributary from the north, Contentnea Creek.

There at Catechna, King Hancock's town, the Tuscarora in council tried these men, first deciding to free them the next day (what difference would it make, given the Tuscarora's immediate plans?), but then, because Lawson lost his temper and exploded in the morning at his accuser Core Tom, chief of the coastal Coree, determining in a second session to put them to death. Baron von Graffenried talked his way out of it, though, by invoking the vicious rain of fury that the great queen across the waters would bring down upon them if they did him in.

They knew Lawson far better than they knew the baron, and they blamed Lawson all the more for what was happening in Chattoka.

So let him be a lesson for all the white people.

Let us be done with him.

Bring him to Catechna's central fire. Let the singing and dancing of war begin. Let the women weave pitch pine needles into the flesh of his forehead and temples, around the back of his head, wherever else on his body they may please.

Then light them afire.

Light *him* afire.

John Lawson of London, England; of Bath, North Carolina; of Chattoka, Tuscarora Nation, lately of New Berne, North Carolina, was dead, tortured to a death by fire by the Tuscaroras and their allies—warriors of the Bay River, Machapunga, Neusiok, Coree, Woccon, and Pampticough tribes— massed for war at Catechna on Contentnea Creek.

John Lawson was only the first victim of this Tuscarora War. On September 22, 1711, the Native Americans rampaged—within days, 130 settlers were slaughtered: 80 infants, women staked to cabin floors, vicious mutilations, and a message of terror supreme.

The next eighteen months . . .

North Carolinians were pitifully unprepared for the Tuscaroran onslaught, yet the Tuscarora themselves would in turn soon feel a wrath they may not have expected either. Twice, forces from South Carolina—Englishmen bolstered by huge Native American contingents hostile to the Tuscarora—came north to help out and fight for the beleaguered Carolinians.

Colonel John Barnwell led a handful of white militiamen and hundreds of Yamasee, Pee Dee, Appalachee, Waxhaw, Congaree, and Wateree natives in fighting the Tuscarora to a standstill and surrender in early 1712.

And when this less-than-complete defeat did not hold, the Tuscarora erupting again by summer, a second army, under Colonel James Moore and with a thousand natives, soon marched into eastern Carolina to put an end to the troubles. Moore's force in March 1713 moved well up the valley of Contentnea Creek and besieged the Tuscarora stronghold there: Fort Nooherooka hard by Fort Run not far from the run's mouth into the creek, just a few miles north of present-day Snow Hill.

Why did the Tuscarora not use their protected water source, Fort Run, as an escape route, and carry themselves away by night?

Why did they wait in place, as if they now knew they were doomed, till Moore mercilessly filled Nooherooka with shot and fire, killing half the nearly one thousand men, women, and children holed up within before overrunning the stockade and capturing the rest? And then sending the captured off to a Bertie County reservation, where they and their descendants lived for the rest of the eighteenth century before moving north to New York and their Iroquois kin, their long-ago presence remembered now only by the name of a township there: *Indian Woods.*

Never again after the fall of Nooherooka would Native Americans seriously threaten the European settlement of North Carolina, as they had up and down this valley. Charred remnants of this horror, pieces of the fort, charcoaled peaches, musket shot lay in the hallowed ground, where so many perished, for 280 years, till the scholars and the students from East Carolina University disinterred it all, found and sifted the shards of this stark past.

Near where the tall, bright arch now stands, twenty-seven miles north and eighteen months away from the Catechna killing of Lawson, the embattled enclave at Fort Run and Contentnea Creek enacted the last stand of the Tuscarora. Three centuries would pass before words and songs in

Longhouse and corn, Tuscarora Memorial

their native tongue were in the air again over this consecrated land. Tuscarora from New York and Tuscarora from Carolina converged and sang here at the arch's dedication, testifying and signifying that this place was not dead and long gone to them, but, rather, that it remained as an abiding sacred space held tightly within—and with a grip hard upon—their hearts.

The Strange Tale of James Glasgow

At Sheppard's Ferry Road, between Stantonsburg and Snow Hill, stands a silver marker with black lettering telling the world just a word or two about James Glasgow, a late eighteenth-century North Carolina politician.

Decades after the Tuscarora War, Colonel Abraham Sheppard—a colonial settler with a plantation along Contentnea Creek and a ferry across Fort Run Swamp—protected his assets by fighting in the Battle of Moore's Creek Bridge and then joining Washington at Valley Forge. Sheppard had met a young factor in Suffolk, Virginia, named James Glasgow, and when Glasgow came down to Contentnea country to visit the landed Sheppard family he in turn met and fell in the limelight of the good colonel's daughter Pherebe.

This pair married, and Colonel Sheppard gave them a plantation, Fairfield, along Contentnea Creek. James Glasgow also fell into politics and Revolutionary War service alongside his father-in-law, was popular with patriots, and in 1777 got himself elected to the brand new rebellious land's office of secretary of state, North Carolina's very first.

So far, so good for this young man on the rise.

Secretary Glasgow would have one main job: doling out huge acreages in what would become Tennessee to Revolutionary War veterans as payment for putting up the good, successful fight against the king. Glasgow would serve in this post for twenty years, during which time his grateful state, in 1791, peeled off a portion of Dobbs County and named it for him:

Glasgow County in the valley of Contentnea Creek.

What a fine ring the name has to it, and we would all know and call it out that way still, but for one thing, one magnificent dark mark:

Secretary Glasgow had certainly been dealing in western lands, just not in the fair, intended way. Deeds that were virtually negotiable instruments, duplicate deeds, signings over of large tracts by veterans tricked by their conniving drinking companions—the tales of systematic, fraudulent technique were hideous, and massive in scope. Glasgow had colluded with other men, including his kin, to defraud veterans of their legitimate claims and to steer between 600,000 and 700,000 acres into the undeserving hands of speculators, including himself.

When a letter bearing witness to this went from the hand and pen of future President Andrew Jackson to Governor Samuel Ashe and the North Carolina legislature in 1797, Glasgow's house of duplicitous cards collapsed.

"An angel has fallen!" the governor declared to his Council of State, moving quickly against Glasgow.

As indeed he should have: Glasgow and his cohorts even attempted to burn down the state capitol and thereby destroy the records that would prove their guilt and seal their fates. Governor Ashe foiled that plot, though, and Glasgow was indicted and convicted of the fraud that has ever since borne his name. Due to this scandal, that name was quickly torn from Contentnea Creek's short-lived Glasgow County, which was renamed in 1799 for the hero of the Battle of Guilford Courthouse: General Nathanael Greene.

As Marlowe said of Faustus, "Cut is the branch that might have grown full straight." James Glasgow and family slunk off to Tennessee, where he had over twenty ignominious years to think about it all before dying in 1820, divorced forever from his state, his standing, and his good name, across a great, permanent divide from Fairfield, from Sheppard's Ferry, far, far away from Contentnea Creek.

Crawfish hole, Little Contentnea Creek at Scuffleton, April 2014

Along the Valley in Spring

We stopped, Ann and I, late one April morning, and pulled the car down toward Little Contentnea Creek, past two old brick churches side by side at Scuffleton, two buildings almost twins with their squared-off towers—the Little Creek United American Free Will Baptist Church and the Little Creek Church of Christ Disciples of Christ, a legend at the latter reading:

"Where Everybody Is Somebody."

Down a short path, a cadre of cypress knees sprouted in the creek's twenty-yard-wide muddy flood plain, and pollen and oak flowers floated lazily by in the slow-moving dark brown water, dappled in the late morning sun. A hatch of water bugs went tearing around on the surface, springtime celebrants of creation and all its attendant energies, cutting concentric circles into Little Contentnea Creek, designing their world just as they wished it.

A good-sized redbud lay all lavendered out on the opposite bluff, an extraordinarily welcome sight after the state's, and the South's, brutal winter

77

of 2013–14, yet my eyes were drawn to a different, smaller creekside sight the likes of which I have known all my life: the two-inch-tall, gray-balled mud of a crayfish tower, a sign of health and hope in the watery world. We tarried a bit in this glade, and then, as we were about to depart, here came one of the grand, archetypal twosomes ever devised: an older, wizened man and a younger bearded one, slowly driving past us, waving, in a red pickup truck with "The Barn King" advertised on its side.

Together, they slid a small green canoe with a pair of fishing poles in it out of the truck bed, and walked it down to the waterside.

And went fishing.

Several miles downstream of Scuffleton, the so-called Little Creek joins Contentnea Creek itself, and Ann and I strolled out to the confluence, the trail to it absolutely littered with the lemony blossoms of yellow Carolina jessamine and, nearby, a big dogwood stood in full bloom, white and delicate as a veil in the woods. The day before, Ann had been out here to Bray Hollow, a nature preserve, on a North Carolina Coastal Land Trust field trip, and she had heard from one of the Brays that this point was where the Tuscarora had done in John Lawson.

That this place was King Hancock's town: Catechna.

No town here now. Nothing but the name Lawson Trail on a board sign even vaguely suggested anything about the great struggle and awful bloodlettings of long ago, the Tuscarora War. Even in all this bright midday spring light, with the jessamine laying its golden twinings into the pines everywhere about, the air so fresh with promise eight ways from Sunday, there were dark threads, too, behind and beneath it all. *If* one but knew of them.

Yet the warblers choiring away in the trees, just back from the Tropics and ready to breed and happy to be, sang not of such things. In song, as in flight, they rose above it all.

Contentnea Creek ran about sixty yards wide at the confluence, and the slower flow of the lesser creek poured steadily into the more rapid downstream motion of the greater. A light westerly breeze came at us at the point, carrying us away into the light, rippling the sun on the water and making diamonds more perfect than any Solomon ever brought forth from his ancient, legendary mine.

Lunch at Ayden's Skylight Inn set us up for the afternoon. From beneath the silvered capitol dome atop the small brick restaurant, we came forth with a pair of medium pork trays, featuring compressed, gnawable, sui

Confluence of Little Contentnea and Contentnea Creek, looking upriver, near Ayden, April 2014

generis cornbread, and the pair of mottos that made the Skylight all the good that it was: "If it's not cooked with wood, it's not BBQ" and "85 Years—Unchanged." We ate out back off the car hood, parked as we were between a fresh collards shack, an eighth-of-an-acre pile of split wood, and an old wagon, the Skylight's parade-symbol of its origins way back when Pete Jones's great-grandfather sold chopped pork off a covered wagon to field hands and town clerks, first come, first served.

Grifton down the road, the former rail- and steamboat hub just above Contentnea's mouth into the Neuse River, was preparing for the Shad Festival, moving small carnival rides and funnel-cake purveyors and a T-shirt painter's booth into place. This gathering had been going on for forty years, and drew its emblematic slogan from a crude yet effective piece of graffiti someone back in the 1970s had painted high on the town's old silver metal bridge, featuring a fish skeleton and the imperative "Eat Mo' Shad." The only shad that visitors were likely to see these days, though, would be frozen exemplars brought out of coolers for use in the big shad toss down by Contentnea Creek, those and yellow construction-paper silhouettes taped up in store windows around town. Essence of the festival's piscatorial stew was catfish, fine enough in its own mustachioed way, but not shad. The tawny, stuccoed, old 1933 St. Jude's Spanish Mission–style chapel, built for Catholics with a New York widow's cash but now serving Free Will Baptists, sat improbably high on a hill at Queen and Highland, and looked down upon it all, silent, bemused.

Valley tourists, we motored on, up Skeeter Pond Road to Edwards Bridge, there to linger watching swallows at work on their nests beneath a steel-girder-and-concrete span, the birds chittering away, high-pitched, and paying Ann and me no mind. Crows called out and cackled constantly. Fishing line dangled off a low cypress limb, and we lazily followed a streamside trail a couple hundred yards upstream to a fishing and swimming hole.

A right nice boat ramp lay just downstream of Edwards Bridge, and a pair of men in a gray camouflaged jonboat came on in to land while we were there. One of them hopped out and backed pickup and trailer down to the river's edge, the trailer far enough into the water for the man in the stern to try and drive on. He sat high up on a bass-fishing seat, and his height and weight and the steep angle of the ramp, as well as the weight of the motor, depressed the transom and pushed it dangerously low and, at moments, under the water—the very landing of the boat threatened to sink it. The pilot tried, backed off, tried again, and again, each time with water sloshing over the transom. No dock committee, no matter how critical, really wants to see a sinking, and after several minutes we eased our car away, saying simultaneously to each other:

"Can't watch any more of this."

Later that day, Ann and I were lounging on a dock at the Hookerton wildlife ramp, being afternoon quiet, not saying much but marveling at Contentnea's broad width and flow, a good eighty feet and moving fast, oak flowers and yellow jessamine flowers dotting its surface this early April day. No less a marvel that, two hundred years ago, this sleepy hamlet somehow boasted three flourishing academies.

We hung out there awhile, dangling our feet just inches above the water, when an old-timer eased up, causing our small dog to leap into action, barking to beat the band, if there had been a band, and waking up this somnolent scene. He said he lived in a trailer just across the street, and he soon made sure we knew he was not a native.

"I'm from New Jersey," he stated flatly. "My daughter married down here, and I followed her."

He was just getting out of the house, he said. Didn't really do any fishing, so didn't know what kind of fish lived in the stream.

"Tell you one thing, though. I came down here not too long ago, saw a great big snake in the water. Eight feet long, sure was. Well, guess I'll be going back to the house." And then he slowly strolled up the modest hill toward his trailer.

No sooner had he ambled off than a middle-aged man with two younger women in tow showed up. This man, dressed in T-shirt, jeans and ball cap, carried a light-gauge fishing rod with spinning reel, a very small rubber worm, about the size of a beetle spin, on his line, and no other bait. The young women drifted on down to the water, while the man genially asked us where we were from and what we were up to. When we told him we were studying the river, and that we had already stopped downstream at Grifton and at the confluence of the Little Contentnea and the Contentnea, and at Edwards Bridge, he seemed genuinely appreciative, and he confided in us, telling us about a big reserve on one of Contentnea's tributaries upstream, outside Snow Hill.

"They say they catch these big monstrous five-pound bream in there," he said, shaking his head, "breaking twenty-pound-test line! But I've lived here all my life and I'm forty-nine years old and it's not been many places I haven't fished, and I never caught no monstrous bream yet! One pound, two pound, that's about it."

Better an agreeable skeptic than an officious braggadocio.

"Well," he said, looking toward the river.

"Good luck," I said, as he turned for the dock.

"Thanks," he said, grinning over his shoulder and giving his rod a shiver. "I'm gonna need it!"

8

The Trent

Nace Brock

In the country of the upper Trent River, south of Kinston, west of New Bern, something there is that is nicely asymmetrical, cockeyed even, about the little community of Comfort, North Carolina, lying so hard by Purgatory Pocosin.

How did one Ignatius Wadsworth Brock, a boy born and raised here in this back-country world during Reconstruction, choose to go off to art school at Cooper Union in New York, and learn to capture the world with glass plates? What brought him back home to work for the Gerock Studio in New Bern, where the Trent joins the Neuse, and to marry fellow Jones Countian Ora Koonce, only then to espy Asheville while on honeymoon and settle there, becoming the famed, innovative, pool-hall-loving photographer Nace Brock? How does artistic genius arise in the way-out-yonder plantations and piney woods be-twixt and between flat-landed comfort and purgatory, only to find and realize itself fully in the great blue hills faraway? Brock was an old-time bohemian, prefiguring by a century the Buncombe beats of the here and now, an artist with an atti-tude, believing it better that a high-flying, wasp-waisted, early twentieth-century socialite wait unattended in Nace's studio at the appointed hour than Nace let a fine game of eight-ball in a watering hole just across the street go unshot.

What about this Brock, this unkempt little blue-eyed, bearded man of whom Doug Reed once wrote: "he slept in his clothes" and made "a bag of peaches a meal"? What sort of man "walked in the pouring rain as though it were sun-shine"? And made hay whether portraying the chivalry of Bun-combe (he shot the Vanderbilt girls) or the landscape of the Smokies (at times he depicted nude women gazing lazily upon great gorges)? If Ashevilleans cussed him for slovenliness and disregard of appointments and protocols, they still paid him royally—at his price, on his schedule—for his art.

Nace Brock's On Scott's Creek, *late nineteenth century, just below the confluence of the Trent and the Neuse at New Bern*

He was a man comfortable with discomfort, and purgatory was neither here nor there to him. Trent River water ran in his veins, even in the land of the French Broad, and something there was in it that made him an artist, a poet too, one who, mountain life and success notwithstanding, also left behind lowland scenes aplenty, homage and echoes of his Trent River youth, where and when he first chalked a cue.

Nice break, Nace Brock.

Brock's Mill Pond

Nace might have been the first of his tribe to make it out that far west. His father Isaac was a lifelong planter in Jones County, and, at about the same late-1890s time Nace was settling in Asheville, his kinsman Furnifold Brock bought an eighteenth-century gristmill (Hatch's, later McDaniel's Mill) in Jones County, and put his own name on it. Brock's Mill Pond is a 122-acre cypress reserve behind a dam holding back both spring waters and Crooked Run Creek, flowing out of the Hofmann Forest, and the old mill still stands on the south side of Trenton, just a few yards west of N.C. 58, all but impossible for travelers to miss.

Unlike the Trent River itself, which flows obscurely above, behind, and

around county seat Trenton. Many who have driven through the small town regularly may never have known that a river wound so close by it, though it certainly asserted itself in the fall of 1999. That was when Hurricane Dennis first filled the basins of eastern Carolina, and then Hurricane Floyd came in on top of that, dropping twenty inches of rain in twenty-four hours and flooding the eastern land wholesale: 18,000 square miles of it.

Water was already starting to sheet the town's streets at daybreak Friday, September 17, 1999, and by that afternoon the whole of Trenton—Brock's Mill Pond and all—was in the Trent River, and no one could have doubted the river's presence any longer, or its meaning in the life of the town.

But floods recede, even high waters as epic and disastrous as Floyd's.

In more recent years the old mill has had its foundation shored up with concrete, its milldam cleaned up, its siding replaced. Children flock to the banks of the millpond to learn how to cast a hook and line. The Friends group sells prints of Brock's Mill Water Ground Corn Meal yellow bags, with emblematic green ears of corn and red print, in two-, five-, and ten-pound sizes, all to raise money to keep up the mill house. And for Jones County's official seal, an artist has caught the whole scene, cypress trees over all and water flowing over the dam and down toward the nearby Trent River, as it has for well over two centuries, seeking its own level.

Brock's
Mill Pond,
tributary of
the Trent

Lower Trent

Many years ago, I spent a hot late spring afternoon snaking down dark, narrow Brice's Creek from the Croatan Forest in the jonboat, emerging grandly into the broad lower Trent River only a couple miles above New Bern, Union Point, and the Neuse. This was the Trent that most folks saw as they glided over its twin bridges, above the broad, beautiful Trent River marshes, verdant in the warm months and a muted golden during the cold, and Lawson's Creek, where the English explorer and town founder lived so long ago. The big, antique brick redoubt of Governor Tryon's Palace faced the Trent, solemn and stern, and, by night, New Bern's four-faced, white-lighted clock tower shone out over this meeting of the waters like a homegrown man in the moon.

Reaching these, then, was Ann's and my quest when we put the jon-boat in on the Trent River just below the Pollocksville bridge and headed downriver. Beneath towering sycamores, she and I shoved off from the small town's landing just before one o'clock one hot July day. An old Chris Craft cruiser had long lain at its dock, its docklines soaked and mossy, and not far downstream of it, a bottle tree reached glassy branches—wine and whiskey bottles, brown, green, blue, and aqua—up to the big blue, cumulus-clouded sky. A bass boat rolled past us, going upstream, and we in turn glided slowly by a quartet of kayakers, the young boy in the group breaking out to surf what small wake we left him. We tarried beneath a big osprey nest high up a dead tree at the mouth of Scott Creek, the elders circling noisily around above, the young still in the nest.

We cruised slowly down the long reaches of River Bend, manicured lawns right down to the river's edge, wild marshes and woods out across from them. One spot, displaying a rather large for-sale sign on its dock rail, had the look of a big, Corinthian-columned Tara down by the riverside, with a runabout on a boat-lift to boot. Not a shred of the fish camp about it: no sale.

Then, on our way to take a look at another osprey nest across the now-broad river from the marshes where Haywood Creek and Rocky Run join the flow, our little, ever-reliable 8-horsepower Johnson conked out. Thinking it only flooded when it would not crank, we shrugged and drifted happily beneath this never-lovelier summer sky and sooner than not were over against the Haywood marshes, looking at wildflowers in the cypress shade. After a time I back went to wrenching away at the pull-rope, more vigorously now, yet still getting no response. Most of an hour had passed, and I was on the verge of calling the towboat boys to come pull us into the nearest marina, when across the open water in a twenty-one-foot Carolina skiff with a big four-stroke 115 came the angels.

The Mantyla family, to be more precise. Two highly genial grandparents—slender, lovely Faye and the captain, stouter, Saint Nicholas-bearded Amos—who had had their brood of three grandchildren out tubing their wake for some time. They had come by us earlier to apologize—saying they had not meant to swamp us in all their circlings with the young tubers. Now they had returned to check on us, having seen us dead in the water, the jonboat snubbed up against the cattails and duck potatoes along the shore.

After some motorboat palaver and Cap'n Amos's also pulling the rope to no avail, to our astonishment he offered to tow us not simply to the nearest marina, but rather all the way back up to Pollocksville—we were then very not far from New Bern.

"That's very kind of you," I said, "but that's fourteen miles!"

"Ah, come on," said Amos, tossing us a towline. "We're up and down this river all the time."

No solution, no provision for the maritime fix we were in, could have been better, or more welcome. We accepted, and off we went, midafternoon now, and only the best of clouds in the sky.

A jonboat in tow, Trent River, July 2014

Cap'n Amos had grown up hereabouts, he allowed, and he just about knew the river by heart. "There's a fifty-foot hole back there at River Bend," he said. "Unbelievable speckled trout. We kept it a secret for a long time, but now . . . word is *out*." In one stretch not far upstream from the ospreys of Scott Landing, he waved his free hand broadly and said, "I learned to water ski on this stretch of the river—that's been a right long time ago." And of another reach he remarked sagaciously and appreciatively, honoring the glorious white perch, "This is a perch-y place—a *very* perch-y place!"

The first time Amos had ever fished the upper section of the river, he and three others put in above Pollocksville and came on down, fishing the channel and the banks. As he recalled the trip, he lowered his face and looked up from under raised eyebrows, his visage belying a certain level of apprehension the wild Trent had once given a quartet of young fishermen on their novitiate trek.

"It was just after *Deliverance* had come out," he said significantly, saying no more.

Then, merrily, he pointed out a small floating dock and recalled a friend and his wife sitting out on it of an evening when a runabout came slosh-ing by, at full speed: "Man, those barrels were really *bucking!*" And as he slowed at last to come up alongside the Pollocksville dock, he said, "Water-skied all up and down the river—we'd come all the way up here to the bridge, and turn around. Wouldn't go up above the bridge—too snaky up there. Well, you all take care, enjoy the rest of your afternoon!"

And then the Good Samaritans turned, waving, and were away ("Don't you be sending us a check," warned Faye good-heartedly, "cause it'll never be cashed"), one of the grandchildren already getting the wakeboard out, now after a fourteen-mile rest all up for more sport as the Mantylas of Trent floated back down the river they loved.

Plantation Days

Not far below Pollocksville, off to the north through the riverside jungle we passed that day, stood the Foscue Plantation house, a fine two-story Flemish- and common-bond brick home dating to the early 1800s. Its cur-rent condition—restored, manicured, artfully appointed, and on the Na-tional Register of Historic Places—could not alone have revealed the his-tory of disappointment, disaffection, alienation, and death that had gone along with the name and the immediate territory. Yet family letters and ledgers in faraway Wilson Library in Chapel Hill, like those of Carothers McCaslin's commissary in Faulkner's *The Bear*, do not lie, and they tell something more of the old antebellum life and times than this fine, well-tended, two-hundred-year-old treasure of a domicile could on its own.

There lay word of Simon Foscue Jr., who found his father's notes ten years before the father's death, notes not yet a will, on division of Foscue property, and what a rift that find occasioned; word of Simon Jr.'s brother Lewis's long upset over the way Simon dealt with their sister Dorcas, who was later, in 1823, called a "lunatic" on the occasion of Dorcas's property drifting to guardian Simon; word of brother Lewis's hoping to make a deal and sell his share of family lands to Simon Jr. and then light out for the far-off territories, declaring he would be happier among strangers out West than "with my only full Brother and others of my relatives"; word of Simon's death at age fifty in 1830, and of his son and heir John's death at forty in 1849; word of monies paid the county sheriff for tracking down and catching the family's runaway slaves and hauling them back; word of John's widow Caroline carrying on at Foscue Plantation with three chil-dren, till she felt forced to flee early in the Civil War; word scrawled from poor, aged Dorcas, her pathetic plea to be allowed to return to her rela-tions the year after the war; and a coroner's juror's word of a branch of family, that of Reaves Foscue, being murdered on the final Friday of June

1867, descended upon in their home by black robbers, the wife shot and left to bleed to death in the house, patriarch Reaves whipped and done in with a maul in the yard, children and grandchildren hiding in a corn-crib and shot through the slits in its side, a young mother escaping and dragging all night through the woods with her wounded infant, reaching a neighbor's place three miles distant at dawn, and finding it then only by the early cries of the fowl, the child dead by that time.

So much blood in the dirt down east, I remember Catherine Bishir, the great architectural historian, saying to us years ago, and here it all was again: the dead never dead, the past never even past, and never a place where blood could not rise up and ghosts might not howl.

Yet a sanguine man and woman in a jonboat slowly passing the jungle that screened the old plantation from the river's traffic that July day—though sensing all this and feeling it keenly—could still be impelled by the current to let the dead bury their dead, and to move on down the high-summer river.

And so we did.

Flat Boat

During the winter of 1989, in a meander not too far up the Trent above its confluence with the Neuse at New Bern, a pile-driver operator at work on a bulkhead along the river's shore spied an unusual collection of timbers in his way, and stopped his work to take a look. He was not entirely sure what he was looking at, but he was certain that the large, timber raft in muddy shambles was something historical and possibly important—enough so that he contacted authorities, who called in a cadre of archaeologists.

Theirs was a quick, significant rescue: in the late winter, these reclaimers dug up and delivered to the North Carolina Maritime Museum in Beaufort the remnants of a flat boat, that is to say, a flat that *was* the boat. What they pulled from the absolute mud was a lengthy side piece—thirty-one feet, hewn from a single cypress log—and most of the flat's eleven-foot-wide bottom.

Renowned maritime historian Michael Alford studied and ciphered over this big relic: had it been a ferry, or had it hauled produce, bales, and barrels for some plantation farther up the Trent? On reflection, he wrote, the "asymmetry of the transverse frames suggest that this flat was a cable or rope ferry" weighing two long tons, sturdy and quite capable of carrying four and a half tons "of cargo, livestock, or passengers." Of the distinct advantages of such shallow-draft boats, historian Alan D. Watson observed:

The Trent below Pollocksville, looking downstream, July 2014

"They were able to come close ashore and by means of an apron or gang-plank unload their passengers on dry land."

In the marine world of colonial coastal Carolina, these ferries had once been common across the region, and the King's Highway had depended on them. Nor were they solely an eastern mode, as such piedmont rivers as the Haw, Catawba, and Yadkin all had them, and upstate roads still bear their names, such as Avent Ferry in Wake County, Jones Ferry in Orange and Chatham.

There were four ferries in eighteenth-century Craven County alone, yet the Trent River ferry flat was the first of these humble, instrumental crafts from the back times ever to turn up. Owing to the keen eye and thought-fulness of one single pile-driving man working the shores of the Trent, the miracle was not only that this proud relic was found, but also that it was saved.

A Tale of Two Waterways

Upper Newport

The Newport River, a serious part of the great central estuary of North Carolina—Bogue Sound and the White Oak to the Newport's south, and the North River and Core Sound to its north—winds down out of the vast Croatan National Forest, where it is a black bottomland water, and becomes tidal long before it broadens at Oyster Point, a swamp stream by then clearly a coastal river. Big rains, though, like those of July 2014 when twelve inches deluged the middle coast, will pour tannin from the boggy Croatan and turn the Newport the color of Killian's ale as far downriver as Mill Creek.

Late afternoon one hot Third of July, Ann and I slid our canoe into the dark waters of a shortcut off the upper, thickly forested Newport, the state wildlife landing just off Chatham Street in the town of Newport. We paddled upriver for some miles, beyond the U.S. 70 double bridges. How shallow and muddy the edges of the stream were, outside its narrow channel, and how the whole affair narrowed quickly above the big highway.

All in all, this was another fine jungle, right in the middle, and then on the edge, of a town we simply could not see from the water. A pair of pileateds chased each other high above the water, and a pair of prothonotary warblers showed their gold as they shuttled easily amidst lower branches. A barred owl spooked down by the river's edge and flew up to a branch on a tall, slender gum, then spied furtively from around behind the tree trunk at us. A second barred owl flapped high up into a sixty-foot pine and posed, a dark silhouette against a burst of golden sun in clouds.

Swamp roses and small white flowers were all about, and cypress seeds hung above us. Palmetto fronds fanned out in the shadows, while others displayed themselves brightly in the evening light, and around one bend Ann spotted a bunch of wild clematis, or leather flower, sporting gorgeous purple-and-white, inch-long bells.

Nearly two hours after the high tide's peak at Beaufort Inlet, tidewater was still coming in and pushing leaves and twigs on the river's surface upstream, though our paddling was fairly effortless both going up and coming back down. Cicadas noisily set off their high winding chorus, and we were definitely up the lazy river of which Hoagy Carmichael wrote and the Mills Brothers crooned so long ago, and Ann, leaning back around toward me from the bow seat of the canoe and smiling at the locust-song, sang languorously herself:

"Does this say 'summertime' to you?"

The Harlowe and Clubfoot Creek Canal

To connect the Newport River—via its tributary Harlowe Creek and a three-mile ditch cut through the land to Clubfoot Creek—and the Neuse River, and thereby to join the ports of Beaufort and New Bern, the Harlowe & Clubfoot Creek Canal was approved by colonial authorities in 1766. The goal was to get New Bern's commerce in and out of the deepwater Beaufort Inlet and to steer shipping away from difficult, dreaded Ocracoke Inlet to the north.

Took awhile: nearly fifty years later, an act of the North Carolina legislature in 1813 reauthorized the canal, and digging began. This ditch was to be four feet deep and fourteen feet wide at the bottom, with sides flaring out a foot and a half for each foot of depth, thus with a surface width of twenty-six feet. Four sidings along the canal, each sixty feet long and twelve feet wide, would allow boats to pass. And the freight boats envisioned as the canal's market were substantial—thirty- to forty-ton vessels, seventy to eighty feet long, drawing three and a half feet.

The canal's early commissioners, or directors, included Elijah Piggott, who often served in the state legislature from Carteret County; Dr. James Manney, who had moved from Poughkeepsie, New York, to Beaufort; Otway Burns, the former privateer, hero of the War of 1812, a shipbuilder, also often a member of the legislature; Joseph Borden; and Jechonias Pigott. Canal collaborators Manney and Burns would later compete against each other in trying to supply bricks to Fort Macon out on Bogue Banks, both losing money, with Manney eventually going bankrupt.

Harlowe Canal work went slowly, bogged down, as it were.

Hamilton Fulton, the state's estimable new chief engineer (he also envisioned the Roanoke Canal and its Chockoyotte Aqueduct to get around the falls of the Roanoke River at Weldon and Roanoke Rapids), took over in 1819 and got things going again. Yet with too few hands on shovels and picks, the canal was only three-fifths of the way by 1823. The problematic Neuse River, being higher than the Newport, rushed its water in through Clubfoot Creek on the north, caving in banks on that end of the canal. Finally, the Harlowe & Clubfoot Creek Canal was open for business by about 1827, and, though it shoaled at both ends, freight did manage to move through it.

Just not enough.

The canal simply did not collect enough in tolls to cover its debts (the state had put $38,000 into the project by 1832), resulting in foreclosure upon it in 1844. No one stepped forward to lease or purchase the canal, and, though the legislature passed in 1849 an act to incorporate a new canal, this never happened either. When a new outfit sprang forth in 1872 proposing a new, parallel route just a few miles east, the state of North Carolina moved its interest in the Harlowe & Clubfoot Creek Canal over to the fledgling New Bern & Beaufort Canal Company. Canal historian Alexander Crosby Brown wrote of it: "This canal made the same connection slightly to the eastward and is the route [Core Creek to Adams Creek] of the present U.S. Army Engineers canal as part of the line of the Intracoastal Waterway."

And the small, original route languished.

In its day, though, the Harlowe & Clubfoot Canal carried water, with periaugers and other small craft easing, poling, and pulling their ways through it. Gideon Bell and his wife Eliza Pigott (the older sister of Emeline Pigott, who would become a celebrated Confederate spy) built a large home beside the canal and took in travelers; it still stands, just northwest of where N.C. 101 crosses the juncture of Harlowe Creek and the old canal, a crossing known in the nineteenth century as Bell's Bridge. Railroad magnate John D. Whitford, recalling this spot long after the Harlowe & Clubfoot Canal's prime, reflected in the *New Bern Daily Journal*, August 6, 1882:

A good hotel was erected at the "haulover," the entrance to the canal from Harlowe's creek, where there was originally a small lock. There too the canal was crossed by a bridge on the old stage road from Newbern to Beaufort. A year ago we visited the place with Capt. Marshal Parks and Mr. Courtwright, his engineer, passing through Harlowe's creek in a boat. After spending some two or three hours with Mrs. Gideon Bell and her daughter, who treated us with great courtesy and kindness, we returned in the same way to Morehead City, some time before night. Mrs. Bell owns the plantation on which was the canal hotel and her handsome residence is part of it modernized. The yard towards the

canal was beautiful with a variety of blooming flowers. Messrs. Editors, if you have never been there, you would be astonished to see such a lovely place, locked as it were, now in the woods. Our fathers failed in their efforts to make the canal useful and profitable by getting it too small.

Harlowe & Clubfoot Creek Canal, looking north from Adams Creek Road Bridge, August 2014

Trying—and Trying Again

Once I had more than a little of a turn of my own with the shoals of upper Clubfoot Creek.

Back in late June 1999, my son Hunter and I had crossed the broad Neuse from Oriental in our Boston Whaler, coursed along Great Neck Point and Great Neck, tried to raise friend and fellow author Janet Lembke on the radio, she who lived out here for years and wrote of this riverine outpost so compellingly in her memoir *River Time*. No luck. The sun cast a bright but diffuse light as we passed inside Great Island, the long grass bed just east of the mouth of Clubfoot Creek, and then into the creek we went.

Sailboat masts clustered in a cove not far inside the creek's mouth, where Mitchell Creek comes down, identified Matthews Point Marina, where the small harbor was all quiet. No other craft but ours was moving this late summer morning, and we plied slowly up the long, narrow, three-mile creek. By the time we made the upper reaches, the waters were a slate gray bank to bank, impossible to read in this light, and I made the wrong call about where the channel into the old Harlowe Canal was, running us up into thick, muddy shallows on the creek's east side.

After a few minutes of poling, Hunter and I decided we would be better off, better equipped for this particular boatman's job, if we first had some lunch, so we sat back and ate sandwiches and took it all in at our ease—until a crabber in a twenty-five-foot skiff came up out of the canal's mouth about a hundred yards distant, and I hailed him:

"Are you going back down the canal?"

"Soon as I check these pots," he called.

"Can I follow you?"

"You'll have to," he said. "You don't know where the stumps are."

Buoyed that we would now have local knowledge helping us work our way south through the old canal, I quickly went back to poling us off the mud, and the crabber called me to hurry up and come on just as I was putting the motor back down to start it.

He was vanishing into the canal just as my starter wound down and the battery died, and we were dead in the water.

Or almost so.

For this week-long trek from Little Washington to Beaufort, we did have on board a little Johnson 8 as a kicker, and now Hunter and I got it rigged up on the Whaler's transom so we could putter back down Clubfoot Creek and see about charging the battery at the marina. Figured if we could get back under way, we would let Clubfoot Creek alone and go on back around the neck and head for Beaufort via Adams Creek and the Intracoastal Waterway. Slow going, but soon we pulled into the Mitchell Creek cove and realized that this was only a private, unattended marina. We sat sullenly pondering our next move for half an hour or so, and then a pickup truck roared up to a garage on the point, the driver got out energetically and went into the garage, and I walked up to ask for his help.

This was Jet Matthews, a very friendly, enterprising fellow (he would ere long take on and accomplish the renovation of the moribund Morehead City Marina) who, hearing our tale, readily loaned me a battery and some cables. When I came back up from the dock not ten minutes later, unsuccessful, he hauled out yet another one, saying:

"For God's sake don't hook it up backwards! This one's for a bulldozer, and if *it* doesn't start your motor, *nothing* will."

It did. Heroically so.

Twelve years later, I tried the two waterways again, this time aiming for a full circumnavigation of the big landmass bordered by the two north–south canals. We were a foursome—Ann, the lanky, lively historian David Cecelski and his daughter Vera, and I—and we put the small Whaler—our friend Jim Rumfelt's old 13′10″ with its Evinrude 30—in at Sea Gate Marina on the Intracoastal Waterway just a mile and a half or so north of the Core Creek Bridge.

We were going in the same direction as had those who dug this big ditch—Frank Furst's Maryland Dredging Company out of Baltimore— from north to south, from the top of Adams Creek through five miles of Carteret County forest to the top of Core Creek. For less than $400,000, Furst's dredges, steam shovels, draglines, scows, and scrapes did the job between September 1908 and mid-November 1910, and once they were done digging "the Beaufort Cut," did they ever celebrate. The revenue cutter *Pamlico* led a parade of one hundred boats up into the new waterway on Old Christmas, January 6, 1911, and twenty-five hundred folks came out

Beaufort Belle *pushes a barge up the waterway into Adams Creek toward the Neuse River, July 2014*

to the canalbank to hear the politicians and deeper-waterways enthusiasts carry on, to bear witness to this new shortcut, and simply, as the *Baltimore Sun* put it the next day, to "jubilate over the canal."

As we passed under the bridge, a high flyover within sight of the maritime array of Jarrett Bay boatworks, David told a couple of bridge stories from the old, lower, drawbridge days here. In one, a gospel quartet that had just done a rousing show in Beaufort came flying east in their van and somehow missed the signals and plowed right on through when the draw was open and sank into Core Creek, all of them losing their lives—David said everyone claimed they were bound for glory and singing for it when they went. In another tale, he recalled a big man who—sick and tired of waiting for all the stalled-out, open-bridge traffic he was stuck in to start moving—got out of his truck, cussed like a champion, and—in full sight of everyone—hauled off and threw his keys over the bridge rail into the water below, leaving his *locked* truck and walking west toward Harlowe. David and his family remembered this one well, because they were sitting on the porch of their farmhouse at the corner of N.C. 101 and Ball Farm Road, miles from the bridge, when the irate man stomped by, still westbound, still furious, still cussing.

We came on south in the boat, then turned west into the upper Newport River where the dolphins and the rays cavort, and coursed over two miles of broad shoals there, pushing the little boat on plane, the wind behind us, and going with the waves. At the near side of White Rock we turned due north into Harlowe Creek, then wound several miles through quarter-mile-wide marshes with a good many egrets, and half a dozen ibis, then through the last of the broad needlerush, under the N.C. 101 bridge—Bell's Bridge, in the old days—and into the Harlowe Canal. So convoluted and curvy is all the canalbank's grapevine growth that if one did not know it, one might well believe he was navigating a narrow river, not a man-made cut.

Several miles in this calm channel and we slipped on out of the old, narrow waterway and into Clubfoot Creek, having left Vera off at the Ball Farm Road bridge across the canal right behind her family's farm so she could walk back to her car there and go off to work at the Maritime Museum in Beaufort. To our left was a creek's mouth leading into Morton's Mill Pond, now a huge maze of marshes coming down out of a cypress swamp in the Croatan Forest. Years before, David had taken Hunter and me kayaking back in there later in the week after we had come a-cropper on the mudflat, and I recall his tasting and testing the water as we went upstream from bright marsh into dark woods, looking, as ever, for the salt line.

This was a blue-sky day, and we enjoyed a light easterly breeze back here in the protected water of Clubfoot Creek. Matthews Point had added a fuel dock in the years since my last visit, so we filled our tank, got out of the boat, and had a sandwich beside the cove there. By the time we boated out of Clubfoot and onto the Neuse River, about 12:30 P.M., we were facing into a fifteen-mile-an-hour wind out of the east-northeast, a right nice chop, so I hugged the shoreline below Great Island and on up Great Neck. David pointed out a little river beach and said that right beyond it was Long Creek, more miles of marshes where he and his brother Richard, the dashing Carolina Beach outfitter-educator, used to kayak for all the livelong day when they were boys.

Great Neck Point afforded us something of a lee, and we got close under it and worked easily up that shore, past where the late Janet Lembke and her husband, the Chief, used to live, but when we got right around the point, between there and Adams Creek, we were in a pretty strong chop again. Soon we would cruise past a host of large brick ruins on that creek's west bank, and wonder about them. We would see several dolphins, briefly, at Marker 13 in the Intracoastal Waterway, and we would make it back to Sea Gate by a quarter to three in the afternoon, a six-hour run along the two waterways that held within them a good two centuries of maritime life hereabouts.

But first, as we were splashing, even thrashing, through the chop over that last reach of the Neuse from Great Neck Point to Adams Creek, through the bow spray Ann exclaimed, laughing,

"It's not a dry boat!"

To which David readily agreed, adding:

"It's not a dry river."

Winthrop Mills

A century ago there would have been nothing lazy whatsoever about either of these parallel waterways, particularly on the northern end of each one, where the John L. Roper Lumber Company of Norfolk, Virginia, had significant industrial presence and pounding, ear-splitting sawmill machinery.

By the spring of 1907 Roper was all over eastern North Carolina in force, like an octopus, with vast timber holdings of 1,250 square miles, comprising more than 2.5 percent of the total land area of the state of North Carolina, with sales offices in Boston, Buffalo, New York City, Philadelphia, and Portland, Maine. In the Albemarle, Pamlico, and Neuse River areas, mills sat like colonies on harborsides and creekbanks, cranking away in Roper, Belhaven, Scranton, and New Bern, with more at James City, Pollocksville, Oriental, and Jacksonville—in addition to those here on Clubfoot and Adams Creeks.

On upper Clubfoot Creek, Roper ran a sawmill and dry kiln, and on lower Clubfoot Creek, another sawmill and dry kiln. At the Winthrop Band Mill Plant on the west side of Adams Creek lay not only a sawmill and more dry kilns, but also an enormous shipping shed, a lumber shed, a powerhouse, water tanks, and a huge railroad logging port right on the creek. When Roper lieutenants and their guests toured these massive field operations, they did so by pulling up here in the sleek, luxurious, teaked-out, fifty-foot motor yacht, the *Lowther*.

Nowadays, for all that effort, all that timber, all those men, and all their work in this little place, all that remained were those brick ruins we had seen on the creek's western side, to which Ann and I returned one hot partly cloudy day in July 2014, jonboating up the Waterway the eight miles from Sea Gate. X-shaped foundation piers stood canted on the creek's beach, or lay fallen over in the creek itself, and one fifty-yard portion of beach lay there simply bricked over by the debris. More piers stood here and there in the cedar and yaupon thicket just above the beach, and dark, rusted iron piping lay partly to fully exposed on the beach or in the woods. In and among all the rubble on the sand were the tracks of deer.

Roper Lumber
Company's
railroad
logging
operation,
Winthrop
Mills on
Adams Creek,
circa 1907

Beyond that beach of bricks and pipes, there was little more, only a name left on the map at the eastern side of the mouth of Adams Creek. Roper's once-great reach and doings here had all come down to just a pair of words on a tiny corner of the enormous estuary:

Winthrop Point.

Crosswinds

Cousin Sal, the colorful large-scale painter, lives just a scant mile or so from White Rock and the mouth of Harlowe Creek, in a small brick fish camp of a home, with bamboo screens and an outdoor clawfoot tub, looking out on all creation. Her place—she calls it Crosswinds—sits way down low right on the Newport River where the water gets big and wide, coming westerly out of the Croatan woods, flowing past the relict, Indian-era causeway still called Cross Rock, and then turning south for Beaufort and Morehead City, for the big ships' turning basin, Beaufort Inlet, and the sea.

Almost straight across from her place, east-southeast, is Lawton Point, and far beyond that, of an evening, are the lights of Beaufort's north side: Town Creek and Gallants Channel. Sally calls her small craft, which once plied the shallows of Bogue Sound, Taylor's Creek, and Middle Marsh, MG, or "the Mullet Grabber," and well she might: she has been eating straight out of the river the entire time she has lived hard by it: fish, shrimp, clams, oysters, mussels.

Sally's and Ann's and my family spent the long, warm afternoon the day after Thanksgiving '12 in a joyful, successful effort at finishing off a bushel or more of oysters from right off the shore. A shrimper lay up a ways out,

Adams Creek ruins at site of Winthrop Mills, July 2014

tied off to a post, his butterfly wings out, nets drying. A slender moon appeared low in the western sky just after sunset and soon sank slowly over the waters beyond Cross Rock.

Who wouldn't give thanks?

Who wouldn't sing praise? Who wouldn't howl, whether the moon was up there to howl at or not?

IO

The South Flows North, the North Flows South

South River

Ann and I slowed our car and asked a man working on a motor grader at the state fisheries dock if he knew where a landing might be here in South River, the small, lowland village in northern Carteret County, almost up to the Neuse River, and he quickly said in full soundside brogue:

"Oi'm not from araound here, oi wouldn't knaow." So we then inquired of the fellows back at the nearby Marine Fisheries work shed and one of them remarked authoritatively:

"Why, go back turn right at the stop sign and on the left after the big curve there's a open place, kind of sandy, between two houses and you can put in there."

"You sure?" I asked.

"Yep, it's my family's ramp, and I haven't heard they'd closed it, so go on in there."

A nice spot it was, too, with a three-dollar ramp-fee honor box on a post. We slipped the two kayaks—a Carolina 13.5 and a Pungo 11—into the water at the pair of docks, L-shaped, flanking the concrete ramp on South River Road. A seventy-five-yard cut led out to Martin Creek, an east-flowing tributary of the South River. While paddling past old docks the quarter mile down the creek out to the river itself, we scared a couple of ospreys off their high pine lookout point on the south side at the creek's mouth, and passed green daymark 1.

A light summer breeze laid a slight ripple on the water, the day overcast when we got under way just before noon. Up-river, more than a mile south of us, a small trawler worked the waters, its diesel thrumming low while we paddled for about half an hour from the put-in to the river's far side, where we were greeted by white signs on leased bottom:

2467111
C. L. Cannon

Live oak,
Martin Creek,
South River,
August 2014

South River's eastern shore showed just a few short sandy beaches but was mostly a stretch of cutaway clay banks with pines towering over the riverside. I made my way up it toward our goal, the last vestige of the disappeared village of Lukens, though Ann hung back in her kayak, intently watching something I could not see for fifteen or twenty minutes. When she caught up with me, she was happy and excited, with a tale to tell.

She had been paddling along the edge of the glassy river, beside a sandy shore with a lot of old tree roots and tangles of trees that had fallen into the water, a pine upland with a couple of small live oaks above and a yaupon by the shore. Suddenly she heard a big rustle in the middle of the small live oaks, and shaking coming from something that seemed to her larger than a bird.

"So I paddled over to it," Ann said, "and after a minute or so a little tail dropped down below the canopy of the oak and then a little head appeared—one raccoon kind of skittered down the tree trunk partway and the other one went up the trunk—and then they just played around— I could see 'em—then, they were playing around on this young live oak and they went out on a limb toward the water and one of them played with twigs and the other one that was behind it somehow leaned backward, upside down, and they were both purring.

"Meanwhile, there was another one on the beach behind the tangle of tree roots and limbs, just checking things out, digging and stuff, climbing on the tree. And eventually the other two came down on the ground too and started climbing around, up and down the little bluff and back up the tree and back down again. The one on the shore got up on the old tree limb where I could see him pretty well and so I wanted to come in and take a picture. I let the boat drift in, but the current pushed it a little too close, so I back-paddled, and when I did, another slightly larger head popped up from behind the driftwood tangle on the beach and looked right at me—took a really good look—and it was obvious that she didn't like what she saw, and that she was *The Mama*.

"So, with no hurry and no panic, she turned around and went back up into the lee of the little bluff, and I couldn't hear her sound any kind of alarm or anything, but the other ones played their way over to where she was, and she very purposefully led them up the bluff and into the pine-woods, away from the boat. The little upside-down thing was so ador-able—I don't know how it did that."

Pushing on for Lukens like Gil Favor, Trail Boss, I had been too single-minded, and had missed out on a very nice show indeed.

Great gray-and-white cumulus clouds now filled the sky, and the shore-line riprap seemed barely able to hold the land beside us—a short, eroding bluff—in place. Swells had begun slowly rolling in and up the South River from the Neuse, and, though gentle, one could feel them nonetheless. A huge pine stood beside the arched white sign on the bluff above:

Lukens Cemetary Est. 1810

We floated in amber waters just above some iron ruins, an old steel hull gone almost totally to pieces in the shallows below the riprap, and regarded all that was left of the little Lukens community that had once thrived here. Ivory and lavender morning glories were twining about each other on the riverbank, helices of life, and the graveyard above us lay in the shade of the big pine and some large live oaks. Half a dozen grave-stones, mottled chalk-white and gray, stood within a coffin's length of the dark, storm- and wave-cut bank.

Soon, back at the Martin Creek landing across the river, we would feast on our lunch on the dock, peanut butter–and-lettuce sandwiches: "In honor of Doctor John," Ann said, referring to her late father, then four years gone, who specialized in this particular repast. Crumbs from our sandwiches would fall on the water, and blue minnows would surface and eat them. A pair of small trawlers coming into the creek would chug on by, going farther up to dock and unload.

But before we left Lukens and its graveyard, I sat there in my kayak thinking of how Hurricane Isabel back in 2003 likely tossed many a massive wave up over these long-lonesome dead as she sent a spectacular surge up South River that September night. They slept through that storm, though, as they will sleep through them all, even the great, future tempest that takes away the bluff and moves them again at last and lays them for a spell in some other estuarine bed.

What do they care, or mind? What of trawlers, out working the river, what of big Marine Corps helicopters percussively thudding the clouds as they flew east for Piney Island, or of a pair of us kayakers floating below them for just a few moments longer?

They have won this riverine promontory and, now, are above it all.

They are the dead of Lukens, mourned by their living kin in the village of South River and by many more well beyond it, prayed over way out here by osprey and kingfisher and crow.

On the first warm day of a false spring, my next time out on South River, we put the jonboat in—our daughter Cary, old friend and fellow mariner David Cecelski, and I—at the same three-dollar ramp Ann and I had used two years earlier. I cranked the 8-horse Johnson and we slowly headed out. A sunny day in the low sixties, and the air was light.

Across the river we beached the small boat, tied its painter to a piece of riprap, and climbed the six-foot bank up into the old graveyard at Lukens. Tall and at home here, David marched thoughtfully through this field of the long gone, aflood with midday light and warmth, delineating the names on the weathered tombstones, saying which people went with the old coastal communities and had ties over the miles-wide Neuse River to Oriental and Arapahoe and even out to Portsmouth Island (the Masons, the Pittmans, the Tostos), and which names were more recent (the Hardys, the Normans) and ran with late nineteenth- and early twentieth-century timbering hereabouts.

Only this old burying ground—nothing else was left of Lukens, North Carolina, and so it had been since the late 1940s, with the demise of its school, post office, and church. We spoke of Tom Tosto of South River, who, starting in 1987, each May had been ferrying relatives of the Lukensians across the broad South River stream to reconnect with the land of their ancestors.

"About twenty years ago," Tosto told the *Carteret County News-Times* in May 2008, "I took two aged widows over there. They wanted to see their home place, though it [the house] had been moved. . . . They cried on my shoulder and told me how much it meant to them. It had a strong bearing on my heart to be able to take them."

Lukens Cemetery, overlooking the South River, August 2014

Now the three of us sat near the edge of the Lukens bluff and had a fine lunch of turkey, cheese, and tomato sandwiches, enjoying our big Edward Hopper view of South River and on out to the Neuse, and noting how smooth the waters had become, the breeze having fallen off. "Dining with the dead," the late Jake Mills would have called it.

A couple of osprey soon flew over the tall pines north of Lukens. Back in the boat heading south, or upriver, we saw buffleheads north of Eastman Creek, and a line of four pelicans just off the mouth of that creek.

"Wonder if they spread a gill net between them," David mused wryly.

What a sight! A hundred wood ducks or more rose beautifully, majestically together as we plied up Eastman, the creek fringed by marsh and short pines, and then I eased us over to the south side of the creek and killed the motor, and for a spell we just looked about and admired the day. David talked about the late Doc Borden, whose medical practice was in Morehead City and who had a fish camp out here at South River, and who had been his and his brother Richard's mentor years ago.

"Doc loved birds," David said, smiling with tender friendliness at the memory. "He kept track of osprey nests and liked to show them off. He'd tramp through the marsh looking for marsh hens, rails, do a call, see if he could find them and see them. And he looked for swifts under little road bridges."

Under way again, going farther up Eastman, I slowed as the creek narrowed to perhaps forty feet, right at a bend with a fallen pine in it—there had been a white-liquor still back in the woods here long ago, a South River fisherman later told me. His two uncles as young men had been standing guard for the moonshiners right here on the creek, but when a Coast Guard cutter came in one night and fired a warning shot above them, they took off, and the still operators lost their lookouts, and that was that.

For a short spell we coursed a gang of switchbacks through the marsh. No more ducks to regard, but we did happen upon a small, four-foot-long alligator, booking away when he saw us, and we him. We looked up another narrow creek on South River's east side below Southwest Creek, this one with a pine forest close in on its south, and we watched a stick start moving swiftly through the water. First and only snake of the day.

Then we followed the river to the southwest into the vast, 57,000-acre Open Grounds Farm (the largest farm in eastern America, so they claimed), under the Nelson Bay Road bridge, where a flock of blackbirds swarmed the marsh. Turtles, large sliders, hit the water, two groups of four, then two more, before I saw one big fellow hanging out, refusing to budge on our account, still in the marsh.

And then there before us lay a six-foot gator, twenty-five feet ahead, aiming, as it were, straight at us, unmoved by us and unmoving.

"Daddy . . . ," Cary, sitting in the bow, said apprehensively.

We slowed to a crawl, yielded to the primitive saurian whose place this was, and turned around.

As we reapproached the bridge, a white pickup went roaring by at eighty or ninety miles an hour, disregarding the fact that the small, narrow bridge had no guardrails. Back at the bridge, we got a view up a drainage ditch of the enormous Open Grounds storage bins to the west, through which millions of bushels of grain flow every year.

A kingfisher flew up, chittered, dropped down toward the ditch, came back up, and artfully inscribed sines and cosines for a few seconds in the air above the bridge, giving us an uncommonly good look at him.

Just south of the mouth of Southwest Creek, as we moved steadily downriver on our return, we looked in upon a clutch of pelicans, three of them taking off together, climbing to thirty or forty feet, then abruptly turning and dropping and hitting the water all at once, a splashy, dramatic show of synchronized fishing. Cary would later tell me that she saw a pelican in the water trying to eat a fish and that, when the fish started wriggling loose, the big bird had simply flipped the fish, caught it anew, and on the second go-round quickly swallowed it.

For miles on either side of South River lay only marshes, pines, and cedars, a scarcely disturbed stretch of the great eastern Carolina estuary, riverine wilds below the totally cleared, totally altered Open Grounds Pocosin of old. I said something about having at last, after our brutally cold winter, the very first sense of spring on this warm day, and how all these birds and reptiles were wanting, and starting, to move—to which David over the hum of the little engine ecumenically replied:

"Including us."

North River

On All Soul's Day 2013, Ann and I spent a good while at the long bridge, taking the late-afternoon measure of the North River, a few miles above Beaufort, and its gorgeous, autumnal sights. Wind out of the north at fifteen was shaking the short cedars and the myrtle alike, the red-berried yaupon too, and a white houseboat that had long been resident near the eastern shore lay canted before the breeze. I turned and looked away downriver, recalling Peter Riggs, who lived for a time at Lenox Point near the river's mouth, and his telling me many years ago about kayaking there amid scores of dolphins, maybe a hundred of them at once.

Small waves washed in quickly, steadily, in scalloped patterns, slapping the riprap of the causeway, and the smell of fish was in the air. Below the bridge, the water was quiet. Only one craft was out, three men in a twenty-one-foot T-top bateau, moving slowly, stopping now and again for one of them to throw a cast-net and pull it back in, then trolling on along.

At Ward's Creek, the North River tributary not far to the east, a dull golden spindrift lay in hanks, blown up onto the small sandy beach above the creek bridge. More yaupon was all berried out, and a big skiff lay up on its side on the far shore. Across the road a hundred gulls wheeled and spun and dove, noisily working the shallows.

We were soon speaking of the river over dinner out at Davis Shore on Core Sound, with old friends Candy Rogers, the cheerful, elegant woman whose place it was, and Elton Ellis, her colorful, capable companion, a jaunty marine construction man whose home was at North River. He remembered years back, when he first moved to Carteret County, that there was a Ms. Yeatman, a farmer and airplane pilot, who lived on 500 acres along the upper North, and that she had a dairy farm and something of a "little village" where her farmworkers lived.

Ward's Creek, a tributary of North River, November 2013

He thought maybe she had picked out her place from the air.

Indeed she had. The MIT-trained architect Georgina Yeatman spied the land of her dreams while flying over the Open Grounds Pocosin in the 1930s, first buying an old hunt club on Eastman Creek and South River along with 25,000 acres of the Open Grounds for less than $1 an acre in 1936. She spent her lifetime farming it, raising dairy and beef cattle, even trying sheep and goats, while steadily increasing her holdings to some 43,000 acres. In 1974 she sold this vast spread for nearly $4 million to the Italian agribusiness giant Gruppo Ferruzzi, which cut, drained, and converted it into the wide-open grain cornucopia it is today.

"She was an Amelia Earhart type," Elton said in admiration, and with appreciative laughter.

The North narrows not too far above its bridge, where it was a mile or more wide, and its upriver marshes were extensive. Elton said he had recently been out mucking about in the marsh, looking for a small, square-end canoe he had left out there quite a while back, stored on a rack. Unable before long to retrace his steps back to that spot, in storing the boat he had simply lost it.

"Finally found it, though," he said, laughing some more, admitting that at first he had hardly recognized it.

"Hadn't seen it in two years," said Elton. "It had changed color."

Ten years earlier, one bright January Saturday in 2003, a bunch of us, directors and staff of the North Carolina Coastal Federation (NCCF), met and had lunch at Mark and Penny Hooper's creekside home and crab-shack and clam-leasehold at Smyrna, in Down East Carteret County.

That was just a little over a year after the NCCF had acquired the nearby 6,000-acre North River Farms, cropland that lay between the much larger Open Grounds Farm and the marshes and waters of the North River estuary, and on this day we were going to see it. The headwaters of the South River flowed north out of the former gigantic pocosin, and those of the North flowed to the south.

And we aimed to use North River Farms as a filter for the agricultural runoffs from the Open Grounds, to slow down the V-ditch waters, to close the gates and stall out as much as possible of what had shut down shell-fishing in the estuary. To that end as well, we were prepared to have heavy equipment come in and carve up land that had been rendered table-top flat for farming, and now to create depressions all over it in which water could sit and percolate—in short, to try to re-create and restore a wetland, to put a pocosin back to right.

These were our dreams many years ago, and we who had signed off on the North River purchase could not wait to get a good look at the place. Its entrance was a gated road just a ways down U.S. 70 from Smyrna, back toward Beaufort from the Hoopers' place and not far from where, as we always told our children, Ann had seen the bear from the school bus on the way to East Carteret High one morning. We now all drove over and into North River Farms, down the straightaway farm roads, through miles of stubble, past big metal buildings that shone in the winter sun, and finally down a long lane that brought us to a water-control structure and a batch of canoes.

We launched, about sixteen of us, and slowly floated southward and eastward down a farm canal in the shade of pines a quarter mile or more, till the canal hit an unnamed creek near its head, then turned south into the creek and went with its wiggles southerly on down through most of a mile of marshes to its mouth, its broad, shallow opening into the North River.

By now it was pushing three in the afternoon, and the cool breeze coming off the river bade us not linger too long admiring the far shore—this was *January*, after all. John Runkle, the great conservationist lawyer who has kept North Carolina's environment out of untold amounts of trouble, turned to me from his canoe with one hand mimicking a rounded grip, though it was empty. "Just doesn't feel right," he said, laughing. "Being in a canoe and not having a cold beer in my hand."

So we turned back upstream but in no hurry, disembarked and stacked

North River, looking east from the bridge, November 2013

the small boats on the trailer, and were then bound back toward town and all the pleasures of the harbor.

What we had just assayed, borne witness to, and floated over would soon become nothing less than the largest wetlands restoration effort east of the Mississippi. What we were about here would make a grand difference. Though we could not know for sure that day and could then only hope, Down East watermen would, ere long, once again be taking clams from the waters of the North River that flows south.

11

Taylor's Creek

Taylor's Creek

The inner shoals, sandbars, and channels among them have shifted greatly and are greatly altered since Blackbeard anchored and lay inside off Beaufort in 1718, before scuttling his ship *Queen Anne's Revenge* in twenty feet of water just off Beaufort Inlet and then heading north to his last stand at Ocracoke. The current tidal creeks and channels scarcely match up with those mapped by the superb coastal hydrographer, John Newland Maffitt, Lieutenant Commanding, of the U.S. Coast Survey's early 1850s charting work in Beaufort Harbor—yet the Beaufort citizenry, all out in layered dresses and top hats filling Front Street near the Ocean House hotel, looking past the waterside warehouses and the beached boats along Taylor's Creek and watching the Union shelling of Confederate-held Fort Macon across the inlet in late April 1862, would have still seen between them and the fort a scant two miles away most all of what Maffitt mapped.

What we take in today, though, does bear a fair resemblance to the Taylor's Creek that Rachel Carson knew and loved, and to the cedar-and-gaillardia dunes and the great slough and tidal flats to its south, where she walked and worked. For she was here *after* the 1930s Corps of Engineers dredging that made the deep cut through upper Taylor's Creek to the mouth of North River, creating in the modified creek a continuous navigable channel from Pivers Island and Gallants Channel on the west to Lenox Point in full view of Harkers Island on the east.

Along the Taylor's Creek shore in downtown Beaufort, the town's current sirens are a fleet of waterfront shebangs: the Dock House, Clawson's, the Queen Anne's Revenge, the Rhum Bar, and the Spouter Inn. The last serves as a direct allusion to chapter 3 of *Moby-Dick*, and Ishmael's experience with the whale-and-ship mural, the trick glasses at the bar, and his sleeping with a harpooner, and also as an admission that just

a few miles across the inlet sound from Beaufort there had once been a whaling community, as whalers and porpoisers worked out of Diamond City on eastern Shackleford Banks. Other watering holes are set back, though not far, from the creek: the dark, funky, low-ceilinged, convivial boaters' Back Bar and the bright, dressy nouvelle Aqua, the two cheek by jowl on Middle Lane; the nearby musical winecellar Cru; and the noisy, rocked-out, unadorned, slate-tabled pool hall on Turner Street, the Royal James—another antique maritime allusion, as this was the name of gentleman pirate Stede Bonnet's sloop.

Something there is that has long made the Royal James powerfully magnetic. Perhaps its secret lay in its abject unpretentiousness, its onions near the griddle, its agreeably aggressive chili sauce, its pool cues ranked high along the north wall to either side of an all-the-hits, all-the-genres jukebox, overall a quality of place that is a great equalizer, like a town park, or a coastal fishing pier—something like that, coupled with a plenitude of good, solid red-blooded spirit. One April long ago, all hands in the RJ cheered Tiger Woods when he took the Masters by storm, and similarly, on a hot July afternoon a couple years later, the RJ's citizenry gave it up for Brandi Chastain when her boot beat China for Team USA and she yanked off her jersey and waved it like the stars and stripes. Something about this place: on a Friday night shooting eight-ball with the ever-ready Scott Taylor, one of the South's finest photographers and, in his spare time, an extreme, hundred-mile-racing kayaker, one could not help but note that the hands pulling the tap behind the RJ bar belonged to a woman wearing a formfitting sequined dress with deep-woods camouflage design.

A block and a half away from the Royal James, on the cloudy Wednesday before Thanksgiving 1987, I found myself sitting in the quiet parlor of Langdon House, the white, double-porched 1730s beauty at the corner of Ann and Craven Streets just a block from the creek. My host was its restorer-owner, Jimm Prest, each of us holding a short glass of sherry as Jimm laid out his inside word on the small-town environs inscribed by Taylor's Creek and the North and Newport Rivers: tales of Hippie Steve and the superb good deals on his used bicycles; of the delusional Cap'n Snap wandering town plinking at tin cans with his imaginary, though patented, nuclear pistol; of shaggy Irving's yearly mane-cutting out on the deck of some sailing craft or another in Taylor's Creek. Big, bearded Jimm kept a small, congenial inn here till his untimely death at fifty-three in 2008, and his widow Lizette carries it lovingly on—he was one of the truly grand, embracing spirits of the old town's current age, well known for greeting all who rang the bell of Langdon House's front door in his bare feet, and with charm to burn.

And, sometimes, with Gosling's black rum.

"What's it like here in the dead of winter, Jimm?" I asked him that day. At that moment, I had spent but one night in the town that has, by now, long been a second home to Ann's and my family.

"I can tell you in a few words," he replied. "Friends and the wind, just friends and the wind."

How often since then have I felt winter's power here, felt winds shift big and fast, heard the very cedars of this place shake and shiver, and thought of Jimm that late November afternoon long ago and his clear, thoughtful, prescient words.

Beaufort's cedar-, sycamore-, and live-oak-lined streets receive a range of weather so forceful and changeable that the elements, seeming frightful, even spiteful, on one day, present themselves as nothing but delightful the next. An early March sidewise nor'easter's forty-degree howling rains and mists, which send townsfolk and visitors alike screaming into the public houses for all due process and protection on one evening, may quickly dissipate overnight, and then the calm, sunny, sixty-ish new day that has followed now has the maritime citizenry afloat by the score in biminied runabouts, kayaks, daysailers, and even the celebrated thirty-four-foot Crestwood rowing gig (a descendant of the Swampscott dory) of the Beaufort Oars. A fierce July hurricane in the night, like Arthur on the Fourth of July '14, blowing 101 out at Cape Lookout and 93 atop the main-mast of a Taylor's Creek sailboat, may yield to a bright, cool breezy morning with little more than a host of downed pecan and sycamore branches to gather up (if, that is, your Ann Street oak did not come down or your thirty-six-foot sailboat did not drag anchor and wind up beached on Town Marsh).

Speaking wryly of the acute, rapid back-and-forths Beaufortians experienced during the dazzling, difficult, hard-freeze winter of 2013–14, one port-town woman sagely observed:

"It was Antarctica one day, and Cuba the next."

A Rachel Carson Slough

When Rachel Carson came to work in North Carolina in early February 1947, she found her way to coastal Hyde and Dare Counties, to the Pea Island, Swanquarter, and Mattamuskeet National Wildlife Refuges, and to the hunting lodge fashioned by the Civilian Conservation Corps out of the old New Holland pumping station just in from Lake Mattamuskeet's southern shore. From this rustic, agreeable quarter she ventured out and met the Carolina coast in all its wintry glory, the big-sky world of scores of thousands of ducks, geese, and swans, the marshes gone tawny, the lake- and streamside cypress gone an antique bronze.

Her second morning at the 40,000-acre Mattamuskeet, our state's largest natural lake, Carson rose and walked the canal, listening to whistling swans and finding their "high, thin" notes to have "almost a woodwind quality." She wanted to find one flock of geese that was laughing, cavorting, and honking out, but she could not make her way to it.

Part of the conversion of the New Holland pump station—which for a generation had pumped up to 12,000 acres of Lake Mattamuskeet's bottom dry enough to farm rice, wheat, rye, and soybeans—into a lodge had involved setting a circular staircase into the building's 120-foot-tall smokestack, and thereby giving visitors a near lighthouse-height view from its top. The look out over the lake country from that prospect was breathtaking When Ann and I first made our way up to this same spot, fifty years after Rachel Carson did, a thoroughly rainy winter's day was drawing to its end, and the back side of a great storm was moving east toward the lake as the sun fell toward sunset—it was clear to those of us at the chimney top that the setting sun would soon fit, and sit, between the bottom of the eastbound cloud cover and the horizon. And when it soon did just that, *Lord have mercy*, the glory of that long slant sunlight rapidly flashing and shooting over the lowlands and sheening them in a bright raw umber made a late-day luminary like none other we have ever seen.

During her own brief stay, Carson found muskrat houses in the marsh, shone her flashlight on deer outside the lodge, heard frogs in "throbbing amphibian chorus" during the mild winter nights.

And then, not too many years after she discovered the wonders of the Albemarle and Pamlico peninsula, she returned to Carolina, in June 1951, to Beaufort, to Taylor's Creek and the sloughs of Town Marsh and Bird

Gaillardia, Town Marsh sandhills along Taylor's Creek, 2009

Shoal. When the Corps of Engineers dredged Taylor's Creek, they had piled the dredge spoil on the creek's south side, across from the town of Beaufort. In no time at all, cedars sprang up on these new dunes, and bright green pennywort and red-and-yellow gaillardia took hold, and feral ponies fed, slept, and bred there.

One stream—Deep Creek—both creates and drains the large central slough and tidal flat, alternately flooding and flowing out into Taylor's Creek with the tides, and a second one, unnamed, does the same with a smaller slough to the west, this one emptying into the main channel from Taylor's Creek down to Beaufort Inlet. These wetlands are full of shorebirds, plovers and willets and oystercatchers, egrets and ibis, of horseshoe crabs trailing along in search of food and mates, and the sloughs, too, have long been the perfect world for shallow-draft boats, kayaks and canoes, jonboats and skiffs.

Rachel Carson fell upon this interwoven web of wind, wave, and tides when she came to work at the U.S. Fish & Wildlife station on Pivers Island, the small toehold island in the western waters of Taylor's Creek, just across Gallants Channel from Front Street's western end. She took to wandering its small dunes and flats, all the way out to the long, thin beach of Bird Shoal, noticing and noting even the least creatures and their works, and here, in *The Edge of the Sea*, she saw the world and she saw it whole. As she wrote at the book's outset:

"The edge of the sea is a strange and beautiful place."

A thought she continued, closing in on this very place:

Wild Ponies at pond on Town Marsh, Rachel Carson Reserve, 2009

To visit Bird Shoal, one goes out by boat through channels winding through the Town Marsh of Beaufort and comes ashore on a rim of sand held firm by the deep roots of beach grasses—the landward border of the shoal. The burrows of thousands of fiddler crabs riddle the muddy beach on the side facing the marshes. The crabs shuffle across the flats at the approach of an intruder, and the sound of many small chitinous feet is like the crackling of paper. Crossing the ridge of sand, one looks out over the shoal. If the tide still has an hour or two to fall to its ebb, one sees only a sheet of water shimmering in the sun.

Ann and I have boated and strolled all over the place for most of thirty years now, our twins often climbing and jumping off the high dunes at Bird Shoal's channel-end in summertime, Cary coming with us by jon-boat and canoe from the little put-in at the foot of Gordon Street, clambering up the ponies' dunes and over onto the tidal flat for the wet, sandy walk to Bird Shoal, the nearly private beach looking out toward Shackleford Banks. The panorama presents Beaufort Inlet's breakers far off in the wind, old Fort Macon, the state port's big cranes, and, around behind us, the rooftops of Front Street houses old and new.

Sailing skiffs, runabouts, and catboats, headboats and dredges and tankers and giant cargo ships all course up and down the channel, and

Scott Taylor and other intrepid kayakers will circumnavigate the whole of Town Marsh and Carrot Island, 2,300 acres of maritime wilds, long since named Rachel Carson Estuarine Reserve for the visionary woman who spent some of her good life watching the ways of this place. From an aircraft at a thousand feet, Scott once put his lens to work capturing hundreds of nurse sharks that he saw feeding in the shallows behind the inlet, between Bird Shoal and Shackleford Banks.

We feast here, too, no less than they. Early and late, coastal light and air play over the stretches of sand, the lush green-grassed shallows, the dark sand- and mudflats, the salt waters covering them. If Bird Shoal and all its collaborative spaces lack the remoteness of Core Banks or Pea Island to the north, or of Hammocks Beach or Masonborough Island to the south, they are nonetheless all related—they have shared sand and water with each other for eons, as they will for ages yet to come.

One who lingers here feels that Bird Shoal may be not only at the center of our coast, but at the center of much else, too.

The sweet mystery of life only deepens, Rachel, as you well knew.

When *Honey Fitz* Hit Town

On the first of June a couple years ago, we put the kayaks onto Taylor's Creek at the small floating dock at the foot of Orange Street, where for decades the ships of Beaufort's great menhaden fleet, big ships with their seine skiffs and crow's nests, would lay rafted up when they were in. We were bound—Ann, our slender, bearded neighbor Bill Garlick, and I—around the corner, as it were, up Gallants Channel to the marina at Town Creek.

A healthy southwest breeze bounced us through a bit of chop as the last of the afternoon's high tide came in, and we paddled past the big Philadelphia yacht on the point, past small boats up on lifts, one of them a Simmons Sea Skiff, one of Carolina's great twentieth-century small craft and a nifty sight at that, in the channel across from Nasty Harbor, which the red shrimp trawlers called home. Then under the little bascule bridge, the Grayden Paul, which will be long remembered and lamented once a high flyover span replaces it, and past the little beach where today half a dozen African Americans were out fishing.

Now we were in the lee of the town, and the water flattened right out. Across the cove, the classic day cruiser *Honey Fitz* lay, tied up bow in at a south-facing dock, and we floated up to her and toured her from the water, stem to stern. At a time when many large craft, the outlandish modern mega-yachts, look like molded plastic toys with dark tinted windows resembling wraparound sunglasses, here was a sterling model from the old days: bright white, long and lean, teak-toned, tawny curtains in her salon windows, a top deck big enough for seventy, a long red stripe at her waterline, her nearly plumb-stem bow reminiscent of old-time Coast Guard cutters, and the Presidential seal on her stack.

From below the squared-off stern, Bill looked up and said, "She reminds me of a railroad car."

Some train! The ninety-two-foot *Honey Fitz* cruised on the strength of a pair of 500-horsepower locomotive engines, and she had seen a wide variety of service since Defoe Boat Works of Bay City, Michigan, built her for Sewell Avery, Montgomery Ward's chief, back in 1931. The Coast Guard claimed her at the start of World War II and put her to work, first as a picket ship off Rockaway Point and Fire Island, New York, then as a trainer for submarine crews. Refitted in June 1945, she became a tender to the large Presidential yachts *Potomac* (165 feet) and *Williamsburg* (245 feet). Ike liked her a lot, naming her *Barbara Anne* and taking her out on the Potomac and on Narragansett Bay. But JFK liked her even more, and he is said to have put her to the most use, rechristening her *Honey Fitz* after his father's father, the Boston mayor, and floating on her in the Potomac, off Newport, and at Palm Beach. Later, Nixon sold her—no salt he.

More recently, a Texas oilman named Kallop (whose grandfather was once a schoolmate of Kennedy's) bought her and completely restored her in West Palm Beach—for over time she had gotten fifteen degrees off kilter. In 2013 Kallop had sent her off raising money for charities, a goodwill tour of the eastern seaboard.

The next day we went back for more, this time with Mike and Corliss Bradley in their runabout, and *Honey Fitz* was as lovely as she had been at first sight. Mike then cruised us over to the state port, where the huge, 554-foot Singapore freighter *Pac Athena* lay docked. The wildlife fellows were out checking licenses in the Intracoastal Waterway near Sugarloaf Island, and we drifted down into the great turning basin, where a massive dredge worked away. The big Olympus dive boat passed us at quite a smart clip to starboard. Thousands of horsepower were out on display this afternoon.

Including ours. I was at the helm now, bringing us around the Radio Island rock jetty, Shark Shoal where the crabs and the sheepshead hold sway, and back up the Beaufort channel and into Taylor's Creek. The day was perfectly balmy, light and breezy, irreducibly gorgeous out on the water.

How many thousands of sloops, schooners, spritsail skiffs, watercraft of all sorts and size, have plied this channel, I have often wondered and always will. As we headed up the creek, I remembered just a few of them: the old long and low oyster buy boat that used to show up here once a

Taylor's Creek, from Town Marsh looking east, 2009

year or so; the 74-foot brigantine *S/V Fritha* out of Fairhaven, Massachusetts, that wintered here more recently; the 184-foot cruising ship *Grande Caribe* from Warren, Rhode Island (bright white with a long blue stripe around her pilothouse and upper deck); the small, teaky yacht *Bounce* that Tommy Thompson, our dear late friend, the champion banjoist and former Mississippi River coast guard patroller, loved so; Commander Tom Harper's catboat *Blue Goose*; the catamaran sailboat *Lookout* that has long shown visitors the banks and the Cape; the blue-and-white doubledecked *Mystery* that for years toured the harbor on hot days and moonlit nights. I thought of a thousand late-night strolls with Ann, and of so many temperate afternoons like today's, the sweet, soft summer air breezing up our way from out of the southwest.

"Days like this make me wonder why I moved away," Mike said. "So what I really need to think about is what it's like here during February."

Friends and the wind, Jimm's voice echoed across thirty years: *just friends and the wind.*

12

The White Oak

Dixon Field to Haywood Landing

Dixon Field Landing was a shady place on narrow water, the White Oak River only a couple dozen feet wide and as much a blackwater river this far upstream—just south of Maysville—as any in the Carolina east. All told, we were a raft of boats, ten strong by the time we got the kayaks onto the water that Sunday morning in July 2011—I had promised Carl Spangler, our old friend and one of the Beaufort Oars, that this was simply going to be a lazy-river day, nothing like the dreadfully hard paddle that I had gotten him in on, going up into the Great Dismal Swamp against Lake Drummond's stern, heavy storm-waters outflow the previous fall.

So we were off a little before noon, easily gliding down the dark, luscious, slender strand. Huge cypress trees loomed over us, much larger individuals than I had expected—one, double-trunked like a tuning fork, stood just below Dixon Field Landing. On this hot day in high summer, the swamp singers sang: a prothonotary warbler flitted its golden way in and out of the thickets, a pileated woodpecker sounding off *kuk-kuk-kuk* nearby and out of sight. The swamp garden was putting out, too: duck potato, frothy white-topped cow parsnip, water arum with their white petals presenting small golden columns, a band of cattails, brilliant red cardinal flower in bloom. All this fecundity and loveliness way out yonder in the wild, whether anyone was looking or not, reminded me of a line in Emerson's *Rhodora*—"Beauty is its own excuse for being"—and it touched me, as it always does.

Just shy of six miles was the White Oak's run down from Dixon Field to Haywood Landing, and who would wish to rush it? Little pockets of freshwater marsh flourished alongside this creeklike stretch of river, and I found it a distinct pleasure to wander off into a glade for a few minutes at a time.

Off to our right for most of the way lay the Quaternary Tract, from Starkeys Creek (the honoree was pioneer settler and assemblyman John Starkey) on down to below Mulberry Creek past Haywood Landing, a 1,400-acre-and-then-some swamp wilderness that a conservation coalition had acquired back in 2004 and then given it over to the state of North Carolina for gamelands. The river that lolled down out of the White Oak Pocosin in upper Onslow and lower Jones Counties was not very long, just forty-eight miles, had little gradient, and was in no perceptible rush on its way to Bogue Inlet and the sea.

Yet it did grand work.

The White Oak, historically, drained nearly half a million wetland acres, three-fifths of which were still reasonably close in nature to what they were at the time of European contact. Much of its eastern flank made up a part of the massive, 160,000-acre Croatan National Forest, and, along with the Morton and Huggins Tracts downstream where the river quickly broadens below Stella, the Quaternary Tract has proven to be a mighty and good contribution toward the preservation of the White Oak's pristine waters.

In late August 2014, Swansboro's *Tideland News* editorialized against the embattled potential sale of the 79,000-acre Hofmann Forest, the nation's largest research forest just to the White Oak River's west, by N.C. State University to a midwestern corporate farm and an Alabama timber firm. Though financing for this particular deal collapsed and the university canceled it in early December 2014, in doing so the chancellor declared the great forest still to be on the block, while sale opponents fought on in North Carolina's Supreme Court.

"Not such a good idea," the newspaper stated, hoping that either N.C. State University would reverse course and keep Hofmann or that the U.S. Forest Service would absorb the tract into the Croatan. Fearing the damage that stormwater runoff from potential development in the forest would inevitably cause, the *Tideland News* put it bluntly:

"Hofmann's Future Is White Oak's Future."

Indeed. With the Hofmann Forest's help, with the altruistic activities of the late Elmer Eddy and his thousands of Stewards of the White Oak River Basin, and with $23 million in public water-quality funding, this little river has kept itself uncommonly clean. May it always remain so.

Not far above Holston Creek's confluence with the White Oak, the river made a sharp, full turn to the south, and from there on, we paddled in long, broad reaches, as the river attained a different character, one reminiscent of the lakelike passages in creeks off the Alligator River in the Albemarle country, or even those in the Suwanee in southern Georgia's Okefenokee Swamp. With both wind and tidal current now coming strong at us, we worked our paddles quite a good deal harder, and I tasted salt in waters that were no longer black.

Ann and I both thought we should have reached Haywood Landing by now, midafternoon, and she wondered aloud a time or two if we might be on the wrong track, if somehow we could have passed the landing. I said that this was a fairly narrow corridor, with only one unbraided river in it, that we were surely heading south, and that the landing was just too big to miss. Still, we had lost sight of our companions, we were paddling harder and harder, and I had started to wonder myself.

We passed one more enormous monarch cypress on the east bank, at a spot that we would learn was about a mile yet upriver of Haywood. Just then the effervescent Patty Davis of Beaufort's Tierra Fina caught up with us, excited that she had just spied an alligator, which, upon spying her, had quickly disappeared into the reeds.

After not too long a while, to our pleasure and relief, as we rounded a slight bend the bluff of Haywood Landing came into view. Two whiskery old boys were getting their Basstracker into the water, and a woman in a skimpy sundress sat in a beach chair beside the boat ramp, a brown-and-white setter lying nearby, the woman languidly smoking a cigarette, watching us with as little interest and as dull a regard as possible while we came in, soon followed by the rest of our comrades.

"I thought you said this was a lazy river," said Carl Spangler, breathing hard and giving me a sidewise gaze, just a bit of a paint-peeler, as we hauled the boats on up the bluff.

"Well, it was," I said, knowing he had me dead to rights about those last two testy miles. "For a while."

Around Haywood Landing

On the Ides of March 2014, nosing the jonboat up Grant's Creek, a large stream coming into the White Oak from the west a couple miles or so below Haywood Landing, we went looking for alligators.

Dark green cedars and winter-bare cypress grew along the tawny marsh, which looked like fine gator terrain to me. Yet, though we saw many slides, no alligators obliged us by appearing. Only large painted turtles on logs, falling off at our approach, and one feral escapee: on a downed tree in the river, studying us coolly, a trepidatious Muscovy duck.

After cruising for a spell in the broad, marshy wiggles (a few hawks and buzzards flying, and a solitary wood duck) in the White Oak on down toward Stella, we came around and headed back up, passing a group of eight or ten marines, all men, setting up a grill at the Long Point landing—many a cooler, but not a boat in sight.

"Party time," Ann said from the bow, and none would gainsay it.

A light-hearted moment, that, and one in marked contrast to the damp morning twenty years ago when a hunter up on a deer stand just a quarter mile back in the Croatan Forest from the White Oak River at Long Point spied something strange and unsettling. The early morning light lit up the dewfall on the grasses of the forest floor, and the man, seeing what seemed to be ranked depressions, had the sudden, eerie feeling that he was hunting in a graveyard.

The Forest Service, investigating his report, discovered 220 graves, yet not a single marker. Who were these dead? Slaves? Victims of an epidemic? Fallen soldiers from a Civil War battle? No one living had any idea, outside of an older African American man who recalled as a boy being walked past this hallowed place (then full of wooden crosses, and a beech tree with hatchet marks to keep count of the graves) by his elders, their quieting him and telling him, "These are the folks you, and all of us, owe our freedom to." Whoever they had been in life, if their last resting places had had wooden gravemarkers, common in the East, a past controlled burn to clear brush and vines from the overgrown forest floor would have easily incinerated such dried, ancient slabs and left no traces. Wiregrass growing up and covering the ground would have obscured the depressions.

Until a lone man up a tree with the right slant of light was given a new perspective on these long-dead. Ground-penetrating radar has fairly confirmed what the hunter suspected, with one reflection even seeming to a forest service official to be that of a metal coffin. DNA testing of the interred who had lain so long undisturbed at newly named Long Point Cemetery may be sought in the near future, and, as ever, one recalled Doctor Thomas Browne's somber truth from his 1658 meditation *Urne-Buriall*:

"Oblivion is not to be hired."

Upriver above Haywood Landing, a couple in a very low-to-the-water craft fished desultorily, as did another pair in a jonboat powered only by a trolling motor. A father and son in a Lowecraft used long, thin stakes, like bamboo, thrust down into the riverbottom to keep them in place, enabling them to move from spot to spot and reset more quickly, and more easily, than they could have with an anchor or two. In the riverside forest, a man in camouflage stood beside his ATV, lost in thought, or perhaps simply lost.

Maybe all of us were guilty of rushing the season. Yet how could it not feel grand to be moving about a riverswamp, seeing who and what else

Creek off White Oak River above Haywood Landing, March 2014

were abroad, what was waking up and coming to grips with the southern world this mid-March Saturday afternoon?

Ann and I had brought Tipper Davis, our good friend from Beaufort, along on this mission, and he seemed not to mind the ride. Tipper—a master preservationist, a designer and builder who has done much work at Mount Vernon—was an avid, skillful boater who owned a featherweight graphite canoe that he paddled double-bladed kayak style. A skillful boatbuilder too: he had built his first boat, an eight-foot pram, when he was eight, and his second, a fifty-eight-foot sailboat, when he was nineteen. He had joined us on a float up in the Great Dismal several Octobers back, when to get up to the spillway and Lake Drummond, we had to fight the powerful, literal outpouring of Tropical Storm Nicole's waters (she had dropped a foot or more of rain all over the North Carolina and Virginia tidewater) coming at us down the Feeder Ditch from the lake.

Tipper had been the very first to reach the spillway.

Now, as we puttered back down to Haywood Landing, we spoke of other boats, other gear. "I'm done with big boats," Tipper said, shaking his head. "Had it with 'em." He was just now renovating a classic, high-shine Airstream behind his Live Oak Street home in Beaufort.

"What about your airplane?" I asked (he used to commute by small aircraft from his house to George Washington's). "Still got it?"

"No," the droll man with the mustache said, smiling. "I wasn't going up to Virginia all that much anymore. Couldn't afford to keep it just to go fly around Cape Lookout Lighthouse once a month. I got myself a new motto."

"What's that?"

"No toys," Tipper said, "that don't live in the backyard."

Stella

Stella, at thirty feet above sea level Carteret County's highest point, and its river bridge at Boondocks Landing lay a dozen broad, looping reaches and bends downstream of Long Point, just an old, closed-up-tight brick fertilizer warehouse and a turn-of-the-last-century white frame general store (closed) with a small post office (open) in its southwest corner. A late nineteenth-century grandee's white mansion just up the bluff from the old store towered over all, and on a recent sunny July afternoon the main enterprise and activity in the tiny hamlet were all wrapped up in the Green River Preserve's coastal base camp: young boaters, middle- and high-schoolers from all over creation, had spent many days taking on our lowland, sound-country waters, and were now busily cleaning salt-encrusted life jackets and washing off their dozen kayaks.

Scott Grafton, the tanned and handsome, happily loquacious fifty-two-year-old owner of the old home and store, sat on the edge of a big barbecue cooker giving genial encouragement to the youths, for whom he was slow-cooking a pair of pork shoulders, and spinning lively tales about his little corner of paradise. First, he gave us the geographics: seven miles downriver to the Intracoastal Waterway, eight miles upriver to Haywood Landing—"But if you take a GPS and straight-line it, it's only three miles!"

Then the weather. Though this one was a real nice hot summer day, Grafton recalled, some years ago, a sudden summer squall coming up out of nowhere, with gusts to seventy—there were a bunch of canoes down by the river, and several of them were snatched up by the wind, blown up into the air, clipping the telephone poles. "It was unreal!" he said.

And then the fishing. He reported that the big red drum were currently laying up in the river one to two miles downriver of Stella. Every Thursday, September till January, Grafton allowed, he staged a fish fry here on

Walking tree,
Upper White
Oak, March
2014

the Stella grounds—"Whoever's got fish brings fish, everybody else brings something else.

"In the fall of the year," he said, "The speckled trout fishing here around Stella is out of this world!"

Jones Island

When the North Carolina Coastal Federation's genial, burly associate director, the fine journalist Frank Tursi, first got onto Jones Island in the middle of the lower White Oak River, he judged its twenty-four acres, seventeen of which were up for sale, to be a little on the wild side.

Its shoreline, pelted by wave action, rising tides, and coastal storms of all styles and seasons, was wasting away. Like most any untended real estate in the sound country, the island was overgrown, a small pine and live-oak forest returning to jungle, in league with yaupon and myrtle thickets. A small junked-up house had no electricity or water, though it did in one room have a special collection of mirrors on walls and ceiling, and appeared to get at least occasional use.

"The love shack," Tursi called it.

The painted bunting flew and nested here, too, and the little island lay just a brief boat ride or kayak paddle from either shore of the river. Tursi and Sam Bland, the skillful naturalist who for years directed Hammocks Beach State Park before joining the NCCF's board, then its staff, both saw the place as a significant opportunity for the group, and for the state park.

In October 2007 came the chance to act: as with Huggins Island just downriver, the NCCF used Clean Water Management Trust funds, along with an Audubon donation, to buy most of Jones Island and then donate it to the park. Nowadays, the grounds and former love shack on the island's north end have gotten some grooming, and, up on the ten-foot bluff there, nearly six acres of Spanish-mossed, live-oak-canopied lawn made a good prospect from which to survey the White Oak. Swarms of volunteers have boated out, planted cordgrass, salt meadow hay, and black needlerush, and set oyster-shell-bag sills in place along the shore—all to help it accrete, rather than erode, and to encourage the return of native oysters. Rising third- to fifth-graders have encamped here on summertime days to learn of island wildlife and ecology.

And April Clark of Second Wind Eco Tours and Sally Steele of the NCCF have been leading kayak-and-yoga treks from Cedar Point Wildlife Landing out to Jones Island from spring to fall.

All in all, a rather good change in estate for the little island, a different fate from the condominium-cluster that might have been imposed upon it, development whose runoff would almost inevitably have fought the river, rather than preserved and restored its health. So seasonal use it was for Jones Island these days, just as the Neusiok made of it, the Native Americans whose potsherds are there yet, and, too, their shell-shaking spirits, and some of their bones.

Clyde Phillips Seafood

During the many years I have served on the Coastal Federation's board of directors, one of the great ancillary joys of it all has been bringing home to Ann the fresh fruits of river and sound and sea.

For quite a spell I made the quarterly trips to NCCF's headquarters, just across the road from the pine-and-wiregrass savanna of Patsy Pond in the southern Croatan National Forest, by way of Beaufort—typically, a drive down late Friday, dinner with Scott Taylor's and Lenore Meadows's bohemian crowd somewhere along the waters of Taylor's Creek, followed by several rounds of eight-ball at the Royal James if I were lucky, and then off to the meeting the next morning, during which our board and staff pondered conservation easements, water-quality initiatives, program expansions, occasional court actions, all in all by my lights the most progressive coastal-policy outfit at work in North Carolina.

As these Saturday sessions drew to a close along about three o'clock, I would ponder my next move. Sometimes I would drive with dispatch to the small blue cinder-block building on the long, broad curve east of the White Oak River bridges, "Shellfish 2000," home of a devoted oyster gatherer whose name I never got—though from him I bought many a bushel he had tonged the day before, usually from nearby in the White Oak (he would tell me by name the hammock or piece of marsh, as the tag only said: "White Oak River"), sometimes from up the coast just a ways, around Middle Marshes, where the North River Channel comes through and meets the Shackleford Slue behind Beaufort Inlet.

Sometimes I stopped at a newer outlet, Runners Seafood at Bogue, for a while my solid depend-upon for oysters. Then after a spell Runners closed its doors, and in more recent years after our meetings I found myself drifting down to the White Oak River fishhouse that dated all the way back to the year of Hurricane Hazel, 1954.

Clyde Phillips Seafood.

Its plain old bold sunrise-pastel 1950s two-story self recalled The Band's musical redoubt of many years ago, "Big Pink," as it sat on the modest, narrow sandbar island between the two river bridges of N.C. 24 crossing the White Oak from Cedar Point to Swansboro. A long, lean dock out back was homeport to shrimpers—the *Capt Phillips* (a big white otter-trawl craft with red butterfly wings, built by Harold D. Varnum at Holden Beach back in 1981) and some skimmer trawlers too.

We watched the *Capt Phillips* come slowly in and tie up late one Thursday afternoon in August, back from a run far up into Pamlico Sound that had begun here four and a half days earlier, on Sunday at 7 A.M. Captain Jimmy Phillips, grandson of the boat's namesake, said they had been shrimping hard up near Englehard, Long Shoal, and Stumpy Point, and were now bringing home pushing three thousand pounds, a hundred boxes, on ice in the hold.

When hurricanes approached this spot, the river waters came right up to the edge of the dock planking and, indeed, right up to the fishhouse doors. A Pepsi machine sat to the right of the front door, and off to the left was maybe a tenth of an acre of free parking. By night, a huge pink neon shrimp on the store wall glowed away and told the story.

Clyde Phillips Seafood Market, White Oak River between the bridges, Swansboro, August 2014

Tipper Davis had an agreeable tale of his own about Clyde Phillips Seafood, from the time many years ago when he and two crew members sailed his self-made fifty-eight-foot schooner from the Bahamas bound for Chesapeake Bay, and anchored here, below the bridge at Swansboro one rainy day. "We had three dollars between us," he said, "so we walked across the bridge and into the fishhouse and said 'How much shrimp can we get for three dollars?' I guess we looked pretty bedraggled. They took a snow shovel, scooped up shrimp and filled a big brown grocery bag, and we went back to the sailboat and had steamed shrimp and beer on deck the rest of the afternoon."

Inside, the store had a few chairs, space for half a dozen folks ("the sideline crew," they called themselves) to mill around, framed fading feature stories about the place on the walls, and current owner Jimmy Phillips, father of the trawler's captain, gray-haired, in jeans and bluish checked shirt, had an easygoing manner as he laconically directed behind-the-counter gutting and fileting of fish, heading of shrimp, and in general satisfying the surf-loving trade that wandered through his door. Red was the color: of T-shirts with a "Between the Bridges" motto scripted on each one below a line-drawing of the *Capt Phillips*; of small, collapsible coolers with the same images.

I never concerned myself with oysters in this particular world—shrimp

and fish was what they did and what they had. (Mill Creek and Down East
oysters were still to be had upstate at Tom Robinson's Seafood in Carr-
boro, near home, after all.) I liked hearing about red drum back in the
old days, fish that had scales so big and thick you could pick a guitar with
them, and, too, I liked the resilient down-home stoicism over how things
do come and go in Jimmy Phillips's remark, "We may have went in the
hole on the cabbage, but we're gonna make up for it on the taters."

Mostly I liked just being on the edge of a North Carolina river buying a dinner's worth of fresh fish, just as I had done as an Elizabeth City boy when my mother sent me down on my bicycle to Mister Crank's fishhouse on Tiber Creek, right where that little stream hit the Pasquotank, and getting real, good food from real, good people in yet another of the loveliest spots in all Carolina, and hearing Jimmy say in farewell "Come back, now," and taking something that slept in the ocean last night home to my baby and laying it on the grill and then putting it on the table for her not four whole hours from right then.

Ain't that, as the all-wise, downhome jazzman Mose Allison once sang, just like livin'?

13

New River

Brim

H. H. Brimley, brought from Bedfordshire, England, to Raleigh, North Carolina, by his parents when he was nineteen in 1880, back when the capital city offered its citizens and visitors only rutted mud streets, took to North Carolina's natural world like a red-cockaded woodpecker to a longleaf pine. This astonishingly gifted naturalist, writer, and photographer, friend and collaborator of Audubon leader T. Gilbert Pearson, along with his own brother Clement, on *Birds of North Carolina*, not only founded and led, for his lifetime, the state's Museum of Natural History (now our Museum of Natural Sciences), he also toured our varied Carolina terrains indefatigably, and created a colorful, learned, and deep documentary portrait of late nineteenth- and early twentieth-century life afield and afloat in the Old North State, leaving behind thousands of photographs from the coast to the mountains.

One of Brimley's favorite coastal haunts, one where he often took Pal, his equally adventurous wife, was the Onslow Hunting Club, an isolated spot with docks on French's Creek, just off the lower New River's eastern side. For years hereabouts the Brimleys in midsummer paddled and poled their small craft, the *Flapper*, in Brimley's words "a skeleton-framed, canvas-covered canoe, fourteen feet long by thirty-six inches beam," with "a seven foot cockpit amidships." Brim, as he came to be called, recorded some of his favorite times on the New in his essay "Flapper Frolics."

Early one morning, as Brim was poling them down toward Goose Creek, which he called "a stinking mudhole, fine for alligators but no good for bass," the Brimleys had a brief but moving moment watching an "immaculate" pair of gray foxes at the river's edge. Once, up before sunrise to go alligator hunting on Cowhead Creek, Brim and Pal at first light surprised a wild turkey and her brood. Near sundown on another day, the pair was

bass-fishing on Jumping Run when, from trees near the creekbank, "seven great turkey gobblers left their roosting place and winged their way back into the depths of the swamp."

Brimley harbored a keen determination to take a gator and, from its hide, stitch up a traveling bag for Pal, and he showed no squeamishness about his means to that end. At the Onslow Club one evening, he took from a setter's new litter a puppy that had died, then hooked it on a line and towed it ("We could not stand it in the boat," he said of the ripe, swollen creature) down to a gut in the marsh above Duck Creek, and rigged the line to a pair of cedars—he tied it fast to a live tree and then lightly hung it across "the extreme end of one of the snaggy branches" of "a dead, partly submerged cedar," "with the bait just above the surface." Back out early the next morning, Brim and Pal got there just in time to see the huge bull gator they sought caught and wrestling with the line, until, as they waited patiently in *Flapper*, Brim holding his Luger pistol to finish it, the gator thrashed heroically and broke free. The Brimleys then hung around half an hour expecting him to resurface before finally admitting he was another one that had gotten away.

The Brimley frolics on the lower New ended with an uptick, though. A big fish in Duck Creek took Brim's bait—"a brand new Shimmy Wiggler with a gorgeous Parmachenee Belle trailer"—and immediately got itself all hung up in sunken brush. Pal nobly set about trying to dig it free with

Flapper's "six foot spruce paddle for a spade," and her efforts were soon rewarded: a three-and-a-quarter largemouth bass "flopping on the floorboards between us."

If this all seems so long ago, a century or more past, and decades before massive Camp Lejeune took over the lower New River and changed that landscape forever, so it was. Let it live in its own spectral time. Yet also let Brim and Pal guide us, and show us the way to go back and linger there awhile.

And let these two good ghosts show us a way to be.

Rich Lands

The New River, this fifty-mile-long stream all of it in the one county of Onslow, is said by some to be the shortest river in the world to be so wide—as it is below Jacksonville. In its upper basin, the sinuous New River was once a highly resinous country, and people in the antebellum days often called the vast longleaf pine stands "turpentine orchards." Well might they have termed them "turpentine *mines*," for the practices dealt the longleaf were thoroughly extractive and unsustainable—yet while the pines lasted, there was enormous money to be made, and thousands of men slashed boxes, V-cut grooves, into the tree trunks, and the longleaf resin oozed down the barkless tree trunks into bowls and pots, from which it was dipped into barrels and wagoned to distilleries and refined.

The Rich Lands: so the Avirett family of upper Onslow County named its nineteenth-century New River plantation, some miles to the north of Jacksonville and Tar Landing. John Avirett, patriarch and squire, held 20,000 acres of longleaf pinelands, a fiefdom of thirty-four square miles, and, with the aid of 125 slaves and a slave named Philip as his lieutenant and field commander, he drained a fortune out of it. Two large distilleries stood on the south shore of Catherine Lake, six miles from Tar Landing above Jacksonville, each with a chimney smoking away while crude turpentine, brought in from the piney woods in barrels by mule-train drayage, boiled below, cut with water pumped into the mills from the lake by a windmill. Thirty thousand barrels of refined spirits of turpentine came out of the Avirett mills each year, and captains and vessels waited on them at the Avirett family's wharf several miles upstream of Tar Landing. Those very captains were ordered to bring with them on their return—when they came back upriver at Christmas-time from Wilmington and Jacksonville—a full complement of New River oysters, as well as clams, shrimp, scallops, mullet, trout, sheepshead, flounder, croaker, wine from the Rich Lands' merchant trading-partners, and stiffer spirits than wine.

The Aviretts hunted foxes with hounds named Fashion and Juno. They shot bear out of trees. They entertained guests from all around the coastal plain, from Clinton, Kenansville, Kinston, and Trenton, from New Bern and Wilmington. They danced quadrilles and mazurkas, while their slaves kicked double shuffles and pigeon wings, chicken-in-the-bread-tray and cakewalks. They all sang out: "Grey Eagle" and "Fire on the Mountain." The Rich Lands rang to the music of banjo and fiddle, piano and guitar, even to the rhythms of the castanet.

And, through all the exuberance and society, through all this New River gaiety, all the while the river of resin ran out of the dying Avirett forests (longleaf pines lasting a mere half dozen years once the boxing and scraping and draining commenced) with nothing to replace it. Four years before Edmund Ruffin pulled the lanyard on the cannon aimed at Fort Sumter, the Aviretts sold off the Rich Lands for a pittance, an average of $2.25 an acre for the whole fabulous place.

No gone with the wind here; no blaming it on The War.

The Aviretts had indeed lost it all, yet they had done it all on their own.

Catherine Lake is still there, and a lane leading to and from it is still called Mill Road. All that remains of the monumental Rich Lands is its name in the record of the squire's son, Episcopal Reverend James Battle Avirett's valuable yet romantic, rhapsodic 1901 memoir, *The Old Plantation: How We Lived in Great House and Cabin before the War,* though the hamlet across the New River from it, known through much of the nineteenth century as Upper Rich Lands, became Richlands in 1880.

And Richlands endures.

My Grandfather's Map

My grandfather, Julius Andrews Page Sr., was born in late January 1886, twenty-one years after Appomattox, to a Confederate infantry veteran and his farm wife, she who wore the same size shoes her husband did and wore his new peg-soled brogans before he did, to break them in for him. Granddaddy came into the world in a tenant farmhouse, just a scant mile west of the New River naval-stores shipping wharf, Tar Landing.

Though he moved to Wilmington with his family in 1900, where he learned all the building trades during his teenage years, in time becoming a master builder of public works, he had incredibly strong memories of his boyhood home, and he often punctuated the endings of his remembrances with "Oh, that was *hard*, son, that was *hard*." He spoke of Catherine Lake and its healing waters (Alum Springs), and of Richlands, where he remembered seeing the intimidating, white-supremacist segregationist Red Shirts parade through on horseback in red union-suits and bearing shotguns, the gun-butts on their hips, in 1898.

He told me of chopping up nails and even lead sinkers for shot, when he was put to hunting squirrels, going down toward the river with the family's old flintlock, coming back with enough for dinner. He told me of the boy about his age who overate unripe chinquapin nuts, a real belly full of them, on one day, only to die the next. He told me of Jake the Indian, a workman by day who was a tent-revivalist preacher by night, right up till the night he asked the sisters to fill his water pitcher with white liquor, whereupon the fire and the brimstone and the love of the Lamb that he laid down that evening caused the biggest collection of souls Preacher Jake had ever had to walk down the sawdust path to Jesus, and he looked himself in the mirror at home later and said, "Jake, you're a hypocrite" and quit the whole revivaling business, never to preach again—all this he confessed to my young grandfather.

And Granddaddy told me of the day in his early teens when he was given the reins to the family's wagon and told to drive up to Kinston with the farm's tobacco crop and sell it, a distance of forty miles, which he did, leaving before dawn and making the sale at the Neuse River market-town, then turning the horse around and riding all the way home, finally falling asleep in the dark, reins in his hands, somewhere near Richlands, and not waking up again till the horse stopped stock still in the dirt yard there before his Tar Landing home.

Early in his ninth decade (he lived through most of his ninety-first year), he sat down and prepared from memory a map of his boyhood settlement, and his small 8½-by-11-inch document carries in its few lines and locations a wealth of Tar Landing society. He shows the house where he was born, another where his cousins lived, where the store and the church were, where barns and stables were, and a cooper shop, a barrel warehouse, a turpentine still, graveyards. The narrow New River comes down from Richlands, and, just above Tar Landing's wharf, oxbows out to the east—the old main stem—while a cutoff carries the flow southerly and creates an unnamed island. Granddaddy's map notes, with an arrow to the landing, that it was 150 MOW (miles over water) to Wilmington from this spot, nearly thrice the distance overland, and reports "for 10 miles from here, no sailing, [cargo sailboats] pushed by men, using wood poles 30 feet long +/- from side of boat." Anyone believing that getting tar, pitch, turpentine, or any other form of resin to market back in the olden times was an easy matter might just linger on those few words. A thirty-foot-long wooden pole is one hefty, heavy tool.

A darker report evinces itself in the last half a dozen lines in his legend to the Tar Landing map, one of violence in the little crossroads and not just violence, but an astonishing variety of it. In one spot, "Langley, a man killed in a house—shot through door." Another was a "Negro tenant log house—baby: killed by hog." One shot, one torn up by an animal. These were violent and strange enough for my grandfather to recall, at seventy years distance, from his early teenage years, and yet a third incident was stranger still. In a house not far west of the Negro tenant's, a "white tenant" was "killed by lightning, cursing God."

Hard times in the country.

The good old days.

Bastille Day at Tar Landing

Just under the bridges and upriver of the parkside ramps in downtown Jacksonville, we headed upstream in the jonboat, floating through the low, marshy, unpopulous reaches, much in the way of tall green grasses and cattails, of the New River. An osprey prowled the marine territory near its west-side nest, and Ann and I in our boat encountered only three other craft late this July afternoon and evening.

Swamp woods—cypress, pine, maple, grapevine—closed in as the river narrowed about three miles up, and, in another mile, we slowed as we passed a high, hundred-yard-long bluff, a pair of docks at the foot of it.

Then not much farther on, we came to a large, swampy, unnamed island. A partially overgrown sign nailed to a tree at the foot of the island read "Keep Left," and so we did. We had the jonboat not forty feet up that reach when here came a big, laden, rolling-wake-making runabout, what the keen outdoor writer Eddie Nickens would call "a floating sofa," sloshing its way along a mite too rapidly, passing us quickly. We followed the straightaway reach on up to the head of the jungly island, then broke off from the river's channel and came around starboard in order to circumnavigate the stout half-mile land. On the east was a narrow, curvy passage, many logs in the stream and much to look out for, both the danger of snags and the grapevine-tangled loveliness of the way less traveled, before the oxbow came back to the main channel.

Again we slowed as we approached the long bluff, for this had once been my grandfather's youthful purchase on the New River: this was Tar Landing, where the small ships pulled in and pulled out, poling all the way, as he noted, this far up. As a black man in a silver jonboat smiled and eased past us southward, we cut our engine and drifted awhile. A kingfisher, and herons both blue and green, awaited us downriver, yet let them wait. For a few moments we could drift in current and drift through time, the evening sun setting a golden glow that seemed to be rolling aslant down the bluff . . . the house in which my grandfather had first seen the light had stood not far west of where we now floated—and seventy years

New River
just above
Jacksonville,
July 2014

after his birth here, Ann was born just a few miles downriver at Camp Lejeune, when her father was a navy doctor on the base, he and Ann's mother loving the wet, wild coastal territory they would bring their family back to half a dozen years later.

Such resonance held within it some features of a Walker Percy *rotation*, a sense of return to a place we had never been before, and a gift indeed it was for us to float this portion of the dark, narrow stream for the first time together on Bastille Day, a day we hold dear.

Something of a liberation.

Something New.

sweetheart stream

Upper Lumber

Down on the Lumbee River
Where the eddies ripple cool,
Your boat, I know, glides stealthily
Along some shady pool.
— from "Sunburnt Boys,"
    by John Charles McNeill (1874–1907)
    of Riverton, North Carolina

On the afternoon of the third day canoeing down the upper Lumber River in 1915, young Leonard Freeman shot his sixteen-foot craft past a fallen tree, grazing the bank and rousing a wild nursing sow, a three-hundred-pounder, that had her brood of a dozen nestled on a spit of land between the dark river and its swamp. Williams Haynes, Freeman's companion, impulsively slid a paddle underneath one of the piglets like a spatula, flipped it to Freeman in the canoe, and off they went, out of the Sandhills longleaf pine country and downstream to Lumberton, where they procured a nursing bottle for their new ward, on down into the cypress jungles of the lower Lumber—fed by Big, Flowers, and Porter swamps, and many more—past Fair Bluff and into a wild country out of our realm, down the Pee Dees Little and Great, to Georgetown, South Carolina, and the Atlantic. The two men, along with a setter named Belle, a Scottish terrier named Dixie, and their stolen piglet, T. Porker, Esquire, claimed to have made the first canoe trip from the Lumber's headwaters to the sea.

    The first in ten millennia or more of humankind moving about in the Carolina east? Well, whether or not Freeman's and Haynes's claim was true, their zest for the river certainly was. In more recent years, the Lumber, particular the upper river with its blackwater lowland look and its hill country rapidity, has attracted and charmed thousands of paddlers.

Lumber River just above Lumberton, looking downstream, September 2013

"Sweetheart stream," Riverton journalist and poet John Charles McNeill, our state's unofficial poet laureate and a favorite of President Theodore Roosevelt, once called the Lumber. He absolutely adored the river that flowed through his boyhood and helped raise him. In 1907, the year he died young, at the age of thirty-three, and was buried in the old Spring Hill Cemetery in Scotland County, McNeill wrote these parting thoughts about the Lumber River:

"She is a tortuous, delicious flirt, but she does not deserve the punishment put upon her by geographers, who have perverted her sweet Indian name of Lumbee into something that suggests choking sawdust, rotting slabs, and the shrill scream of the circular saw."

When Ann and I ventured out early one May with our seventeen-foot white Mohawk canoe, the Lumber's headwaters were running high and heavy. We took a late-morning look at the U.S. 15-501 bridge over Drowning Creek. There were turkey feathers along the roadside and dandelions two feet tall, and the air was redolent of smoke from a controlled burn in the piney woods north of the creek.

Some hold that the Lumber is born at the confluence of Drowning and Naked Creeks above here, while others say at Drowning and Buffalo Creeks below. Either way, in its upper reaches this is its aspect: a thin, dark stream, one of short stretches and sharp, slaloming turns ("cow faces," Haynes said was the native name for these bends) varying from twenty to forty feet in width and almost always canopied by cypress, gum, maple, and occasional pine.

A bay tree at the 15-501 bridge was all abloom with white flowers from the bottom to the top. A pileated woodpecker cried out, and we saw swallows curve and cruise about the bridge, then watched two wood ducks slide back and forth across the river near a downed tree upstream, one duck having the temerity to step out of the water and onto the tree for a few moments. The path on the south side, though well worn, was a mite steep for a put-in, and the river a bit cinched up, so we rambled farther downstream and slipped in at the ramp beside the old 401 bridge.

"There must've been a big hatch this weekend," said Ann, bemused by the bottle-green damselflies that were aswarm on overhangs, lily pads, everywhere. We paddled around in a cypress grove above the bridge, then boated on upstream some miles, a task not difficult but rather steady against the swift springtime flow of the rich black stream. When at last we reached a blow-down barricade, we turned around and rode the river back down.

Under the bridge were the wild sculptures of cliff dwellers, tubular villages of the mud dauber wasp, and the neat half-cone nests of swallows, the birds upset and all aflutter over our short intrusions. Ann and I glided the canoe behind the root-ball of a recent cave-in, through a chute so narrow we might have lodged, but we were so inspired by thoughts of three-hundred-pound sows and no-shouldered wildlife that our negotiation of the scant channel was brief.

This was woodpecker heaven. Pileateds kept sounding off—*kuk-kuk-kuk-kuk-kuk-kuk*—and trees they had pocked, scarred, and dug out well were plentiful. We watched a hairy woodpecker on a slender bankside tree work his way from the ground up nearly to the crown, while the hollow tattooing of some other woodpecker carried clearly all across the bottom. I got many glimpses of large birds out in the forest, flying dark, steady and, somehow, unobtruded through the jungle.

The songbirds, too, were in here, back from the tropics, bold yellow prothonotary warblers busily shuttling about. A kingfisher scooted down-river, with his percussive, *coming-through* cry, but the loudest music came from none of these—it emanated from the swirling song of the waters steadily eddying, rippling, and whirling around the fallen trees that lay in every reach.

On our way back up to the 401 bridge, we stopped to admire a pair of dramatic downfalls—two pines, each of them three feet thick, one lying prone, its rusty crown in the shallows of the stream, just high enough above the Lumber for us to slip beneath, the other a little upstream of the first, lodged at a forty-degree angle, awaiting its fate.

"The down and the doomed," Ann spoke drolly of them, and a short while later my own sweetheart and I sat on boat cushions beside the swift, dark stream, laughing and filling up on sardines.

Later that day, Ann was catching minnows in her hand in the shallows by the N.C. 71 bridge, while I stared at a twenty-foot section of cypress blown down out of the top of a tree beside the road. Again we paddled upstream, where there were more prothonotaries, and a red-bellied woodpecker this time.

Everywhere water was in the woods. We cut a hundred yards or more off the river by slipping through one drowned grove, but when we came back down, the Lumber took its turn with us—the current was so swift and forceful that it kept pinning our craft against one tree or another, and we had a hard time getting the boat aimed to where we could reasonably steer, no matter how much ferrying, prying, and drawing of the canoe we did.

Our time on the Lumber that long-ago day was a thoroughgoing lark, though, and I later thought of serendipitous stories I'd heard about the river, of law students from Carolina coming down from Chapel Hill and launching at night, un- or ill-advised as to where and when to do so, and sallying forth in a torrent in the dark, one of them at least having enough sense and savvy to find them a pine stump for a midnight fatwood fire in the rain. And of Corliss Bradley, the artist and Lumberton native who, out once in a canoe with her young son, talked herself blue saying no, there was *no*, there was no *way*, they were miles from anywhere, to his constant requests for a soda, only to hear after an hour a jonboat puttering upstream and, when it came around the bend toward them, find that its pilot was a friend of theirs, whose very first words were,

"Hey, y'all—want a Pepsi?"

Turnpike

The waters of the thin, dark Lumber powered around a switchback near the landing where I put a kayak in on another morning in May, twenty-odd years after Ann and I first floated the stream. This was at Turnpike Bridge on the Hoke and Scotland County line upstream of Wagram, on a road more informally called "the Turnpike."

This spot was well known locally as the place Sherman crossed the Lumber as he moved northeast from Columbia, South Carolina, toward Fayetteville in early March 1865. The downpour that day and night when they crossed the Lumber, March 10, was phenomenal—Sherman's staff officer George W. Nichols called it a "deluge," and remarked on the "solemn woods and sandy plains" of the "cussed sand country" he passed through in this awful weather in order to bring reports to the Union commander. Nichols wrote:

"I found the General, stretched at full length asleep on the floor in the pulpit of a church." When Sherman bade Nichols to stay over in Bethel Presbyterian Church, Nichols demurred: "Notwithstanding the kind offer made me of a vacant pew for a bed-chamber," the officer preferred a wet ride back to camp, there to get a dry shirt and to sleep five hours "between comfortable blankets."

March 11, 1865, dawned bright and sunny, lifting the spirits of the Union soldiers and teamsters, so Nichols reported, who had been battling the weather and the "wretched swamps." General Sherman, before departing Bethel Church, left an instruction for the preacher inscribed in its Bible:

"Mr. McNeill will please preach a sermon on the illusions of pleasure and hope.
"Mr. McNeill will please prove the absurdity of the Universalist doctrine.
"Mr. McNeill will please preach a sermon from the First Epistle of John, 4 Chapter.
"Mr. McNeill will please pray for Old Abe.
"By order of W.T. Sherman, Major Genl. Comd. U.S. Forces."

No record apparently exists as to whether Reverend Mr. McNeill and his congregation followed these very particular instructions from the Union foe—the Confederacy would still be alive for another few weeks, and some of Sherman's men had gone off for sport while in the neighborhood and shot up the Temperance Hall, an octagonal brick meeting- and schoolhouse a few miles south. The general's command about praying for President Lincoln just then may have been honored far more in the breach than the observance.

Nearly 150 years later, nobody had to explain the remark "This is where Sherman crossed." Any southerner knew who that was, and when it was, and what it had meant. The Lumber and Cape Fear river basins had been thoroughly full at the time his four columns made their ways over the Lumber, and the spring flooding of 1865, the highest anyone then alive had ever known, has for generations been referred to, pregnant with extra meaning, as "Sherman's Freshet."

I paddled hard against the current of this May morning's high water. The river was only forty feet or so wide at the Turnpike, and its strongest flow only about twelve feet across. Outside this stream within a stream it was easy to maintain position, but inside it, something of a bear. The Lumber's rule for boaters intending to return to the same landing from which they had departed was simple: for every minute going downstream, figure two minutes coming back up. I went up a ways and down a ways, got a very good look around at the quiet, shady place where Sherman had brief purchase on this river, and crossed it.

Last of the Lowries

With a population of over fifty-five thousand, the Lumbee Indians of the Lumber River swamp country are the largest tribe of Native Americans in North Carolina, and no single member of the Lumbee tribe has lodged so strongly in public mind and memory as Henry Berry Lowrie.

All during the Civil War, the Lumbee—free people of color—had been conscripted—in essence stolen away and forced—by the Confederacy and its Home Guard to go dig and work up the big sand ramparts and shelters of Fort Fisher between the Cape Fear River and the sea. In March 1865, hidden by jungle cover, Lowrie at the age of just twenty witnessed the swamp slaying of his father and his brother by the Confederate Home Guard. After these murders, Lowrie and an already-established gang of kin and runaway-slave confreres, hiding out in a collage of Lumber River swamps above Lumberton, an area called Scuffletown, waged seven more years of guerrilla war against the Confederates and ex-Confederates, against the white slavocracy that had abused the Lumbee.

"The Indian Robin Hood," some called Lowrie, who was reputedly armed with five revolvers, a lever-action Henry rifle, a flask, and a banjo, which he played in the swamp depths of Moss Neck and beyond. By sympathetic report, the Lowrie Gang would not steal from the poor; would not ride off with everything a man owned; gave a man a signed receipt for whatever they had confiscated, pledging to rob no more from him, at least for a spell; and would restore a man's goods to him, once they were of no further use to the gang.

"Terror gang," said others. "The audacity of these outlaws out-Herods Herod and is unparalleled in the history of any state," wrote the *New York Herald*. "The notorious swamp outlaw," the *Louisville Courier-Journal* called Lowrie, with even the *New York Times* opining from afar on July 22, 1871: "These events, we learn, have plunged Robeson County into a state of terror. . . . Such a state of things, however picturesque, is simply disgraceful to any civilized community."

No less controversy surrounded, and still surrounds, Lowrie's mysterious disappearance in February 1872. Had Lowrie died while hiding out in a barn from the discharge of his own gun as he was cleaning it, a self-inflicted blast to the head that took away part of his face and the front of his head? Was he secretly buried beneath a corncrib, then reburied way off in some hidden spot in a Lumber River swamp?

Journalist Ben Dixon MacNeill, who called the career of the Lowries "a carnival of plunder," posited in early 1926 that there may have been a strong connection between (a) a February 1872 nighttime Lowrie Gang robbery (in which $22,000 cash disappeared from the Pope & McLeod store in Lumberton), (b) the disbanding of a cadre of anti-Lowrie troops a mere two days later, and, (c) the story of Lowrie's accidental death that raced through the Lumber River country one week after the robbery. MacNeill reported the deathbed declaration of an aged Indian "not many weeks ago," which told of his seeing Henry Berry Lowrie two days *after* the story of Lowrie's death came out, and of Lowrie's swearing the man to secrecy, revealing only that he was about to leave Robeson County forever.

Had the $22,000, none of which was ever recovered, financed the outlaw king's escape, with half of it going to reward those soldiers for getting him out of the state of North Carolina, the other half underwriting a new life for Lowrie in Mexico, "where he lived until very recently"? MacNeill seemed to believe it so, and yet . . . if so, why had Lowrie's wife Rhoda never slipped away too, and joined him south of the border?

Who knew for certain?

On May 16, 1935, the *Lumberton Robesonian* ran a story about one John Dial, who at the healthy old age of eighty-three, before a gathering on the Lumber River's Jennings Beach, had gone and gotten himself baptized. Dial was said to have ridden and fought with the Lowrie band sixty-odd years before, was further said to have had two murders pinned on him by his former band and to have turned state's evidence against them, and now at this late date the last living member of Lowrie's band seemed to want a cloak of good, old-fashioned Christian protection as he prepared to meet the Real Man and to give his testimony, unmediated, to the One who has seen and heard it all before.

This seemed to make a certain sense.

Until eleven days later, when, on May 27, the *Robesonian* ran a letter of "correction" from Mrs. James L. Dial, who alleged that Frank Lowry, according to her the source of the first story, "had no stable foundation for the information he gave." What really happened, she said, was that fifty-odd people came to John Dial's home to surprise him and wish him well on his birthday, bringing him gifts and baskets of food.

"A very nice table was set," she wrote.

"Every one had a lovely time.

"All wished Mr. Dial many more happy birthdays."

As with the mysterious disappearance or death of leader Henry Berry Lowrie in early 1872, the late-in-life conversion of the "last of the Lowries" had quickly assumed its own aura of contest and mystery, as if certainty about at least two of the swamp outlaws was simply not to be.

As if they had been suffused with something of the swamp's *will o' the wisp*, not only from the old days when they careened through the Lumber River lowlands together, angry young men on a violent tear against a Civil War that was not theirs and a ruling social order that was not theirs either, but always and forever, all the way right on up to the very pearls of Heaven's Gate.

Margaret French McLean and Her Castle

What sort of lady was the late governor's widow, Margaret French McLean, and what sort of place did she elect to build and spend her time in, miles from downtown Lumberton on a short bluff above a white sand beach on the cypress-lined Lumber River?

In 1937, two years after her husband, the former North Carolina governor Angus McLean, had died, Margaret McLean met up with the German immigrant who had recently built a celebrated wall for St. Francis Catholic Church in Lumberton's downtown, at the corner of Sycamore and East Fifth. His wall featured concrete formed, striated, and decorated in such a way as to resemble wood—one end of it looked like a sheaf of cordwood, and atop it, bordering a long flowerbox lay what appeared to be split logs.

Would this same immigrant build her a retreat, a camp, out in the riverine wilderness north of town?

He would.

Would he enlarge upon the ideas he designed into St. Francis's wall, and lay Margaret McLean's place up in such fashion that one latter-day journalist would judge it a "Bavarian-looking alpine hunting lodge"?

He would.

Would he craft it with leaded windows across the river-facing front; arched, barred, eyelike windows on the gable ends; here a concrete tree, there a concrete stump; concrete flower boxes along the narrow front

*McLean's
Castle
and dry
watercourses,
Lumber River,
September
2013*

piazza; and, inside, a half wall of concrete logs and great logs holding up
the second floor, a massive stone fireplace and hearth?

He would indeed make all this—and Margaret McLean's riverside retreat would be ready for her by 1940. Hers was an odd lodge, fashioned of
gray concrete faux logs, which many called, if she did not name it so herself:

McLean's Castle.

One recent September afternoon, after a pair of feisty dogs chased our
car onto the eight-acre grounds of McLean's Castle and then just as quickly
lost interest, Ann and I slowly wandered this pine- and cypress-shaded
park, marveling at the concrete fountains, the concrete well-house and
bucket, and the odd artfulness of it all. No doubt of it: the whole place was
a sculpture, one sufficiently unusual that it may strike Lumber River pad-
dlers, coming downstream and happening unexpectedly upon the bright
beach and the quiet, tawny-gray, unpopulated place above it, as a blithely
haunted neverland.

No waters now flow through the paths and watercourses our state's
former First Lady designed, with their tabby, shell-encrusted footbridges
and fountains, their tiny brick-cribbed islands. The sight of these must
have brought delight to all, from children to old folks alike, as they sur-
veyed Margaret's small streams and water-world, much smaller than
the Lumber that lay below it, all testaments to the simple, wisely voiced
notion that the state of happiness always involves, if not depends on, a
proximity to water.

Archway and
concrete logs,
McLean's
Castle,
September
2013

Princess Ann and Griffin's Whirl

Down on a river bluff below Orrum lay the village of Princess Ann, North Carolina, established in 1796 back when the whole of the Lumber River was still called Drowning Creek. All that is now left of Princess Ann is her name on a road, and yet that road leads to one of our state's truly great natural treasures. North Carolina has one and only one blackwater stream with the federal government's "national wild and scenic river" designation, and this is it—eighty-one miles of the Lumber hold that honor. In 1989, the state of North Carolina declared the Lumber River a state "natural and scenic river" and made a goodly portion of poet McNeill's "delicious and tortuous flirt" into the Lumber River State Park.

Nowadays, a number of primitive campsites await campers at the park's two key facilities, upstream at Chalk Banks near Wagram, and at the larger, main headquarters here at Princess Ann about fifteen miles downstream of Lumberton. More overnight ports for canoeists and kayakers lie along remote stretches of the stream, and their names—of traders and landings from bygone days—serve as a roll call of the river's history: Chalk Banks, Jasper Memory, John Culbreth, Tom Avent, Buck Landing, Piney Island, Pea Ridge, and Princess Ann.

A river with such a gracious plenty of twists and switchback turns, reaches and bends, once and future oxbows, cutoffs, lakes in the woods out of sight, like this one, may haul off somewhere sometime and perform in a way that is passing strange. Where the Lumber flows into the Princess Ann park grounds from the east-northeast, it suddenly turns and runs south with only a couple of bends for a mile or so, and at that abrupt southward turn moves a rarity, a real river oddity:

Griffin's Whirl.

Mary Griffin was the widow of one of the large Federal-era landowners hereabouts, and on at least one old map the rise at Princess Ann was called "Griffin's Bluff," and a settlement over the river in Columbus County was named, simply, "Griffins." Mary and her second husband, William Ashley, before their marriage joined forces and created Princess Ann, and then her first husband's name rolled away, right off the bluff, though not off the whirl.

At that southward bend, a reach of river backs up to the north (over the right shoulders of downstream-bound boaters) and forces the Lumber to spin in reverse flow, creating an eternal, slow-moving counterclockwise pool, Griffin's Whirl, some fifty feet across. Further, this dynamic hydrology spins off many much smaller eddies within the larger one, little three-foot spins, ever shifting within the larger formation, the way little dust devils dance around each other on a dirt road. To some this feature's name (the very sound of it almost Beowulfian: *Gryphon's Whorl*) may conjure up a malevolent maelstrom that lies in wait, a riverine demon that never sleeps and is always ready, day or night, to devour canoes, skiffs, bateaux, even steamboats, but that sort of fancy has to be indulged in at a mythic distance.

Griffin's Whirl, the real thing, has a much gentler aspect to it, and is far more appealing than fearsome.

Leaves and twigs on its surface turn slowly with it, and if a big, round piece of river could creak, this portion of the Lumber certainly would, like an old overshot millwheel with only a little water running down its race and spilling onto it does. Frogs in a floating grass bed just to its north periodically set up howls of alarm. A boater cannot fail to notice the feature, for it will turn one's bow with the force of a great hand, and right down close to it, Griffin's Whirl is a fascinating and nearly hypnotic feature to regard, unmatched anywhere in eastern Carolina.

Fair Bluff

Fair Bluff, lovely little crossroads town, sat in the lowlands where the Andrew Jackson Highway joined the Swamp Fox Highway and low-lying N.C. 904 crossed the Lumber on an antique concrete bridge. It was the last civilization along the Lumber River in North Carolina—below Fair Bluff lay only two or three miles of wilderness riverswamp jungle, and then nothing—nothing but South Carolina, where the Lumber finally joined Ashpole Swamp and flowed on as the Little Pee Dee.

One of the state's and South's grandest writers, journalist Joseph Mitchell, grew up in the 1910s ranging about a lower Lumber tributary, Pittman Mill Branch, at neighboring Fairmont, a scant fifteen miles northwest of Fair Bluff. How amazing it was that much later, when Mitchell labored at the *New Yorker* in New York City, he could still read the river's level at Cutlar Moore Bridge in Lumberton—reported regularly in the *Robesonian*, to which he subscribed—and know at once how high or low the waters stood in all the riverswamps back home.

At the corner of Main and Orange Streets in Fair Bluff, the Powell House, a small one-story affair, operated as a trading post hard by the Lumber River starting in 1803. It was L-shaped, with Doric posts along its front porches, shaded by hanks of Spanish moss hanging from the great waterside cypress. This ancient coastal cottage predated builder John Wooten's laying out of the town of Fair Bluff by four years, and does not even carry trader Wooten's name—for he sold it to Absalom Powell, a longtime legislator and farmer, in the 1820s, and the place stayed in Powell's family for a century and a half and then some.

The slow-motion, swampy pace of the river here made for a general quietude, though folks said it jumped to life for a barbecue on the bluff in late April, and again for a watermelon growers' festival in late July (the watermelon being well known in North Carolina as the "July ham")—and the Southeastern North Carolina Agriculture Festival sets up at the beginning of October.

I was kayaking on the river upstream of the N.C. 904 bridge at the end of an early May day, lazily watching the late-day sunlight as it struck the moss growing low on the tree trunks, soaking it and lighting it up and giving it an emerald glow. On the long boardwalk above the water, a couple unhurriedly walked a mini-Chihuahua, while, along the east bank below, three black men were fishing.

The Lumber was full of robin red-breast, perch, largemouth bass, catfish, eel, all manner of panfish, the river and its wet woods home to mink and otter and beaver and more. It was a small river where husbands and wives, whole families and cohorts, fished together at day's end, where small boats rode in the backs of pickup trucks, and where it was never very hard to get on the water.

When one of three men got a strike, I paddled over to take a closer look and wish them luck. As the fisherman reeled the fish in, one of his cohorts called out excitedly:

"That's a flat-head—hold *on* to *that cat*!"

And so he did.

Sunset was falling over the lower Lumber, and I lingered in the kayak and reflected: who was it that had really made the first Lumber riverine trek from its headwaters to sea? and so what if the Lumber did finally wind up in the lower Carolina? The river was all ours for 115 miles, and one of the very best reasons to get out and afloat anywhere in our state was the dark, alluring water of this spellbinding sweetheart stream.

15

The Black

Ivanhoe

Almost twenty years ago, in late March 1996, Ann and I first floated the middle Black River at Ivanhoe, land of blueberries. Down Riverbend Lane, near an enormous high-crowned loblolly pine, lay the landing—then unimproved, now a state wildlife ramp—we put in and paddled from there, our children so relatively small (Hunter at eleven, Cary at four) that we could run a good ways up the dark river with all of us in our white flatwater canoe as a foursome.

The bright, sunny spring afternoon could not have been lovelier, the celebrated river was flowing swift and high, and we were able to drift off into dappled, flooded woods and push about, the black water now lightened by the sun in the shallows to an even amber. A pileated woodpecker announced itself, pronouncing that we were once again at large in a Carolina riverine paradise, one that belonged to him. A white-throated sparrow and a towhee moved ahead of us as we snaked about in a gum swamp north of the Doctor Kerr Road bridge. A huge sawdust pile up on a bluff bore mute and solitary witness to sawmilling days gone by; a couple hundred palmettoes fanned out about us told the tale of the here and now.

In the there and then, though, not everyone was as taken as we were with this grand waterway. One Thomas T. Newby, journeying overland from Indiana to the Carolina coast, passed harsh judgment and wrote caustically in his diary on December 9, 1856: "Arrived at Black River pretty soon this morning; a terrible place; water black as tar . . ."

Not so terrible, Mister Newby. As so many thousands do, messing about in boats here, we had ourselves a ball that spring day on the Black. We ate cheese sandwiches and pecan sandies. We lazed about a large, lakelike cove on the river's southwest side. We studied the stick-built work of some master lowland builders, a beaver lodge. We gazed through a huge hollow cy-

press there by lining up holes where branches had fallen off high on opposite sides of the tree—and we saw, magically, right on through the shell of
a tree that had taken hundreds of years to grow, on off into a Carolina blue
sky that seemed to know no end.

Black River Chapel

Just across a field and around the corner from the Ivanhoe landing stood
Black River Chapel, home of the very first Presbyterian congregation in
North Carolina.

The Reverend Robert Tate looked back over the decades during which
he had preached and worshipped here, and, from his vantage point of
about 1840, he penned the story of this meeting's first hundred years. Tate
wrote of Highland Scots coming into this wet southeastern Carolina country well before 1775, followers of Bonnie Prince Charlie, whose hopes were
dashed by his defeat at Culloden Moor in April 1746. Compared to Scotland and its Sabbaths and sacraments and holy communions, they found
that here in the Black River country there was none of that, according to
Reverend Tate, nothing but "a howling wilderness . . . a desert land."

They met in a log building. They sorely missed, wrote Reverend Tate,
the "land of Bibles" they had left behind.

Enter, about 1760, Reverend James Tate, an indefatigable Irish Presbyterian, a man who lived in Wilmington yet managed to minister to the upriver Scots for a couple of years till illnesses in his family ended his labors.
Reverend Robert Tate picked up the fallen mantle in 1799, finding the residents up Black River "kind-hearted, hospitable, and polite," yet also judg-
ing "that very little discipline had been exercised in the church." Dancing
was popular among everyone high and low, and at weddings the whiskey
flowed—"gallons, or more truly barrels of spirits," he remembered. The
Lord's flock up this way also favored gambling and horseracing, and cakes
and spirits at funerals.

When Black River Chapel was dedicated in 1818, Reverend Tate
preached from Matthew 2:11—"And when they were come into the house,
they saw the young child with Mary his mother, and fell down, and worshipped him: and when they had opened their treasures, they presented
unto him gifts; gold, and frankincense and myrrh." In 1829, a Temperance
Society formed within the church, and at first had only two or three takers.
Yet the cause against drink waxed in the early 1830s, and by 1834 Reverend
Tate felt confident enough about the drift of things to ask, after thirty-five
years of service in the spiritual vineyards of Black River, to be relieved of
his labors here.

The Greek Revival chapel that now stands was built in 1859. Edwin

Black River
Presbyterian
Church, the
1859 chapel
at Ivanhoe,
November
2014

Alderman, president of the University of North Carolina from 1896 to 1900, worshipped here, and so, too, did Joseph Wilson, father of President Woodrow Wilson. When Black River Chapel celebrated its bicentennial on June 2, 1940, the postcard invitation to the sermon, the historical speaking, and the box lunch noted dryly and without elaboration that "much history centers around this old Church." There is no record of cards and dice, of contests on the turf, or of any cakes and spirits on the occasion. Perhaps the wilderness was not howling in the Scots, now so long removed from the Highlands, as once it had been.

Cone's Folly and Three Sisters

Cone's Folly is an 8,000-acre longleaf pine stand that fills a long piece of territory on the east side of the Black River, south of Ivanhoe, and west of Atkinson. Ben Cone, a piedmont North Carolina textile magnate, bought the then-unnamed, deforested tract next to this stretch of the Black in 1931, as the nation began to plumb the depth of the Depression. Why? What for? people asked. What good was it? Hence the denigrating nickname Cone's big woods soon acquired.

Yet forests do recover and return, and, as the Cones over time managed carefully and planted with both timber and wildlife in mind, the holding that Ben Cone Jr. came into in 1982 was a folly in name only—it was full of mature longleaf, and as a game preserve, it was full of quail.

The stretch of river that runs down south alongside it is as wild as the Folly's bear-, bobcat-, bobwhite-, and turkey-filled forest: Squalling Bluff Cove is about a third the way down the tract below Beatty's Bridge, and the now-renowned braided section of Black River called Three Sisters lies just below that bluff.

In this wet bottomland, the oldest trees east of the Mississippi, and, likely, east of the Rocky Mountains, have long made their home. Two Arkansas professors—Malcolm Cleaveland and Dave Stahl—found them in the 1980s, took core samples and proved it out: here were thousand-year-old, even fifteen-hundred-year-old cypress, biding their time in the Three Sisters fastness. One of them they dated to A.D. 364 and tagged *BLK69*.

Methuselah, in local parlance—a tree growing in this place since before the Fall of Rome.

Most of us could take in that sort of antiquity, imagined and measured in human generations rather than hundreds of millions of years, the vastness of time the Colorado took to sculpt the Grand Canyon. Here in the middle Black River lay a cypress grove that—if hominids had been in this country twelve millennia—had grown up and grown old witnessing a fair portion of human history in this precinct of eastern America: Native American cultures now called Archaic, Woodland, and Mississippian.

One bright warm November afternoon last year, Ann and I put our white flatbottomed canoe in at the backwater of Hawes Cove on lower Cone's Folly, paddled 150 yards down to the Black and into a gusty breeze coming at us out of the west, and then headed upriver. Crows cried out in the distance, and a pileated woodpecker flew over high above us. A short spell of digging at the wind-driven waters and we were staring right into the mouth of the Three Sisters, the Black's narrow main stem off to the right, a yawning central sister opening dramatically before us, another slender stream off to the left.

Already we could see them: an eighth of a mile away, the great cypress trees played dramatic leads in this treasured waterscape, their rusty golden crowns spreading out high above all. We entered the wide central channel and soon found cypress magnificently buttressed, six to eight feet across at their bases, and the biggest knees one might ever see anywhere, some as tall as a man or woman. As we followed the flows farther up into Three Sisters, we were often poling with our paddles—the water level was a couple of feet or more down, so read the marks on the tree trunks, and we remembered hearing many a tale of kayakers and canoeists at even lower water having to get out and drag their boats across sandbars and swampy shoals.

A flock of a dozen or more wood ducks, the males gorgeous and green-crested, flushed several times at our approach and moved ever deeper into the swamp, drawing us in. A mile and a half across, a foot and a half deep, Three Sisters was our kind of place all right, one of the prize low-

Southern entrance to the Three Sisters Swamp, where the big, old cypress trees are kings and queens, Black River below Beatty's Bridge, November 2014

lands in the whole eastern Carolina province, a marvel and a glory where the big old trees still reigned as kings and as queens.

Black River Steamboat Days

Roan Island, at the confluence of the Black and Cape Fear Rivers, comprises four square miles of low, low ground beset by several flows: of the two rivers themselves, of the Thoroughfare connecting them at the island's head, and of the Atlantic Ocean, whose ebb and flow makes tidewater of it all, though it starts its great floods and falls over forty miles away. Rafts, pole boats, and raft trains of logs clamped together, and the men who guided them down to Wilmington, ruled these waters for generations, till the coming of steam—and even then some hung on quite a while, for the river's flow was free. The Marshall brothers, Milvin and Hailey, worked up timber in the Roan Island wilds and regularly rafted it down to Wilmington, taking three or four tides to get there, well into the twentieth century.

The Black River, particularly in its upper reaches, was said to have been

half a century behind the Cape Fear in getting anything like regular steam-boat traffic to run its rosin and turpentine barrels, and its people, down to the port city. Hundred-ton steamers built for Wilmington-to-Fayetteville trips on the Cape Fear were simply too big for the Black's turns and sand-bars and shallows, and it was not until five years after Appomattox that Captain Paddison put the first steamboat, the *Little Sam*, into the Black River trade, plying the Point Caswell–to–Wilmington route.

Ten years later, in 1880, Captain Paddison had the steamboat *John Dawson* running the Black, and when he docked her in Point Caswell one day in 1882 and called on a pair of teenaged boys, one white and one black, to help him get the boat unloaded, in one fell swoop he made those boys river men for life. D. J. Black, the white, spent forty-five years as a steam-boat man, most of them as a captain on the Black River; his comrade Henry Cromartie, the black, spent his life, too, on this river, most of it as an accomplished pilot, making a pair with D. J. Black.

By the late 1880s four steamboats worked the Black: the *Lisbon*, with Captain Black and Pilot Cromartie, a thirty-ton sternwheel steamer built in 1887 by Point Caswell boatwright Luther Sherman; the *Excelsior* (its screw propeller adjustable for water as shallow as thirteen inches); the *Susie*; and the *Delta*.

At 2:30 A.M. on April 19, 1887, the *Delta* was bound upstream when, off

Steamboat Lisbon (built at Point Caswell for Captain D. J. Black, 1887), McEachern's Wharf, Wilmington, circa 1900

Patrick's Landing three miles above Point Caswell, her boiler blew up, rocketing through the length of her hold from bow to stern and blasting out into the swamp, sinking the boat. Her fireman was blown sixty yards from the boat and found dead in the lowland woods. A deckhand standing in the bow was blown eighty yards out, alive but scalded, and he died not long thereafter. The boiler lay all bent and wrecked in the swamp in plain view of Black River travelers for fifty-five years, right up to the day it was salvaged for scrap metal during World War II.

No other Black River steamboat ever met this fate.

During the freshet of September 1891, the Black grew to a width of several miles, and the *Lisbon* went gliding and coursing through treetops, over drowned cornfields, Captain Black and Pilot Cromartie rescuing people off rooftops. One stranded African American man, seeing them coming his way, proclaimed biblically as he cried out, "Here comes Noah's Ark! Here comes Noah's Ark!" and the *Lisbon* acquired a heroic new name in the valley of the Black.

Pilot Cromartie stayed ably at the wheel many a night with a bottle beside him at his feet, laid there for him by Captain Black. Cromartie was that rare drinking man who seemed to gain a preternatural alertness from the spirits, and he was well known for it. When challenged by a sandbar, he was also well known for turning his craft around, throwing the stern's paddlewheel into reverse, and chopping his way through the bar, cutting a new channel and staying more or less on schedule. No one had ever seen anything quite like this partnership and friendship, but here it was.

Black, Cromartie, and their kind have been gone from the Black River for most of a century now. Boaters should from time to time pull in for a few moments at the old landings, Peachtree, Heading Bluff, Point Caswell, Patrick's, Longview, Beatty's Bridge, Clear Run, and Lisbon, and once again say their names out loud:

Captain D. J. Black, Pilot Henry Cromartie.

And imagine, perhaps even conjure, steam whistles shrieking through the swamp-river wilderness, paddlewheels splashing and churning dark waters, those days, and those nights.

*Unnamed
island in the
Lower Black
several miles
below The
Borough,
April 2012*

The Lower Black

Following the steamboat *Lisbon*'s upstream route, Ann and I launched the Coastal Federation's twenty-two-foot bateau at Dram Tree Park, Wilmington, one late April morning, and were away up the Cape Fear, quickly under the highway and then railroad bridges, past the power plant. By eleven, we were at the southern tip of swamp-forested Roan Island and had made the mouth of the lower Black River, of which our late, great friend Jake Mills had once told me, "There's a famous plenty of red-breasted bream there, big catfish and a lot of bass for jigger-poling, which is the popular method of jonboaters in the area." I recalled that another much-employed style of Black River fishing in times past was bow-netting for shad, with over a hundred folks still out dipping for them up and down the river in the ancient, Indian way only a couple of generations ago.

The fish were certainly feeling no pressure from Carolina anglers this particular spring morning—we saw only two other boats as we pushed slowly along up toward The Borough, where the east-flowing Black turns

due south for its last dozen miles. This was a low, slow-draining wilderness, except for the few chunks of high, dry land distinct enough from the dark waters to become known as bluffs and landings, spots the great hands that carved it all were kind enough to give a bateau, or in times past a steamboat, a place to get a purchase on the watery world. We snubbed up against the bank at Heading Bluff, a small clearing with a lone chimney standing not far from the water's edge, and for a few moments watched a bee at play in a wild iris flower.

The Black splits itself repeatedly in these lower reaches, so we were negotiating a succession of islands as we moved on above Roan Island itself: Raccoon Island, Cross Way Island, D Island, Thorofare Island, Birds Cove Island, and then up into the mouth and lower reach of tributary Moore's Creek, where sits the small fish-camp and jonboat community called The Borough. Here we came around and started drifting back down through the cypress and maple and endless brambles, tying the bateau up in the side creek on the east side of Thorofare Island and having ourselves a slow lunch there: club sandwiches, sparkling waters, *déjeuner pour deux sur la rivière*.

Later that afternoon, as soon as we came out of the Black and back into the Cape Fear again, we immediately noted far more reeds, flotsam, and planks in the big river than in the morning coming up. Last night's rain up the valley had caught up with us, but even so we did not sense the full implication until we drew close, very slowly, to the railroad bridge above the Brunswick River distributary. Where we had had a foot-and-a-half's clearance beneath the bridge when we were heading upriver, both Ann and I could see we were going to be cutting it much closer this time—and with a rented boat. I slipped the engine into neutral and we coasted at the river's speed toward the bridge, both of us wanting to hold our breaths, to clinch and, somehow, to get small.

Ann, from the bow platform, determined we *might* have six inches headroom above the bateau's T-top, and I put the motor in gear and we ever so slowly inched and eased beneath the big bridge and its rails. A few moments later, eighty yards downstream and breathing easier and wanting to say grace to the rainmaker, the bridge tender, or whatever being by whose tender mercies we had cleared the bridge, we turned to a great rising sound, and found yet another reward: the vision of an iron horse, a diesel locomotive lumbering heavily and rumbling through the marshes and pulling half a dozen cars over the big river bridge, full of muscle and purpose, southbound.

shelter Neck

Shelter Creek

The landing and canoe-rental spot for one fine, dark tributary of the Northeast Cape Fear, east of Burgaw and not too far
north of Wilmington, bore the name Holland's Shelter Creek
Restaurant, Boats & Cabins. Just when Ann and I pulled up, another car did too, from which a little girl hopped out shouting
"Mama, *look*!" as she pointed up at three-quarter-scale Santa
Claus posing with staunch authority in a deer stand twenty feet
up a nearby pine.

When you walked in the door to tell them what boat you
wanted and settle up in advance, a six-foot-tall black bear,
stuffed and raring up on his hind legs, greeted you. He wore
a sign with the legend "Do not touch." Nearby sat an ice machine and, beyond it, shelves upon shelves of wine, a posted
menu featuring catfish and frog's legs. Just outside, beyond the
canoe racks, stood a small barnboard concert stage with a ban-
ner on it: "Margaritaville." All in all a very nice Carolina spot,
one where, the bear's admonition notwithstanding, folks came
to have a good time.

So we were lazy and down home now, hanging about on the
water on this bright, sunny, gorgeously cumulus-clouded May
afternoon, southern hot, but only in the eighties. Our canoe, a
fifteen-foot Mohawk chosen carefully, *artisanally* even, from
out of the dozens of inexpensive, much-used twenty-five-
dollar rentals on hand, floated us nicely for miles downstream
and back. Lilies greeted us, and so, too, did hanging lavender
garlands, wild native wisteria, and new cypress needles made
faint green feathers on the old creekside sentinels. A late spring
paradise we had found.

I said as much of it not long afterward to Pender County
native Patrick Wooten, our tall, jaunty friend who had simply,
if surprisingly, appeared one afternoon from out of the Neuse
Sport Shop's circular clothing racks, just burst out and loomed

not two feet away from where I stood regarding camouflage vests. He had stopped off in the popular Kinston life-afloat-and-afield epicenter and found just what he needed:

An ample pair of snakeproof boots.

Hearing about our recent float, Patrick then talked about growing up down Pender way, recalling when Maple Hill Road was still dirt and when he and his young friends were learning to swim in the dark waters of upper Shelter Creek. "We used to spend all our time playing around Shelter Creek in hot weather," he said, with a shudder and a shiver and a shake, tightly clutching his box of snakeproof boots. "Swimming around with all those cottonmouths . . .

"I wouldn't put my pinky into that water now!"

Shelter Neck

The V of low country between Shelter Creek and the Northeast Cape Fear long ago gained the name Shelter Neck. The same Hurricane Floyd waters

Lost Soul Tree, Shelter Creek, May 2013

that flooded Holland's Shelter Creek frog and catfish emporium over its windowlights in the fall of 1999 also rose and swept through the small campus at the nearby Shelter Neck community, the chapel and classroom building of the historic, early twentieth-century Carolina Industrial School there, sloshing a foot or two of muddy mess over the old wooden floors. Within weeks, the Unitarian Universalists, a forerunner of which (the National Alliance of Unitarian Women) had built this progressive academic institute hard by the Northeast Cape Fear swamps nearly a century earlier, were issuing appeals for donations to help restore the severely damaged campus, this now-antique monument to practical education which they had set there, running it from 1902 till 1926 to teach young girls bread-making, to train young boys in shoe repair.

One imagines a new faculty recruit, the young teacher Mary Elizabeth Sanger who journeyed here to Shelter Neck from Detroit, Michigan, back about 1920, with her master's in religious education from Boston University. What a journey, and what a lot of trains! Detroit to Toledo to Cleveland, then down to Columbus to Parkersburg to Charleston, through the eastern panhandle of West Virginia then and on into Union Station, Washington—down the Atlantic Coast Line to Richmond, Rocky Mount, Wilson, and on down lower and deeper into the outer terrace of the Carolina coastal plain, to Burgaw, where she is met by a man with a buggy or a light-gauge car or truck from the school, and then carried miles east to the neck of land that lies between Shelter Creek and the Northeast Cape Fear River.

Most Saturday nights there would be a square dance, and their upright piano would ring out. The new schoolmarm from the North is a favorite; they all want to dance with her, the older boys, the young men from over on the river, or from Shelter Creek. She is the youngest of the teachers. She is the prettiest, everyone says. She has come from farthest away, Michigan, and when they speak her hometown's name they accent its top and go long on the *e* sound, *Dee*-troit, and add city to it, acknowledging that it is, or must be, everything Shelter Neck is not—*Dee*-troit City.

And yet she is here with them and comfortable with it, happy even, and not way back in the incomprehensibly distant, big Michigan town.

Everyone wonders about her, and she wonders about herself:

How long will she stay?

Will she meet a Carolina man and marry?

And what is it like to be a proper young woman from way off, a bringer of light, one who has left her cold Lake Erie home and come to find these youths thirsting for knowledge in a steaming southern jungle?

Perhaps she is bold enough of a Saturday to venture back into Burgaw, maybe buy on her day off a roundtrip on the train for the short trek down to Wilmington, still in that day North Carolina's one claim to a great city, watch a matinee in the jewel-box theater of old double-balconied Thalian Hall, see the house from which Cornwallis once led an army and served King George, see the fountain at Fifth and Market, the Baptist spires there, the Bellamy family's mansion, choice spots of the city that, as the last open port, had helped keep the Confederate rebellion alive most of two years past the twin, early-July 1863 falls of Vicksburg and Gettysburg. A girl from Detroit might want to see all that—she lives too close by not to—and then still be able to retreat back out to Shelter Neck, where all the crickets and tree frogs and barred owls in the eastern Carolina world could drown out cities and even the memory of cities.

They start at dawn.

They eat well.

They garden, and they do so with originality: a strain of strawberry raised here comes to be called "the Peterson" after the down-from-Boston headmistress Abby A. Peterson.

Yet Carolina Industrial will not require Mary Sanger's services for too very long. The scrapes and graders are making the North Carolina roads better now, and the public school bus will soon be able to get out to the Neck from Burgaw and fetch the Carolina Industrial School students and deliver them to the public school in town, and in 1926 the last graduates

*Former
Carolina
Industrial
School,
Shelter Neck,
November
2014*

will take their certificates and enjoy their last dinner on the ground and the pretty young teacher will soon stand in the station at Burgaw again and buy a one-way ticket, now back to *Dee*-troit City, where she will soon be an Extension Service student in the College of Literature, Science, and the Arts at the University of Michigan, far away from the tiny, vibrant community and the children she will never forget, the corner of eastern Carolina along Croom's Bridge Road called Shelter Neck.

Ghost Savannah

A few miles northwest of Shelter Neck grows one of the natural wonders of eastern Carolina: the Ghost Savannah. Discovered in 1997 by Richard Le-Blond, a Natural Heritage botanist working from a 1938 aerial photo, this 117-acre preserve proved to be a small and precious remnant of the legendary, long-lost wildflower phantasmagoria called simply Big Savannah.

In 1920 B. W. Wells, the respected North Carolina State University botanist-ecologist, had seen the extraordinarily diverse and beautiful Big Savannah spring floral display through the window of a moving train, fell in real love with it at very first sight, and prayed a lifetime for its protection and preservation. Though Big Savannah's 1,500 acres of wildflower wealth were plowed under in the 1960s, the botanist LeBlond detected on the old aerial photo silty, sandy Liddell soils, the same type as were in the Big Savannah, several miles to the north of the property Wells had nicknamed "the Garden of God." Hiking this newfound Liddell land, LeBlond then discovered the same sort of diversity of wildflower species Wells had touted in the Big Savannah—LeBlond's keen eye had found and seen a living ghost, a telling and preeminent find, most of it lying beneath a Carolina Power & Light transmission line.

Ann and I got our chance to see this wonder one bright Sunday in June 2011. We were guests of Carrie and David Paynter of Wilmington, and of their group, the North Carolina Wildflower Preservation Society, which, along with the North Carolina Coastal Land Trust, the North Carolina Natural Heritage Program, the Conservation Trust of North Carolina and others, had bought and preserved the little savannah.

Near the beginning of our walk, off to the side of the powerline, we saw red root and yellow wort, and everywhere sundew underfoot. Titi, pepperbush, and leucothoe. Bamboo vine, so sharp it helped keep pocosins impenetrable. And here, too, grew fetterbush, yellow pitcher plants, a purple pitcher plant in one tire track, savannah milkweed (a favorite food of monarch butterflies trying their level best to be quite literally distasteful to birds) in another.

"Hatpins!" called out botanist John Taggert, reading the landscape as our small group walked slowly behind him, pointing out thin green stalks each with a tiny white flower atop it. Sweet bay young were out in the powerline area, where the savanna grass was a jumble. Here was black snake root, there were yellow and purple *Rexia*, the same genus as meadow beauty. Fortunes of pitcher plants grew grouped together in clumps.

Up a lane to the north of the powerline stood a forest of loblolly and pond pine, one crooked member of which, at forty feet, was fully mature. Someone remarked of seeing pond pines in the Croatan National Forest just three or four feet high and, even so, a full hundred years old.

We might have seemed a curious lot to someone driving by and glancing up the way, just eighteen folks in ball caps and floppy hats ambling and meandering about the middle and the sides of a powerline lane cut through the otherwise forested landscape. Who could have blamed that passerby, either? Nothing here seemed spectacular at a distant glance; nothing presented you glorious rewards until you were almost right down at eye level with the grass and the delicate, subtle flowers. The wonder was not that there was so little of this left, but that there was *any* of it left at all.

Big Savannah was a marvel.

Ghost Savannah, named in memory of B. W. Wells, as its remnant, its heir, and its legacy, is no less.

Across Holly Shelter

Shelter Creek, also known as Holly Shelter Creek and long ago as Shelter River, flowed west and south out of the vast, 48,000-acre pocosin Holly

Shelter Swamp. On its other side, watercourses south and east of Holly Shelter fell into the Intracoastal Waterway, up north of Wilmington.

One November weekend in the late 1990s, I called my old friend Linwood Taylor—the big, jolly, expansive theatrical and film scenic designer who had grown up around Gause Landing in coastal Brunswick County, fishing and camping on marsh islands all over the Southeast—as soon as I got to Wilmington. Couldn't find him at first—it was a Friday night about ten, after all, in a bistro town—but left messages wherever I could, and about midnight he rang me back.

"What're you doing here?" he boomed. Even over the phone he was as grand and noisy as if he had been standing right there in the Coastline hotel room, overlooking the Cape Fear River.

"Playing some music. Hoping to catch up with you tomorrow."

"Well, I'd like to," said Linwood, "but I'm going to be out at my fish camp at Hampstead."

"Okay."

"Drying bluefish."

"Okay."

"I got all these fillets need drying. Otherwise I'd be glad to get together."

"Linwood," I said. "You haven't said anything yet that would stop me."

"You'd come *all the way* out to Hampstead?"

"Tell me how to get there."

Late the next morning I drove out to the fish camp, just beyond Hampstead and just below Sloop Point on the Waterway, a small frame plywood sixteen-by-twenty-four shanty that looked like a pair of veterans might have slammed it together not long after they'd come home from winning World War II and were ready to go back to doing what they'd been doing when the war interrupted them, fishing and having a big time out on the water. Linwood heard my car and appeared, laughing from the start, amid a gaggle of big white and blue and orange coolers, twenty or more, stacked against the front of the little house. A pair of skiffs lay up on nearby trailers in the shade.

"How you like it?" he shouted as I got out of my car.

"You're living right, Linwood," I said. "You got coolers."

"Well, you know, there's a few times in the year when a man's worth around here can be reckoned by how many coolers he owns. Come on in."

If his place were indeed a single man's pad, it was no stern old bachelor's little sod shanty, for he had made it as inviting as all get-out: a few well-worn ladder-back chairs, fishing gear leaning up everywhere, a bottle on the shelf. A tall, multitiered, Linwood-designed dryer was humming away in the minuscule kitchen, dealing with several dozen bluefish fillets. If heaven had a smell, this had to be it.

"This'll take a little while yet, then I thought maybe we'd go fishing. You got time?"

Indeed I did; I had time.

Now, the skiff we rolled down the ramp and launched was not just any open boat: it was a twenty-two-foot Sea Skiff, a boat crafted down the Waterway twenty-five miles or so at Sims Simmons's woodworking shop on Myrtle Grove Sound back in the 1950s and 1960s—both locally famous and well-known way beyond North Carolina. I had long heard of them but am not sure I had ever been around one before, and cannot recall how much of the craft's lore I heard from Linwood that day, how much I've picked up since.

There is no doubt that Simmons's light, bobbing wave-buster is one of the truly fine boats of Carolina, inspired by the commercial fisherman who in 1946 asked Sims to build him a boat he could use to net fish beyond the surf, one that could get out and back through the breakers without swamping. The fisherman had no drawing, just the idea in his mind, and the only way he could get Sims to see it was to lead him to a muddy derelict, a New England Down East dory gone to pieces in a New Hanover County marsh, her sharp, high prow easily visible, proudly on display.

A boat just like that, the fisherman said, just like that forward and then flattening astern. And so that is just what Sims Simmons built, laying a raked-back, curved-top transom out for her stern and pulling the engine forward into a well inside the craft, calling it a "Sea Skiff" and putting his name on it and sending it and ultimately a thousand more just like it out into the world. Over forty years now since Sims boarded up his shop in the days following his son's—his partner's—death on the water, and made nary another, yet one would hardly know it, so many restored Sea Skiffs are still plying the waters, and so many newer versions too, made up from easily available plans.

Quite the craft, and now Linwood was piloting his own Simmons, gliding us along down the Waterway and then through the broad tidal marshes, this warm, golden November day, the midafternoon light aslant upon us from behind, angling over the Holly Shelter Swamp country off to our west as we cruised out into New Topsail Inlet.

Out to the breakers so we could test the prow, doing what it was designed to do—Linwood was a gentleman of the theater, after all, and breaking out of an inlet into open ocean is one of the best shows there is. He didn't go far, just showed me how she handled, then piloted her back just inside, where we spent an hour or so drift fishing, each of us pulling in a couple of blues.

"Now we don't have to eat dried fish for supper," he shouted over the engine roar, before he cut it and just drifted, tide and wind soon pushing us against a long sandbar an eighth of a mile in from the breakers, and holding us fast to it.

"You see how people get *shipwrecked*?" Linwood shouted and laughed, as he cocked the engine up and we both of us poled the skiff foot by foot along the water's edge till we got off the sandbar and fished a little more. Linwood pointed out Lea Island, where a single cottage stood nakedly on the beach within easy reach of the tides, and then we went on back into the marsh and as dusk fell puttered onto the Waterway and in the early winter cold made our way back up to the warm shelter of the fish camp, where the whiskey came down off the shelf, the blues went into the pan, the talk ran more east than west, and two men, two children of paradise, were as happy with the world as any two ever were.

A simple Carolina afternoon and evening.

Such stuff as dreams are made on.

17

To Move a House

Cottage Mover

Fifty or sixty years ago my second cousin once removed's uncle by marriage, Uncle John Ferebee, was a legendary cottage-mover on the Outer Banks of North Carolina. He specialized in sliding cottages westward, back away from the encroaching ocean, though he also moved them north and south up and down the beach. Over on Roanoke Island, any numbers of homes in Manteo now stand on foundations they were not built on, thanks to this man's work. There was nothing he couldn't move—why, I believe he once moved a small hotel.

Uncle John had gotten into the business back during the war—an airstrip was to be built just west of Kill Devil Hill, in the shadow of the Wright Brothers' monument, and several small houses were to be torn down to make way for the strip. "But those are perfectly good houses," said Uncle John to his fellow county commissioners. "Well, what would you do with them, John?" they asked. "I'd move 'em," he replied. "But you don't know anything about house-moving." "Well, then," he said, "I'll learn."

And so he did, and that was his start at it, and before long, he was in big demand and had a business and trucks that said Ferebee & Sons, with their motto painted on the side: "No job large or too small."

Down on Hatteras Island, back in the 1950s when the moving of the Cape Hatteras Lighthouse first got talked about, they even consulted with him to see how he would do it, and, though it wasn't till 1999 that the light retreated from the Atlantic, old-timers say that some of the cottage mover's suggestions and methods from forty years earlier were put to use. Uncle John was extremely well-known, famous even, as the man who could move anything.

Famous, that is, in Dare County and parts of eastern Hyde and southern Currituck Counties, and probably not unknown over in swampy Tyrrell. Yet, once that we know of, his fame transcended the Carolina sound country and made it all the way up to Manhattan.

An old lady from Manteo decided she needed to take a trip and go see New York City one time in her life. So she got there and signed up for the Gray Line "Historic Sites" Tour right away. Got on the bus in the morning, along with thirty or so other people. First place they went was to see the Old Dutch House, a little two-story affair down on Wall Street dwarfed by the towers of commerce, and, after the tour guide's spiel, the old lady from Manteo was unimpressed and said from the back of the crowd,

"We got one of these back home."

The tour guide was peeved, but held his tongue. And then they went over to St. Mark's Place and looked at the beautiful commercial buildings along Second Avenue, the Italianate details of the roofs and windows, and the little old lady thought about the antique buildings in downtown Manteo and said, a little louder this time,

"We got some of these back home."

Then they drifted down to South Street Seaport and studied the historic ships there, the square-riggers and the dories, and the old lady, reminded of all the weathered boats, schooners, and juniper skiffs back in Shallowbag Bay at Manteo, said firmly:

"We got some of these back home!"

And so it went, all through the whole half-day tour, the tour guide getting more and more steamed by the old Manteo lady's refrain but never responding, till they finally reached the last site of the day: the Empire State Building. They went up to the Observation Deck, and the tour guide pointed out features of the New York skyline, showed them all the yellow cabs in the world down below. And then, slapping his hand on the great skyscraper's side, he preempted the little old lady from Manteo, saying,

"Well, *madam*, I know you don't have one of *these* back home."

"No," she said. "But we got somebody can *move it*."

The Experts at Wrightsville

Some other somebodies who can move it showed up at Wrightsville Beach in June 2013: the Expert House Movers of Virginia Beach, Virginia. Fourteen summers earlier, in 1999, the Matyiko family—the Experts, four-generation owners and operators of the company—had rolled the five-thousand-ton Hatteras Lighthouse almost three thousand feet back from the encroaching Atlantic Ocean, which had for quite some time been threatening to undermine and topple the great black-and-white striped tower, much beloved all across North Carolina and well beyond. For this majestic feat, the Matyikos won the "Move of the Century" nod from the International Association of Structural Movers.

They were here in Wrightsville to move a cottage for the North Carolina Coastal Federation, though perhaps cottage was too modest a word for the place. The historic Palmgren-O'Quinn House—built in the late 1940s near the foot of Harbor Island between the Intracoastal Waterway on the west and the seaside barrier island of Wrightsville Beach to the east—was a gray-shingled home at the beach with a veranda facing east, from which porch sitters for decades had been looking across a broad lawn at the dock out over the waters of Banks Channel. New owners, though, wanted a larger place, and, hearing the NCCF needed a new regional headquarters, decided to donate it to the environmental group (at a $500,000 value) rather than tear it down.

The gift's given: it would have to be moved.

The first catch was that the NCCF had to find a place to put it down, and in a hurry. Once they found it—a piece of a Department of Interior plot on the other side of Harbor Island—there came a second catch: it would have to be moved most of the way over water.

Some boats are not to be missed, and this venture was one of them. Along with NCCF senior scientist Tracy Skrabal and several others, Ann and I boarded NCCF's twenty-two-foot bateau, captained by NCCF's Mike Giles, midafternoon on Wednesday, June 19, at the Bridge Tender docks on the mainland side of the Intracoastal Waterway, beside the Wrightsville Beach bascule bridge. Mike ran south down the waterway not quite a quarter mile, swung us east into Mott's Channel and then once up that winding channel of docks, cottages, and vast marshes, and turned left, or north, on Banks Channel for a couple hundred yards, and there, on steel beams and four big sets of aircraft-size wheels, sat the Palmgren-O'Quinn cottage on a barge, with the tugboat *Roughneck* cranked and almost ready to go.

The pilot, down on deck level, waved our way and warned Mike good-naturedly:

"No pictures of me working. I'll have to charge you for that."

And then he went aloft, ordered the big yellow crane on board to pull his spuds—the two fore-and-aft vertical metal shafts—that went down through the barge and served as his brakes and maneuvering tools. He blew a loud, fat blast of his air horn, backed out, and was away with this enormous houseboat.

3:48 P.M.

Not only away, but away with what the theater calls "obstructed sightlines." The pilot was pushing the barge with *Roughneck* and could not see anything but the Palmgren house directly before him. But he still had eyes. He had a GoPro video camera mounted on the port side of the barge, and he had a dull gray launch sporting around ahead of him and calling him with steering directions.

The sky quickly darkened. A huge pall of dark, low clouds moved in rapidly from the north, and a light rain began to fall.

A month earlier, Ann and I had scouted this route and the marsh environs to the south in a jonboat, gliding up Mott's Channel, then heading down choppy Banks Channel toward the inlet, where the Carolina Yacht Club's races started running, back in the 1870s or '80s, with Captain John Newland Maffitt, the retired Confederate blockade runner who was then a Wrightsville resident, and his craft, the club's number-one registrant, the *Carrie*. A south wind's waves were banging us royally, but, for our pains, this lovely, rare sighting: a pair of dolphins leapt together entirely out of the water in the channel between the inlet and the Waterway. At the Bradley Creek marina, most boats were tied up, few craft out moving late that May afternoon—a blue heron hunched over, fishing one of the creek's mudflats, about the most active mariner we saw.

Not so today. Several other boats and a couple of kayakers joined in the house-moving maritime parade, and Mike got our bateau down Banks Channel and into Mott's ahead of the barge. More small craft lay in wait down Mott's Channel, paddleboarders too, and scores of people stood in the rain out on docks, on the bulkheads, on cottage porches, and on the balconies of the chalk-white Seapath high-rise.

The pilot and his charge were making six to eight knots, and, seen from the water from off the barge's starboard, the great gray moving house, with only a fortune of marsh behind and beyond it, looked like something dreamt up for a Terrence Malick film, some mythic home drifting past a vast unpopulated prairie as if it had mind and will and force of its own.

We made it back up the waterway to the Bridge Tender docks well ahead of the barge, and regarded it coming to the mouth of Mott's Channel, where the pilot abruptly halted and hung there for most of ten minutes.

And then just as abruptly he pulled on into the Waterway and steamed for the bridge, the draws opening into the gray sky none too soon, and then, as coolly as if this happened every day, *Roughneck* pushed the Palmgren cottage through and beneath and past the open spans.

Perhaps two hundred yards past the bridge, *Roughneck* turned right, into Lee's Cut, which ran along the north side of Harbor Island, and he

Palmgren-O'Quinn house pushed by Roughneck, Banks Channel, Wrightsville Beach, June 2013

was churning a right smart as he made that move. Soon, in a sharp, reverse C curve, he dropped a spud and let the tidal flow pivot him and help him negotiate this tight spot beside a shoal. Mike Giles motored the bateau on up to docks next to the empty lot (the *only* empty lot left anywhere along Lee's Cut, hence the only place the house could possibly land) toward whose bulkhead the barge was advancing.

More than a hundred people had gathered here to watch the ship come in, and when it did, the pilot did another smart shift or two before dropping a spud again and letting the tide drift him into position, squared up with the docking spot, and then moving straight in and blasting the air horn and powering down.

The whole transit had taken just under an hour.

It would be a few hours before the cottage rolled very slowly off the barge and onto the empty lot at 53 Pelican Drive, so in the meantime Ann and I caught a ride back over to the Bridge Tender docks and the Fish House outdoor bar, where fellow Coastal Federationists drank beer and cheered the day.

When Tracy Skrabal and Mike Giles—whose planning and execution of this complex event we were celebrating—showed up at the bistro to much applause, and, when I remarked, "That was some sharp piloting," Tracy took me aside and smiled and said:

"Well, there *were* four problems along the way."

"When he held up at the mouth of Mott's Channel," I said.

"Right," she said. "That was the first one. He couldn't raise the bridge tender on Channel 13 and he kept trying and finally he found her number in his cell phone and called her and said:

"'Hey, what's the matter with you? You're not answering on 13—I need you to open the bridge!' and she said,

"'Where are you?' and he said,

"'I'm down here at Mott's Channel fighting the tide, *in reverse, with a house*!' and she said,

"'I can see you!' and he said,

"'Well, *of course you can—open the bridge*, I'm coming on!' And he did, too."

"The second problem?"

"Going into Lee's Cut," said Tracy.

"All that churning?" I said.

"Yes—the barge only draws a foot, so it got in fine, but the tug, much deeper draft, was pounding on the bottom!"

"The third, at that shoal?"

"No, he was all right there. Three and four were coming in at the empty lot—he lost his right engine, but he said that was all right, that happens, but right on top of that he lost his throttle and it takes a couple minutes to come back up—and *that* was when he dropped the spud and let the water swing him, and by then he had throttle again and came on in."

"Man," I said.

"Yeah," Tracy said, flooded with relief, tired, happy, hand around a bottle of beer.

"Still and all," I said, "pretty nice work."

The next morning, which dawned still and steaming and flat-out hot, Mike Giles showed up at the site at 6:30 A.M., and, as he later told us, the barge and tugboat were "gone, long gone."

The Matyikos glided, as it were, the Palmgren-O'Quinn House across Pelican Drive and onto north Harbor Island's main cross avenue, West Salisbury Street, now aiming (as best one can aim a house) for its choice spot on the Department of Interior property, next to Wrightsville's visitor center and museum a couple hundred yards or so to the west.

How the cottage moved: one stocky man, walking backward while running with a lever on machinery above him the hydraulic motors built into two of the four giant wheel-sets, "drove" the house slowly forward, inches at a time, he backing up by the inch and half-step too, only occasionally looking over his shoulder to see where the whole gigantic affair was going, while other men from the Matyiko platoon moved along the sides, tightening the chains on one side of the rolling building, loosening them on the other—doing the steering. Once in a while, the driver would stop the progress, put the lever in neutral, and walk beneath one front corner or the other of the house and use the bottom of the house's side to sight his course, exactly like a hunter drawing a bead, or like a boatbuilder looking along the gunwales, fashioning the craft by rack of eye.

On neither day had I yet seen a tape measure, or a level.

As the Palmgren house came up on street signs, Jim Matyiko walked over to them casually with a ten-pound hammer in hand and, as necessary, slammed and broke the bolts and laid the signs aside in the grass. When thickly woven live-oak branches were in the way along the roadside, he leapt into the driver's seat of a front-end-loader, and the house-drover got himself up astride the forktines of that machine, with chain saw (no glasses, no helmet), and Jim lifted him swiftly straight up into the tree, and the branches came down. NCCF scientist Skrabal, off to the side, asked the town's mayor if this were going to be a problem.

"No," His Honor told her, "we were going to prune 'em anyway."

And so it went, again with scores of people lining the road, taking pictures, talking about the game that was afoot before them, the Wrightsville denizens' interest in the event running higher than high.

"This is big," said an older man way down the road ahead of the house, his telephoto-lensed camera on a tripod. "This is *really* big."

*Rolling
up West
Salisbury
Street,
Wrightsville
Beach*

A seven-year-old boy on his bicycle said he had never seen a house being moved before, adding with conviction and volume: "I'm *excited*!"

Only a middle-aged blond in pink shorts and a visor cap, out with her small schnauzer and doing a slow-motion jog, seemed behind the curve on news of the move, drawling as she trotted past, "Well, *this* is a suuuu-prahz."

And the only disparaging word heard was that spoken to NCCF's cool, unflappable deputy director, Lauren Kolodij, who said an older woman had come up to her earlier in the morning, complaining about the amount of money that was being spent on this, and how it could be so much better spent somewhere else. When Lauren assured her that this move was being accomplished with private, nonprofit money, *not* government funding, the woman shifted topics at once and went off noisily recounting the evils of Obamacare.

A little before noon, the drover turned off the generator on the house, which had now stopped just short of the turn into the Interior property. One Expert House Movers man roared off in a white diesel pickup to go get sandwiches for the firm. Jim Matyiko climbed into the cab of a flatbed truck, bearing the long, bevel-ended steel panels that had functioned as runways for the house onto and off of the barge, and pulled the flatbed into place close by where the house would have to come onto the lot. To do so, the rolling stock would have the advantage of the two-vehicle-wide driveway, though it would need a good deal more width.

Awaiting sandwiches, the Experts started building a bridge across a

not-inconsiderable swale next to the driveway. The front-end loader, now manned by the main drover, lifted the long steel panels off and placed them side by side over the swale, along with a pair of huge steel road-plates. A large Bobcat, working simultaneously from the opposite side of the flatbed, snagged big batches of ten-by-ten-inch squared-off tim-bers about six feet long and moved them over and dumped them into the swale, whereupon men on foot, one of them a toothpick-thin black man who had been one of the Experts for decades, set about building them up neatly, together—the bridge would really be a causeway, solid, with no gaps for the great weight to sag into.

Then sandwiches appeared and everyone ate during a lunch break that might have lasted ten minutes.

Ann and I repaired to rocking chairs on the visitor center's covered porch, best seats in the house, as the bridge- and causeway-building went on and the house, once fired up again, started making the turn and head-ing for its last hurdle and test. As it came on, there was almost an insou-ciance among the men on foot as they moved about, adjusting and re-ordering the timbers based on where they saw the house weight's hitting and heading, none of them ever seeming to look at the heavy machinery moving near them yet knowing at all times right where it was. This ballet proved to be a magnificent pas de deux between brute force and preci-sion, sometimes alternating, sometimes working vigorously together.

An O'Quinn, son of the former mayor who had bought the house from the Palmgrens, a man who had spent many happy younger days therein, stood in the sun and despaired over "the lack of foresight" on the coast in the age of sea-level rise, while cheering approvingly of the new location and purpose of the old place. A Palmgren granddaughter the evening before had said that, though some of her kin "just wouldn't come and see this," she herself, as the house passed by on the waterway, had "felt a great sense of peace."

And the house, listing and sinking just a remarkably small tad as it crossed the swale, rolled with inch-by-inch inevitability toward the field of pilings that was its future resting place, till it came to rest and was home, less than twenty-four hours after the *Roughneck* tug cast away from the Banks Channel bulkhead.

This may not have been the Hatteras Light, emblem of the firm, yet the Experts had now successfully moved the Palmgren-O'Quinn House for the North Carolina Coastal Federation—whose motto, "Working Together for a Healthy Coast," was a very real beacon—and in so doing had done real magic, for they had helped turn the old Banks Channel cottage into a lighthouse, all the same.

18

The Boats of Carolina

The halls near the lobby of the Asheville's grand old mountainside Grove Park Inn filled with the woodland-spiced, aromatic scent of Atlantic white cedar. It was coming from juniper planks that men were laying into place on the frame of a small craft they were building just outside a set of double doors. All the way from Marshallberg on the mainland of Down East Carteret County, just north of Harkers Island, they had come, here to show the curious and the uninitiated just what went into the making of a sixteen-foot skiff, how swiftly and well it could be done by those who had long had the craft in their heads and hands, and in their hearts too, as if they had been born with it. What witness would have said they were not? On they worked, across a winter's weekend and without a single plan in sight. Just when the skiff was looking sharp and nearing completion, a stranger paused, asking skeptically,

"Will that thing float?"

To which a proud Harkers Island woman standing at the stern said coolly, yet with sound-country vigor:

"Yes, she will, darlin', and she'll come ahead on, too."

We have been building boats in what is now eastern North Carolina for many thousands of years. Cypress dugout canoes, wonders given up by Lake Phelps, date back to at least 900 B.C. Since land-bridge pilgrims first found that big pond and its wealth of fin, fur, and feather some eleven thousand years ago, we can be sure there were dugouts that were ancient well before the ones we now call ancient, small craft that time long ago rendered into dust and settled in mud. Artist John White watched the natives on Roanoke Island working up dugouts, and, though he sketched and painted them at it, he could not have known what a lengthy, extensive heritage those smoldering logs stood for—both the artifact and the pursuit. European colonists, the early Carolinians, went to school on the

Three young women in a punt, Milltail Creek at Buffalo City, early twentieth century

Indian boats and enlarged upon the simple, functional design of the dugout, in time bringing forth the kunner and the periauger, longer and broader-beamed boats rigged with sails, yet possessing clear kinship with those age-old, hollowed-out log craft of the natives.

An East Lake boatwright named George Washington Creef moved to Manteo just before the Civil War, then down to Wanchese not long after it, and left a deep shadboat-building legacy among the Creefs and beyond, for he also taught Otis Dough how to build them, and Dough taught his three sons, and so on it went. The round-bottomed shadboat, now North Carolina's official boat, is as much a bequest, an inheritance, a practical lineage, a hands-on hand-me-down through the generations, as it is a set of planks on frame for to float and fish.

So, too, is the Core Sound sharpie, the round-sterned Long Island Sound craft imported by Connecticut Yankee George Ives to our central coast. In 1876 Ives's sharpie *Lucia* carried the day against a fast local boat in the waters behind Shackleford Banks, and suddenly everyone wanted one: only three years after that now-famous race, there were said to be 599 sharpies along the Carolina coast. James Allen Rose, the late, legendary Harkers Island boatbuilder, recalled how his grandfather George M. Rose "sailed up and down Core Sound in this type of boat."

Boats and the building of boats in Carolina have twined men's names, their work, and their places together like scuppernong vines in riverside woods. In the nineteenth century, Sutton Davis of Davis Ridge in Down East Carteret County built schooners beside Jarrett Bay. Ben Basnight fashioned many a skiff in his shop hard by the dark Pasquotank River, and Joel Van Sant's fleet, skimming juniper sailboat, also first crafted there, is now known the world over (a competitive class in the Olympics, no less): the mothboat, or, to its devotees, simply *the moth*. Brady Lewis put flare into a skiff eighty years ago, and now the flare bow is synonymous with the name of the place where he did it: Harkers Island. Fowle of Little Washington, Whitehurst & Rice of Beaufort, Devine Guthrie and his Shackleford Banks whaleboats, Ambrose Fulcher of Atlantic and his sweeping sheer, the Varnums and Varnams of Varnumtown on Lockwood Folly River down in Brunswick County—these are but a few names from the roll of legendary native boatwrights. Men like Alex Willis of Harkers Island, Bryan Blake of Gloucester, and Jimmy Amspacher of Marshallberg—premier boat-

Prow of the
20' pound-
netting
juniper skiff
Pounder
(built by
Walter
and Ray
Davenport,
early 1970s,
rebuilt
by Willy
Phillips),
Fort Landing,
Tyrrell
County,
September
2013

builders of the modern moment in Down East Carteret County—have the old lines in their hearts and minds, and can craft most anything most anyone might ask of them.

The wind that once blew for George M. Rose still blows, now out of the southwest, now out of the northeast, and the proof of such a craft as the twenty-two-foot sailing skiff Jimmy Amspacher built not too long ago was less the graceful look of her than how she would fare before the wind. "Once she was finished," he said, "I couldn't wait to take her out." So he set sail from Marshallberg one day, single-handed, with only three cans of Vienna sausage, a box of Ritz crackers, and a jug of Bojangles tea. No telephone or radio—GPS only.

Amspacher, a keen, energetic, and ready man, sailed up the west side of Core Sound, past Davis Island and Davis Shore, past the villages of Stacy and Sea Level and Atlantic, the old Hunting Quarters, plying east of Cedar Island through Chain Shot Slue, past Harbor Island and Wainwright Island, and into the Nine Foot Slue of lower Pamlico Sound. Waterbirds regarded him from the little islands, and, because the sailboat made so little sound, gliding by so quietly it was as if he belonged there, the birds did not spook and fly away. Now and again he would reach down in the shallows and pull up a scallop, open it with his pocketknife, and eat it raw not a minute out of the water. He made eight to nine knots easily, and at times sliced through the waters at eleven. He stopped only at Casey's Island behind Portsmouth, and at a dock on Portsmouth, where he picked up a passenger—then he stood for Ocracoke across the inlet, sailed into the little harbor as men have for centuries, and spent the night.

"Over the last thirty years," he said recently, as we talked near Harkers Island's Shell Point, "it was just about the best day in my life."

Thanks be to good, true friends who have taught us much as they let us in on no end of pleasure upon the waves, a deep sense of our forebears' maritime history always percolating all about us. Veteran Pamlico Sound ferryboat Captain Dennis Chadwick took Ann and me on a slow circumnavigation of Browns Island, a marsh-girt, forested spot just north of Harkers Island, in his big Brady Lewis twenty-six-foot skiff one gray summer day years ago. Alligator River crabber and fisheries leader Willy Phillips had us out thrumming along on that blue-sky September Sunday in his shadboat *Heart*, one of the last two built in North Carolina, out on Hatteras in the early 1980s. Captain Ernie Foster, at the helm of *Albatross I*, got Jake Mills and me out onto the blue water fishing for Spanish off Diamond Shoals one bright July afternoon, and we enjoyed, nay, *absorbed*, "the *Albatross* roll" as Foster's round-sterned beauty met inlet waves and ocean troughs and swells, handling them all easily and well. *Albatross I* was a wonder, a craft that no Outer Banks boatbuilder would consent to build for Ernie Foster's father Ernal back in the late 1930s—so adamant were they that Ernal's design was all wrong and would not be worthy that he had to take himself and his plans down two sounds and into the Straits at Marshallberg before he could find a willing boatwright and get Hatteras village's first sportfisherman built. Now, having led the way, the *Albatross* fleet is central to the legend of the boats of Carolina.

From very early spring till very late fall, in every harbor and marina on our coast, sleek sportfishermen with outriggers and flying bridges take their places, like schoolchildren awaiting recess, against the predawn moments they will throw off lines and head for blue water, top-flight boats turned out by the likes of Albemarle in Edenton, Hatteras in New Bern, and Bayliss in Wanchese, along with other widely respected fishing craft by Grady-White in Greenville, and by Parker north of Beaufort near the Core Creek Bridge.

One recalls other, earlier classics: smart lapstrake runabouts like the Silver Clipper from Barbour Boats in New Bern, the kind one saw coursing sound-country rivers back in the 1950s and '60s; and the sharp, rising prows of T. N. Simmons's Sea Skiffs, which he built for thirty years on Myrtle Grove Sound, hulls so uncommonly good at busting through inlet rollers and chop that making replicas of them is a popular amateur boatbuilders' pursuit to this day.

Beyond all these small boats, we also have the deep, lingering, collective memory of much larger craft that have over time come out of our watery world: revenue cutters built in Wilmington in the 1790s for our new nation (two of which, *Governor Williams* and *Diligence*, remain the subjects of an ongoing search where they sank behind Ocracoke Inlet, along with at least twenty-nine other vessels, in the fierce hurricane of late September 1806); warships that kept Cape Fear River shipwrights busy decades later, though for a new, different, and doomed nation, the Confederate States; lumber schooners launched onto the Pasquotank at Shipyard Landing in Camden; side- and stern-wheel river steamers pounded together at Point Caswell on the lower Black River; and more Wilmington ships for two epic twentieth-century conflicts, concrete craft for World War I so top-heavy that when they were launched abeam they heeled over so far they nearly sank, and then great steel ships bound for service in World War II, as were, from farther up the coast, minesweepers put together at Barbour's in New Bern and salvage and landing craft from the Elizabeth City Iron Works, outbound for the seven seas.

Skiff, schooner, shadboat, sharpie, oyster sloop, shrimper, sink-netter, ship—all of them, and so many more, are boats of Carolina.

In December 2012, during the ever-genial gathering of Waterfowl Weekend at the Core Sound Waterfowl Museum on Harkers Island, bright-eyed James Allen Rose and I sat and talked for a spell, and he rhapsodized

Starboard side of shrimper Capt Phillips (built at Holden Beach by Harold Varnum, 1981), White Oak River, Swansboro, August 2014

about Core Sound sailing craft and the old days. He pointed to his model skiff nearby. "I built myself one of those when I was fifteen. Used to go out to the ocean, out to the menhaden boats when they were working close in. Get up on the ship, just so I could watch, and listen to the men singing. Prettiest thing."

A merry man, he smiled steadily as he gazed at the model, seeing beyond it a whole fleet of memories. "Everything on those boats was white—hull, mast, sails, oars. They were just beautiful, when you'd see 'em sailing down the sound, and if they were coming through a fog, they looked just like a bunch of ghosts."

A few years earlier, a skipper had carried me from a back-creek Belhaven marina way up the Pungo River on a big flare-bow sportfisherman, gleaming iceberg-white in the September sunlight as we cruised upriver at good speed, a long bright wake playing out behind us. "She's a James Allen Rose boat, built in the '60s," he said. "Had a different name back then—I renamed her." Back at home a couple of nights later, I called James Allen and told him I had just taken a fine ride on one of his boats, then described her and our trip to him. He knew precisely which one it was, remembered her well. "I'd not heard anything of her for a good while. Wondered what'd come of her. How's she doing?"

She was trim and trig and doing just fine, I had said. A beauty when she was tied at the dock, Captain Rose, and lovelier yet when she came ahead on, too.

coda

The little rivers will run, they will roll and flow, whatever we do or do not do—and yet they would not choose to be left alone. They want their headwaters, whether in swamp or brushy seep or forest spring, to run clean and clear, and their courses sheltered. For if they remain fresh and clean enough that one might scoop a handful and drink it, so will the broad streams they feed, till those are in tidewater and salt is in the mix.

People of a province with five thousand miles of interior coastal shorelines and over 2 million acres of estuarine waters must needs be full of love for every bit. If the Lord sees the least sparrow when it falls, and He does, then let us keep our eyes on every rivulet and rill, every creek, crick, branch, run, stream, prong, fork, river, pocosin, swamp, basin, estuary, cove, bay, and sound, and help them all.

Our purpose must be health. As poet Wendell Berry wrote in *The Unsettling of America*: "To be healthy is to be whole. The word health belongs to a family of words, a listing of which will suggest how far the consideration of health must carry us: heal, whole, wholesome, hale, hallow, holy."

Let us keep our little rivers healthy, and holy, and hold them close in the deepest chambers of our hearts. And part of that care, that health, will surely be to turn our vision ahead, *clearly*, toward what the sea's steady rise will mean, especially to those streams on the outer coastal plain and the people near them, in this century and beyond.

Let us make our many waters living models to the world.

We will come back to them all again, and float upon many another, the Meherrin and the Wiccacon, the Lockwood Folly and the Shallotte, Indiantown Creek and yet another North River, and yet another South. The waters never end, and there is no story without them, and this is why the first question those with the most powerful lenses and sensors and probes ask of cosmic landscapes is: where is the water, or the proof of water past, or the nature of liquid present, like the methane seas of Titan?

The little rivers of eastern Carolina are precious as veins, givers and bringers of life, home of oldest trees and newest songbirds, of great black bear and least newt, and of tiny glutinous eggs bound to become great fish in the sea and to return and spawn. Anyone looking in on our waterways from as close as a boat afloat upon them, or from as far away as an unknown orb in the thrall of some distant star, will see no less than the sweet wondrous mysteries of life, as if through a glass brightly, now face to face.

selected sources

Throughout this work, we have often consulted *The North Carolina Gazetteer: A Dictionary of Tar Heel Places and Their History*, 2nd ed., edited by William S. Powell and Michael Hill (Chapel Hill: UNC Press, 2010); Catherine W. Bishir and Michael T. Southern, *A Guide to the Historic Architecture of Eastern North Carolina* (Chapel Hill: UNC Press, 1996); *GMCO Chartbook of North Carolina*, various editions (Springfield, Va.: GMCO); *North Carolina Atlas and Gazetteer* (Freeport, Me.: DeLorme Mapping, 2003); Paul Ferguson, *Paddling Eastern North Carolina*, 2nd ed. (Raleigh: Pocosin Press, 2007); Roger L. Payne, *Place Names of the Outer Banks* (Washington, N.C.: Thomas A. Williams, 1985); William S. Justice and C. Ritchie Bell, *Wild Flowers of North Carolina* (Chapel Hill: UNC Press, 1968); and two by Dirk Frankenberg: *The Nature of the Outer Banks* (Chapel Hill: UNC Press, 1995) and *The Nature of North Carolina's Southern Coast* (Chapel Hill: UNC Press, 1997).

1. The Upper Pasquotank

John Richard Jordan Jr. of Winton and Raleigh, dear friend since my birth, told me about the time his father met Edna Ferber in Bath, when she came to catch up with the *James Adams Floating Theatre*, and their subsequent correspondence. More about the life and times of this remarkable peripatetic theatrical venue may be found in W. J. Overman III, "*The James Adams Floating Theatre*," *Pasquotank Historical Society Yearbook*, vol. 3 (Baltimore: Gateway Press, 1975); C. Richard Gillespie, *The James Adams Floating Theatre* (Centreville, Md.: Tidewater, 1991); "Salt-water Showmen Roam the Chesapeake: Floating Theater Makes Week Stands, Playing Popular Bills at Towns along the Shores of Bay," *Baltimore Sun*, November 27, 1925; Richard Gonder, "In Memories . . . the *Adams Floating Theatre* Makes Its Rounds on Tidewater Waterways," *Norfolk Virginian-Pilot*, May 30, 1954, a PDF copy of which was provided me by Troy Valos, Sargeant Memorial Collection, Norfolk Public Library; and Mark A. Moore, "Edna Ferber and the *James Adams Floating Theatre*," posted at www.nchistoricsites.org/bath/edna-ferber.htm. For the UNC Center for Public Television, Jim Bramlett directed and Mike Burke shot our August 2005 trek aboard the *Bonny Blue*, from the Elizabeth City waterfront to the Dismal Swamp Canal lock at Deep Creek, Virginia; it is posted at http://redclayramblers.com/bland-simpson-unc-tv-the-great-dismal-swamp/. I spoke with the distinguished boatbuilder Captain Merritt Walter in the pilothouse at that time and, later, by phone, in June 2013. In August 2012, with Captain Bill Welton at the helm and his friend and first mate Enno Reckendorf standing by, I was given a fine ride aboard the small cruiser *Miss Martha*. Noted underwater archaeologist and explorer Phillip Madre and I spoke at my March 2009 reading for the Beaufort County Friends of the Library, Washington, N.C.; before the year was out, the *Norfolk Virginian-Pilot* would run Lauren King's story about Madre et al.'s success: "Shipwreck in Pasquotank ID'd as *Appomattox*" (November 10, 2009). Classic Moth Boat Association leaders Greg Duncan, Beans Weatherly, and Erky Gregory

welcomed us to the 2013 championships on the Pasquotank; see http://www
.mothboat.com/. John Brothers of the Causeway Marina, Machelhe Island,
Elizabeth City, generously got us on the upper river in October 2013. How often I
have referred to all three volumes of the *Pasquotank County Yearbook* (volume 3
is cited above; volumes 1 [1954–55] and 2 [1956–57] were gifts from my great-aunt
[and family historian] Jennie Simpson Overman); William A. Griffin's *Ante-bellum
Elizabeth City: The History of a Canal Town* (Elizabeth City, N.C.: Roanoke Press,
1970); and Thomas Butchko's *On the Shores of the Pasquotank: The Architectural
Heritage of Elizabeth City and Pasquotank County, North Carolina* (Elizabeth City,
N.C.: Museum of the Albemarle, 1989). Some passages in this chapter appeared, in
different form, in my essay "Water Everywhere," in *Amazing Place*, edited by UNC
professor Marianne Gingher (Chapel Hill: UNC Press, 2015).

2. Cashie River Days

Two government documents helped illuminate earlier times than ours on the
Cashie: U.S. Army Corps of Engineers, *Report of the Chief of Engineers U.S. Army*
(Washington: Government Printing Office, 1897); and Dwight F. Davis, Department
of War and Committee on Rivers and Harbors, *Examination and Survey of Cashie
River, N.C.* (1926). See www.roanokeriverpartners.org/ and visit the Roanoke/Cashie
River Center on the Cashie in Windsor. Julia Ridley Smith and Glenn Perkins hosted
us at the Hope Plantation Ball in the fall of 2006, an event that enjoyed gracious
support from my late aunt Jean Simpson Sharp. The late Holley Mack and Clara Bell
shared with us their extensive knowledge of Hope, the Cashie, and Bertie County.
This chapter originally appeared in the 2011 edition of the *North Carolina Literary
Review*, edited by Thomas Harriot College of Arts and Sciences Distinguished
Professor Margaret Bauer of East Carolina University.

3. Scuppernong

Wilson Angley's *A Brief History of the Scuppernong River* (Raleigh: Research
Branch, North Carolina Division of Archives and History, 1986) and the more
recent *Scuppernong River Project, volume 1: Explorations of Tyrrell County Maritime
History*, by Nathan Richards et al. (Research Report 21, 2012, East Carolina University
Program in Maritime Studies) are comprehensive explorations of town, river, and
region. Columbia's historic district has been listed on the National Register of
Historic Places since March 1994, and much about the town can be gleaned from
its successful nomination document, a 2012 adaptation of which is posted at http://
www.livingplaces.com/NC/Tyrrell_County/Columbia_Town/Columbia_Historic
_District.html. J. W. Branning and Branning Manufacturing received much notice—
of both social and industrial nature—in Edenton's *Fisherman and Farmer*
newspaper all across the nineteenth century's last decade. See, for example, "Big
Fire in Tyrrell," March 9, 1900. Notice of Branning's death ran in the *News and
Observer*, March 22, 1901. Administrator B. S. Midgette filed a successful negligence
and damages suit on behalf of W. S. Leary, deceased, against Branning, the chilling
details of which appear in *Midgette vs. Branning Mfg. Co.* (64 *SE Reporter N.C.*,
April 17–July 17, 1909, 5–11), the lower court's judgment in plaintiff Midgette's favor

being upheld by the North Carolina Supreme Court, March 24, 1909. H. T. Corwin's retirement from Branning was covered by the *New York Lumber Trade Journal*, September 15, 1917. Information about the riverside boardwalk that runs past the Branning mill site is at www.fws.gov/PocosinLakes/public.html. Accounts of the launching of the steamboat *Estelle Randall* ran in both the *Washington Post* and the *Baltimore Sun* on December 15, 1897; further description of the *Estelle Randall* appeared in the *Post* on February 23, 1898. The strange case of William Crowley's death and uncertainty over Captain Harry Randall's possible role in it ran in the *Washington Post* on July 17, 1905, and elsewhere, including the very brief notice of Randall's exoneration in the 1906 Annual Report of the Supervising Inspector General, U.S. Steamboat-Inspection Service. Captain E. S. Randall's informative obituary appeared in the *Washington Post* on April 18, 1908. "The *Estelle Randall*" by Dr. Mark Wilde-Ramsing, Underwater Unit, North Carolina Office of State Archaeology, appears in the *Newsletter of the North Carolina Archaeological Society 2, no. 4* (Winter 1992) and is available at http://www.archaeology.ncdcr .gov/sites/estelle.htm.

My cousin Nancy Meekins Ferebee told me the story of Frederick Schlez some years ago and kindly allowed me to read her manuscript remembering him and her youthful experiences at his moviehouse. Virginia Spruill Yerby Wade, my late first cousin once removed, first led me to Pocosin Arts in April 1993, and we salute its longtime founding director, Feather Phillips, and current director, Marlene True. Portions of this chapter appeared, in different form, as "The Scuppernong" in *Our State*, October 2014.

Edmund Ruffin described the canals and drainage patterns of Somerset and Bonarva in *"Jottings Down" in the Swamp* (1839), found in *Nature's Management: Writings on Landscape and Reform, 1822–1859*, edited by the signal historian Jack Temple Kirby (Athens: University of Georgia Press, 2000). What went into those all-important, slender lanes is vividly discussed by the groundbreaking David S. Cecelski in "A March Down into the Water: Canal Building and Maritime Slave Labor," chapter 4 of his book *The Waterman's Song* (Chapel Hill: UNC Press, 2001). The fate of the schooner *Lawrence* is briefly described in U.S. Army Corps of Engineers, *Annual Report* (1886). A river map from that time may also be of interest: the "*Upper Portion of Scuppernong River, N.C.* from survey made under the direction of Capt. C. B. Phillips, Corps of Engineers, U.S.A., September 1878," http://dc.lib.unc .edu/cdm/ref/collection/ncmaps/id/2316.

4. Little Alligator and Milltail Creek

This chapter draws on stories from my mother, Dorothy Page Simpson, my aunt Evelyn Spruill Burdette, and my cousins Virginia Wade and Nancy Meekins Ferebee. Distant Spruill cousin Jim Muse recently sent me latitude and longitude coordinates for the location of the burying ground near the Little Alligator where both Colonel Hezekiah and Rhoda Spruill are both interred. Our substantial debt to Willy and Feather Phillips now includes the old marker at Millers (now Ludford) Landing on the Little Alligator River in Tyrrell County, which *may* be marking the 60,000-acre Collins Patent referred to in *Richmond Cedar Works v. Stringfellow* (U.S. District

Court, Eastern District N.C., September 20, 1916) (236 *Federal Reporter*, p. 267). Suzanne Tate packs a good lot of history, memory, and lore into her short *Logs and Moonshine, Tales of Buffalo City, N.C., as Told by Former Residents* (Nags Head, N.C.: Nags Head Art, 2000). The photographic collections of the Outer Banks History Center (Roanoke Island Festival Park, Manteo, N.C.) contain a small fortune of images relating to the timber-town world of Buffalo City and Milltail Creek. *My Biography*, an unpublished typescript transcribed from a handwritten account by Benjamin Nathan Basnight (1895–1971) of Tyrrell County and, later, Elizabeth City, is included in the Basnight Boatworks Collection MS0142 at the Mariners Museum, Newport News, Va.; I am thankful to Willy Phillips for the copy he gave me of this clear, important record. My "Writing on the Natural World" classes at UNC–Chapel Hill for years made nearly annual spring floats into Sawyers Lake and Milltail Creek, as well as walks at Pea Island, Nags Head Woods, and Run Hill, wonderful, lively outings for which I am eternally grateful.

5. Out on Ocracoke

The literature of Ocracoke is rich and eclectic, like the place itself. Two works explore the *hoi toide* coastal brogue so closely identified with the island: *Ocracoke Speaks* (Ellen Marie Cloud, Ocracoke Preservation Society, 1999; with Becky Childs and Walt Wolfram, North Carolina Language and Life Project) and Wolfram and Natalie Schilling-Estes, *Hoi Toide on the Outer Banks* (Chapel Hill: UNC Press, 1997). Fred Mallison Jr. wrote the compellingly charming 1930s memoir *To Ocracoke! Boyhood Summers on the Outer Banks* (Columbia, N.C.: Sweet Bay Tree Books, 2000); Earl W. O'Neal covered *Ocracoke Island: Its People, the U.S. Coast Guard and Navy Base during World War II* (Ocracoke, N.C., 2001); Carl Goerch created the diverse, observational midcentury scrapbook *Ocracoke* (Winston-Salem: John F. Blair, 1956); Dare Wright's posthumously published collage of prose and photographs *Ocracoke in the Fifties* (Winston-Salem: John F. Blair, 2006) comes close to being a poem of the place, as does Ann Sebrell Ehringhaus's *Ocracoke Portrait* (Winston-Salem: John F. Blair, 1988). Pat Garber leads us afield in *Ocracoke Wild: A Naturalist's Year on Ocracoke Island* (Asheboro, N.C.: Down Home Press, 1996); Philip Howard's inviting, personable *Digging Up Uncle Evans: History, Ghost Tales, and Stories from Ocracoke Island* (Ocracoke: Black Squall Books, 2008) is a highly spirited, informative collection. Alton Ballance's *Ocracokers* (Chapel Hill: UNC Press, 1989) stands as the single most comprehensive evocation of the island and iteration of its history. Gene Ballance's map of Ocracoke, a copy of which hangs on the wall of the Pony Island Restaurant there, is a phenomenal work of geophysical and social record, and of cartographic art. Molasses Creek's song *Waterman* is an anthem to the island's way of life, a story further told by Ann Green in "Local Catch: Watermen Save Ocracoke Fish House" in the Holiday 2007 issue of *Coastwatch* (SeaGrant, N.C. State University, Raleigh). We are deeply indebted to Scott Bradley and Robin Payne of the Ocracoke Foundation and to Hardy and Patty Plyler, as well as James Barrie Gaskill, of the Ocracoke Working Watermen's Association.

6. An Occurrence at Bear Creek Ford

Jake Mills first told me the bones of this tale not long after he and his wife Rachel moved to Little Washington in 1996. The rest I found in the old ledgers, including word from General Grimes's widow, "Sketches of My Life" by Charlotte Emily Bryan Grimes (Bryan Grimes Papers, Southern Historical Collection, Wilson Library, UNC Chapel Hill, #00292, Subseries 2.2, Folder 133 undated). A transcript of the first trial, typed from a manuscript copy, of *State of N.C. v. William Parker* (dated December 7, 1880, author unknown) resides in the Bryan Grimes Papers at Joyner Library, East Carolina University; I am grateful for the copy provided to me by John R. M. Lawrence, director of ECU's North Carolina Collection. Contemporary coverage of the six-day second trial of William Parker in Williamston, Martin County, appeared in the *News and Observer*, June 23 and 24, 1881. Of interest: Captain J. J. Laughinghouse, in a *News and Observer* essay, "Pitt County's Ku Klux Klan of Reconstruction Days" (November 12, 1922), implicated General Grimes— over fifty years afterward—as an "advisory" member of that group at the time of its 1869 organizing. Manley Wade Wellman's short account, "The General Dies at Dusk" in *Dead and Gone* (Chapel Hill: UNC Press, 1954), dated Parker's lynching to the night November 2–3, 1888, in order to involve it in election politics, though the actual date of Parker's demise was March 13 of that year, as reported in the *New York Times* on March 14, 1888. Jan Barwick published "Murder of a Pitt County Civil War Hero" in *Olde Kinston Gazette*, January 1999. Fuller discussion may be found in these two books: Thomas Harrell Allen, *Lee's Last Major General: Bryan Grimes of North Carolina* (Mason City, Iowa: Savas, 1999); and Michael William Coffey, "Bryan Grimes: Power and Patronage among the Nineteenth-Century Planters of Eastern North Carolina" (PhD diss., University of Southern Mississippi, 2002).

7. Contentnea Creek

Basic movements of the Tuscarora War are covered in Herbert R. Paschal Jr.'s *A History of Colonial Bath*, with a short adaptation at www.nchistoricsites.org/bath /tuscarora.htm. Most impressive is the focus of the very first *North Carolina Literary Review* (Summer 1992): "John Lawson and the Tuscarora." I was fortunate enough to see and study the exhibit of Tuscarora and Fort Nooherooka artifacts at the Greene County Museum (Sharon Ginn, Director) in Snow Hill, occasioned by the three hundredth anniversary of the fort's fall. More information about these grave events may be found at *Nooherooka 300 and Beyond*: http://blog.ecu.edu/sites/nooherooka /and at DocSouth's Commemorative Landscapes site: http://docsouth.unc.edu /commland/monument/369/. The late anthropologist Professor David Phelps of ECU led the thoroughgoing, revealing excavations of Fort Nooherooka/Neoheroka, which began in the 1990s. With design consulting from the Tuscarora Nation and the Greene County Museum, sculptors Jodi Hollnagel-Jubran and Hanna Jubran of East Carolina University created the remarkable Tuscarora monument north of Snow Hill, and landowner George Mewborn granted stewardship of it to the Museum. I am grateful to Larry E. Tise, Wilbur and Orville Wright Distinguished Professor of History at ECU, for much information about Nooherooka in recent years. My passage on sometime Contentnean James Glasgow draws on Charles R.

Holloman's entry on Glasgow in the *Dictionary of North Carolina Biography*, edited by William S. Powell (Chapel Hill: UNC Press, 1988), and Russell Scott Koonts, "'An Angel Has Fallen!': The Glasgow Land Frauds and the Establishment of the North Carolina Supreme Court" (MA thesis, N.C. State University, Raleigh, 1995). Bray Hollow in southwest Pitt County is the site of the Bray Hollow Nature Conservancy, *A Time for Science*, and the Pitt County Environmental Education Center: www .atimeforscience.org.

8. The Trent

Dick Brown wrote the entry on Ignatius Wadsworth Brock in the *Dictionary of North Carolina Biography*, vol. 1, *A–C*, edited by William S. Powell (Chapel Hill: UNC Press, 1979), and more narrative about Brock is in the Nace Brock Photographic Collection (P0044) in the North Carolina Collection Photographic Archives. North Carolina Cooperative Extension Agency's Jones County agent, Ivy Reid, wrote "Brock Mill History" about the Trenton landmark. The Foscue Family Papers, 1753–1869 (Collection #04643 in the Southern Historical Collection, Wilson Library, UNC–Chapel Hill) are quite relevant and revealing, as one looks past the bricks and mortar of storied, and some say haunted, Foscue Plantation and into human lives thereabouts. John Eddy of Waterway Stewards US and Jones County Manager Franky Howard gave us excellent, specific local knowledge of the Trent between Trenton and Pollocksville. In *Living Waters* (Chapel Hill: Chapel Hill Press, 2004), Ben Casey created an evocative photographic survey of the Trent. Michael Alford discussed "The Ferry from Trent: Researching Colonial River Ferries," *Tributaries* (North Carolina Maritime History Council) 1, no. 1 (October 1991), and Alan D. Watson assayed "The Ferry in Colonial North Carolina: A Vital Link in Transportation" in the Colonial Records Project, vol. 51 (North Carolina Office of Archives and History, 1974).

9. A Tale of Two Waterways

Clifford R. Hinshaw Jr.'s "North Carolina Canals before 1860," *North Carolina Historical Review* (January 1948), tells of the old waterway, and Alexander Crosby Brown filed a profile of what he called "Clubfoot and Harlow's Creek Canal" with the Canal Index Committee of the American Canals Society on January 9, 1974. I have learned much about the Harlowe canal from David Cecelski, whose family has for a very long time had a farm bordering it. News of planning and budgeting for the "Beaufort Cut" of the Intracoastal Waterway appeared in the *Baltimore Sun* on February 26, 1907 ("Inland Waterway: Conferees Agree to Construct First Section, Beaufort to Pamlico Sound"); coverage of the opening of the Core Creek-Adams Creek cut ran in the *Washington Post* on January 6, 1911 ("Statesmen to Open Canal") and in the *Sun* on January 7, 1911 ("Jubilate over Canal: Tarheels Celebrate Completion of First Link"). The late Janet Lembke wrote wonderfully of Great Neck Point, where she once lived on the Neuse River between the northern mouths of these two waterways, in her memoir *River Time: The Frontier on the Lower Neuse* (Lanham, Md.: Rowman and Littlefield, 1989). More useful information about this area is in Ruth Little's *A Comprehensive Architectural Survey of Carteret County*

(Raleigh: Longleaf Historic Resources, 2012). Notes about the substantial Roper works at Winthrop Mills, N.C., near the mouth of Adams Creek, were drawn from "A Trip through the Varied and Extensive Operations of the John L. Roper Lumber Co. in Eastern North Carolina and Virginia," *American Lumberman*, April 27, 1907.

10. The South Flows North, the North Flows South

A story of the May 2010 twenty-fourth annual picnic and visitation, by barge, to Lukens Cemetery, written by Melinda Penkava, with photography by Ms. Penkava, Keith Smith, and Bernie Harberts, is posted at http://towndock.net/news /descendants-visit-lukens-cemetery-by-sea?pg=1, and more about the area is in Dollie C. Carraway's *South River: A Local History from Turnagain Bay to Adams Creek* (Fayetteville, N.C.: M&L Designs, 1994). An overview on the Open Grounds Farm, "High-Yield Investment" by Edward Martin, appears in *Business North Carolina* (September 2011). Two *Coastal Review Online* pieces tell more of the North Carolina Coastal Federation's efforts here: Christine Miller's "North River Farms: Making the Land Work Again," March 21, 2012, http://www.nccoast.org/Article .aspx?k=59c23ef8-82d2-4e91-a252-929fee18923f, and Brad Rich's "Putting the Pieces Together at North River Farms," June 28, 2013, www.nccoast.org/m/article .aspx?k=869991d6-b1fa-4b60-9f5a-fd102569d132.

11. Taylor's Creek

I have written elsewhere of the exemplary U.S. Coast Survey hydrographer Lieutenant John Newland Maffitt (*Two Captains from Carolina* [Chapel Hill: UNC Press, 2012]); his immaculate work can be seen in the North Carolina Maps Project, in *Preliminary Chart of Beaufort Harbor, N.C.* (1857, and also on succeeding charts of this area, drawing on his command's early 1850s work here), at http://dc.lib.unc.edu /cdm/singleitem/collection/ncmaps/id/599/rec/95. Rachel Carson named a huge portion of the Carolina coast "the sound country" early in her first book, *Under the Sea-Wind: A Naturalist's Picture of Ocean Life* (New York: Simon and Schuster, 1941). She had spent ten days in Beaufort during July 1938 and returned to North Carolina nine years later to write *Mattamuskeet, a National Wildlife Refuge* (Conservation in Action Number 4) by Rachel Carson (Washington: U.S. Fish and Wildlife Service, Government Printing Office, 1947), posted at http://digitalmedia.fws.gov/cdm/ref /collection/document/id/1028. Linda Lear's *Rachel Carson: Witness for Nature* (Boston: Mariner Books, Houghton Mifflin Harcourt, 2009) covers Carson's Mattamuskeet trip on pp. 139–40. Rachel Carson returned for another week in June 1951, just days before the publication of her masterful book *The Sea around Us* (New York: Oxford University Press, 1951), which was followed by *The Edge of the Sea* (Boston: Houghton Mifflin, 1955). For further information on the Rachel Carson Estuarine Reserve at Beaufort, see www.nccoastalreserve.net/web/crp/rachel -carson. The *Honey Fitz* passage is drawn from our observations afloat, with further information about this craft from a short feature in *This Week* (Morehead City, N.C., May 30–June 6, 2013). Two pieces by Carlos Frias about the *Honey Fitz* in the *Palm Beach Post* preceded the yacht's early summer 2013 visit to Carteret County, N.C.: "Company Restoring JFK's *Honey Fitz*," September 17, 2010, www.palmbeachpost

.com/news/news/company-restoring-jfks-honey-fitz-the-historic-woo/nL93q/ and "The *Honey Fitz* Is Back in Business," March 18, 2013, www.palmbeachpost.com /news/news/the-honey-fitz-is-back-in-business/nWst2/. We often, and gladly, consult such works on the town, the creek, and the county as Jean Bruyere Kell's *The Old Port Town Beaufort, North Carolina* (Beaufort, N.C.: Kell, 1993); Mary and Grayden Paul's *Carteret County, N.C. Folklore, Facts and Fiction* (Beaufort, N.C.: Beaufort Historical Association, 1975); and Neal Willis's *Beaufort by the Sea* (Beaufort, N.C.: Seaside, 2000).

12. The White Oak

Many stories, letters, and editorials about the Hofmann Forest have appeared in the *News and Observer* since the N.C. State University College of Natural Resources fundraising arm—the Natural Resources Foundation—resolved unanimously to sell the forest on January 19, 2013. Brad Rich has done excellent reporting on the resulting Hofmann Forest controversy in the *Tideland News* (Swansboro, N.C.), reprinted in the NCCF's *Coastal Review Online*, archival samples of which include [at http://nccoast.org/Coastal-Review-Online.aspx]: "Hofmann Sale Attracting NCCF Attention" (November 20, 2013); "Rallying for Hofmann Forest" (August 27, 2014); "Hofmann Forest Case Goes to Supreme Court" (October 16, 2014); and "Some See Opportunity in Latest Hofmann Twist" (December 10, 2014). David Killette and Amanda Dees-Killette told us of the lost cemetery near Long Point on the White Oak River and the older man's childhood memory of it; Zone Archaeologist Joel Hardison of the Uwharrie and Croatan National Forests provided us with further information about this remarkable discovery. A Coastal Federation fact sheet on Jones Island is at www.nccoast.org/uploads/documents/factsheets/FS_JonesIsland .pdf. Frank Tursi graciously helped arrange our shoot at Clyde Phillips Seafood, Swansboro, in August 2014, and Jimmy Phillips, amid fish-fileting and the arrival of the shrimp-laden *Capt Phillips*, kindly allowed it.

13. New River

H. H. Brimley's jaunty "Flapper Frolics" appears in *North Carolina Nature Writing, Four Centuries of Narratives and Descriptions* (Winston-Salem: John F. Blair, 1996), edited by Richard Rankin. I first learned of the Aviretts and "The Rise and Fall of the Rich Lands" from David S. Cecelski in *A Historian's Coast* (Winston-Salem: John F. Blair, 2000). The map drawn by Julius Andrews Page Sr., my maternal grandfather— "Tar Landing, Onslow County, North Carolina, the Community I Was Born and Reared, Sept 16, 1968"—depicts this village circa 1900; thanks to my first cousin Joseph Bryan Burdette, who provided me with my copy of this map in 1998, one is now also in the North Carolina Collection, Wilson Library, UNC–Chapel Hill.

14. Sweetheart Stream

A brief portrait of John Charles MacNeill appears at his North Carolina Literary Hall of Fame site: www://nclhof.org/inductees/1998-2/john-charles-mcneill/. "Sunburnt Boys," McNeill's hymn to boyhood, was among his *Songs, Merry and Sad* (Charlotte: Stone and Barringer, 1906); Temperance Hall and the John Charles MacNeill House stand very near each other just outside Wagram, Scotland County, N.C. Williams Haynes published his 1915 adventure in New York's *Outing* magazine as "Through a Jungle to the Old South: The Story of the First Canoe Trip from the Headwaters of the Lumbee to the Sea." Ann's and my first trip on the Lumber is recorded as "Sweetheart Stream" in *Wildlife in North Carolina*, September 1990. Reportage on the moment when Sherman and his army crossed the Lumber River is in *The Story of the Great March: From the Diary of a Staff Officer* (New York: Harper and Brothers, 1865), recorded by Sherman's aide-de-camp, Brevet Major George Ward Nichols; Sherman's orders to the preacher are reported in *North Carolina: A Guide to the Old North State*, by the Federal Writers Project (Raleigh: North Carolina Department of Conservation and Development, 1939). David Hardy and his UNC-TV *Our State* crew (Mike Burke, Mike Milstead, and Karen Pearce) got me afloat on the Lumber at various spots during our shoots there during May–June 2013, and Lumber River State Park Superintendent Neil Lee helped us in many ways and introduced us to Griffin's Whirl. My old friend Jeffrey Neelon has answered innumerable queries from me about the river, and he also arranged our fall 2013 visit to McLean's Castle. The Robin Hood code of the Lowrie Gang was reported by William McKee Evans in his entry on Henry Berry Lowrie in the *Dictionary of North Carolina Biography*, vol. 4, *L–O*, edited by William S. Powell (Chapel Hill: UNC Press, 1991). The *New York Herald* and *Louisville Courier-Journal* comments about Lowrie come, respectively, from the February 20, 1872, and March 8, 1872, editions of those papers. Ben Dixon MacNeill's series "Riddle of the Lumbee Indians" ran in four succeeding Sunday editions of the *News and Observer* (January 31, February 7, 14, and 21, 1926). N.C. Central University Professor Randolph Umberger Jr.'s drama of the Lowries, *Strike at the Wind!*, opened in Pembroke, N.C., in 1976 and ran for years. Josephine Humphreys created *Nowhere Else on Earth*, a rich novel around the lives of Rhoda and Henry Berry Lowrie (New York: Viking Penguin, 2000). Scholarly work on the Lumbee people includes Professor Theda Perdue's and Professor Christopher Arris Oakley's *Native Carolinians: The Indians of North Carolina* (Raleigh: North Carolina Department of Cultural Resources, 2010) and Professor Malinda Maynor Lowery's *Lumbee Indians in the Jim Crow South: Race, Identity, and the Making of a Nation* (Chapel Hill: UNC Press, 2010). The Native American Resource Center is an impressive part of the University of North Carolina at Pembroke, scarcely a mile from the Lumber, or Lumbee, River's banks. See Maud Thomas's *Away Down Home: A History of Robeson County, North Carolina* (Lumberton: Historic Robeson, 1982) and Judge Henry A. McKinnon Jr.'s *Historical Sketches of Robeson County* (Lumberton: Historic Robeson and Friends of the Robeson County Public Library, 2001); the judge, a friend of my father's, was kind enough to give me an inscribed copy of his book, one of my treasures, at the Neelons' home in March 2002. The great *New Yorker* writer Joseph Mitchell grew up ten miles from the Lumber, on Pittman Mill Branch; "Days in the Branch," the recently published chapter (*New Yorker*, December 1, 2014) from his unfinished memoir, is priceless.

15. The Black

Lawrence S. Earley's report on this grand stream appears as "Exploring the Black River" in *Wildlife in North Carolina* 50, no. 9 (September 1986); I am indebted to Larry for identifying the source of Thomas Newby's sharp comment as *The Heritage of Sampson County, North Carolina* (Newton Grove, N.C.: Sampson County Historical Society; Winston-Salem: Hunter, 1983). More about our family's 1996 float on the Black River around Ivanhoe appears in "The Big Empty" in our *Into the Sound Country* (Chapel Hill: UNC Press, 1997). The tale of an old riverine congregation's first century is found in *Rev. Robert Tate's History of Black River Chapel: A short and imperfect sketch of the rise and progress of the Black River Church, commonly known by the name of the Black River Chapel* (Publications of the Scottish Institute of America, Bulletin No. 1, September 1925). In "Cone's Folly" (*Wildlife in North Carolina* 24, no. 1 [January 1960]), Sam F. Poole observed the tract's excellent management for both pine timber and wildlife; in the *Seattle Times*, October 25, 1995, Dr. John A. Baden discussed heavy ironies concerning the red-cockaded woodpeckers at Cone's Folly in his article "The Adverse Consequences of the ESA" (Endangered Species Act). We are thankful to B. C. Cone, who graciously granted us access through Cone's Folly to the Hawes Cove landing in late 2014, and to Bo Adams and his son Cody, who got us there on the ground that day. Expert paddling guide Paul Ferguson's 2007 essay *Searching for Methuselah* is an excellent look at the miracle of the Three Sisters swamp: see www.pocosinpress.com /Methuselah.pdf. F. Roy Johnson's *Riverboating in Lower Carolina* (Murfreesboro, N.C.: Johnson, 1977) has been a treasured, and most useful, gift to me from the superb novelist Michael Parker. First-tier maritime historian Paul E. Fontenoy, ever a source of expert advice and counsel, wrote a full analysis of Captain Black's craft in "A Case Study: *Lisbon*, A 'Model' Steamboat" (*Tributaries* [North Carolina Maritime History Council], no. 17 [October 2012]). Cape Fear Riverkeeper Kemp Burdette gave us good counsel about the lower Black, and NCCF Coastal Education Coordinator (Wilmington office) Ted Wilgis set us up with a boat for our April 2012 run from Wilmington to The Borough.

16. Shelter Neck

Notes about the Carolina Industrial School at Shelter Neck, N.C., appear in the July 30, 2014, issue of the *Christian Register*. Richard Rubin's "Shelter Neck School Gave Poor a Chance to Learn" ran in the August 29, 1988, edition of the *Wilmington Morning Star*. The Pender County Public Library contains a photographs and documents pertaining to the school, including a picture of teacher Mary Elizabeth Sanger, whose name then appears in the 1926–27 *Register* of the University of Michigan (Ann Arbor, 1927). At the Ghost Savanna, we were pleased and appreciative to be guests of Cary and David Paynter of Wilmington, and of their group, the North Carolina Native Plant Society; for more on this, please see the North Carolina Coastal Land Trust's article "Lessons from the Ghost Savanna" at www.coastallandtrust.org/guides/. Michael Hubbard wrote the "History of the Simmons Sea Skiff," posted at www.simmonsseaskiff.com/SSS%20history/index .htm. Our great friend Linwood Taylor (who created remarkable sets for our shows

Life on the Mississippi, 1982, and *Cool Spring*, 1989) was a gentleman of the theater and a child of paradise, and I am forever grateful to him for many things, and so glad we went bluefishing and sea-skiffing together that November Saturday long ago.

17. To Move a House

In June 1996 Nancy Meekins Ferebee first told me the short tale that I later dramatized as "The Cottage Mover," published in UNC Center for the Study of the American South's *Southern Cultures* (16, no. 1 [Spring 2010]). NCCF Wilmington staff members Tracy Skrabal (Coastal Scientist), Mike Giles (Coastal Advocate), and Ted Wilgis (Coastal Education Coordinator) worked tirelessly to make the Palmgren-O'Quinn house move a reality, with great help too from Karen Dunn (then an NCCF volunteer, now Clean Communities Coordinator), graduate fellow Catie Ford-Smith, and photographer Melissa Wilgis, and with full support from NCCF headquarters, particularly in the rapid fundraising work of NCCF development director Sally Steele and development officer Sarah King and committee chair Olivia Holding. We are most grateful for having been invited onto the NCCF boat tracking this extraordinary floating move on June 19, 2013. See Tess Malijenovsky's piece about this house's becoming the Fred and Alice Stanback Coastal Education Center, "Grand Opening Unveils a Special Dedication," in the May 7, 2014, *Coastal Review Online*, http://nccoast.org/Coastal-Review-Online.aspx.

18. The Boats of Carolina

This chapter initially appeared as an essay in *Our State* (May 2014). Our shelf of books about our native watercraft includes these important works: Sonny Williamson, *Sailing with Grandpa* (Marshallberg, N.C.: Grandma, 1987); Bob Simpson, *When the Water Smokes: Tides and Seasons on a Wooden Boat* (Chapel Hill: Algonquin Books, 1990); Louis D. Rubin Jr., *Small Craft Advisory: A Book about the Building of a Boat* (New York: Atlantic Monthly Press, 1991); Richard and Barbara Kelly, *Carolina Watermen: Bug Hunters and Boatbuilders* (Winston-Salem: John F. Blair, 1993); Michael B. Alford, *Traditional Work Boats of North Carolina* (Beaufort: North Carolina Maritime Museum, 2004); Tom Carlson, *Hatteras Blues: A Story from the Edge of America* (Chapel Hill: UNC Press, 2005); Neal Conoley, *Carolina Flare: Outer Banks Boat Building and Sportfishing Heritage* (Wendell, N.C.: Carolina Flare LLC, 2007); Scott Taylor, *Coastal Waters, Images of North Carolina* (Wilmington: Coastal Carolina Press, 2000); and Lawrence S. Earley, *The Workboats of Core Sound: Stories and Photographs of a Changing World* (Chapel Hill: UNC Press, 2013). In Carteret County, we have long enjoyed and appreciated the best of talk, advice, and counsel about boats from boatbuilders James Allen Rose, Jimmy Amspacher, and Bryan Blake; mariners and oarsmen Carl Spangler, Nelson and Patti Owens, and Joann Yue, all of the Beaufort Oars; maritime historians Paul E. Fontenoy and David S. Cecelski, and William H. Thiesen, Atlantic Area Historian, U.S. Coast Guard; Captain Dennis Chadwick of Straits, longtime skipper of the ferry *Cedar Island*, as well as of his own Brady Lewis twenty-six-foot skiff; and, likewise, in Hatteras, from Captain Ernie Foster of the *Albatross* fleet, and in Manteo, from Captain Ladd Bayliss of the NCCF's *Spartina*. As there are many boats in and of Carolina, there

are many captains to salute: I have been night-shrimping on Bogue Sound with
Captain Todd Miller of Ocean; Cape Lookout fishing and Harkers Island clamming
with Captain Jim Rumfelt of Salty Shores and Beaufort; and Newport River harbor
touring with Captain Mike Bradley of Beaufort and Raleigh; I have ventured up the
Thoroughfare with Ann's brother, Captain Tad Kindell, crossed Core Sound with
Ann's father, Captain John R. Kindell of Sea Level, crossed Currituck Sound with
Captain Jim Seay of Chapel Hill, crossed Roanoke Sound with Captain Hunter Sharp
of Harrellsville and old Nags Head, crossed Ocracoke Inlet with Captains John
Weske, Norman Miller, and Scott Bradley, gone up Little Alligator River with Captain
Willy Phillips of Fort Landing, collected a wounded duck at Portohonk Creek with
Captain Russell Twiford of Elizabeth City, and for over forty years moved across
Big Flatty Creek, Conaby Creek, Roanoke River, Core Sound, and many a lake and
pond with my great cohort, the late Captain Jake Mills of Burlington, Chapel Hill,
and Little Washington. I started this lifetime of boating Carolina waters long ago in
a skiff on the Pasquotank River. At the helm then was, and there yet is, my father:
Captain Martin B. Simpson Jr. of Elizabeth City, cosmos mariner, whom I follow.

Acknowledgments

Nancy Meekins Ferebee of Camden, my wonderful second cousin, has been an incredibly good and encouraging friend to me my whole life through; we have had scores of conversations about the natural and human landscape of eastern North Carolina. Likewise, Ann's aunt, the inimitable Elizabeth Green Anger Skulstad of Beaufort, has also been a constant source of information and inspiration to us. Our three children—Hunter, Susannah, and Cary—have all come of age covering many a Carolina waterfront, and we are deeply, abidingly grateful to them for their wonderful spirits and companionship.

Great friends up and down the coast who have helped us immensely in this pursuit include David Perry of Chapel Hill, my longtime editor and publisher at UNC Press, who loved the idea of this book from the beginning; David Stick of Kitty Hawk, who has been a great friend to me all my life and who, in addition to all his wonderful coastal books, quite literally gave our state a coastal library of great merit and note, that is to say, his own; Scott Taylor, my collaborator on *The Coasts of Carolina* in 2009–10, and his wife, composer and artist Lenore Meadows, and Tipper and Patty Davis, all White Oak float companions (Beaufort); Jack Herrick, my fellow mariner and co-owner of our Whaler Montauk seventeen-foot runabout *Wahoos 3* (Chapel Hill); George and Blair Jackson of Elizabeth City, who took us on a Pasquotank cruise aboard their skipjack *Applejack* at sunset in late July 2002; Jim Dean and Larry Earley, each of whom edited *Wildlife in North Carolina* for many years and who published the very first piece of this book to see print, about the Lumber River twenty-five years ago; Corliss Bradley, who coached us about the Lumber all along; Barbara and Wilson Snowden (Currituck); Penny Leary (Camden); Rachel V. Mills (Washington and Chapel Hill); Bill Massey, Thomas White, Charles and Rebecca Evans, Tom and Bettie Blanchard, Jan and Jeff Smith DeBlieu, Fountain and Carmen Hooker Odum, and Lindsay Dubbs (Manteo); Bob Oakes and Sophia Sharp (Nags Head); Ernie and Lynne Foster, and Susan West (Hatteras); Alton and Trisha Ballance, Scott Bradley, Kelley Shinn, Hardy and Patty Plyler, Donald and Merle Smith Davis, James Barrie and Ellen and Morty Gaskill, Rudy Austin, and Robin Payne (Ocracoke); Gerry Barrett (Atlantic); Bob and Carolyn Meadows, Al and Ann Goellner, David and Allison DuBuisson, Alison Pratt Brooks, Charles and Deborah Llewellyn, Jeff Adams, Ed and Jill Harner, Jeff and Anne Lovett, Eddy Myers, Cynthia Safrit, Tory Faherty, Sunny Newton, and Fishtowne Seafood's Bill Rice, Chris Conklin and Chuck Just (Beaufort); author-musician David Robert and the late marine-sciences champion Steve Desper (both of Chapel Hill and Beaufort); Pam Morris (Smyrna); Martin and Anne Bernholz (Harkers Island); Dennis and Robin Chadwick (Straits); David and Lida Pigott Burney (Gloucester); Candy Rogers (Davis) and Elton Ellis (North River); Donna Sykes, Altar Cross Farm (Ivanhoe); Cousin Betsy and John Leonard (Wilmington); Ed Strong and Laurel Durst (New York); Buck and Kay Goldstein (Chapel Hill); and Lockwood Phillips of the *Carteret County News-Times* (Morehead City). We have learned much about

ACKNOWLEDGMENTS

the waters of the Roanoke basin from Lucia Peele of Haughton Hall (Williamston) and her mother Lucia Peele Powe of Durham (author of *Roanoke River Muddle*). Bill and Jean Anne Leuchtenburg (Chapel Hill) gave us their copy of *Exploring the Little Rivers of New Jersey* at just the right moment, and I also have drawn a certain inspiration from sculptor-author Robert Gibbings and his *Lovely Is the Lee*, found in an old bookstore in downtown Statesville during a break from the North Carolina Writers Conference there years ago. Our good Carolina mountain friends Frank Graham Queen of Haywood County and Michael McFee of Buncombe and Durham Counties have long been highly encouraging about all our coastal pursuits. Boatbuilder-musician Bryan Blake and Barbara Garrity-Blake of Gloucester, author of *The Fish Factory* and coauthor (with the highly knowledgeable Hatteras Islander Susan West) of *Fish House Opera*, understand the glories and complexities of the coast and coastal plain like few others, and are great friends and counselors.

We wish to thank, for their great assistance in many ways, Bob Anthony (Curator, North Carolina Collection), Keith Longiotti (University Library Technician, Wilson Library), and Jason Tomberlin (Head of Special Collections, Wilson Library), University of North Carolina at Chapel Hill. Further archival help has come to us from Mike Hill, Research Branch Supervisor, Kim Andersen, Audio Visual Materials Unit, Special Collections Section, and Mathew Waehner, Photographer, Collections Management Branch, North Carolina Office of Archives and History, Raleigh; Carla Heister, Forestry and Environmental Studies Librarian, Yale University Library Center for Science and Social Science Information, New Haven, Conn.; Patti Hinson, Library, and Claudia Jew, Director, Photo Services, Licensing and Publications, Mariners Museum, Newport News, Va.; Linda Markham, Assistant Librarian, Tyrrell County Public Library, Columbia, N.C.; KaeLi Schurr, Curator and Site Manager, Outer Banks History Center, Manteo, N.C.; and Paul E. Fontenoy, Curator of Maritime History, North Carolina Maritime Museum, Beaufort. UNC–Chapel Hill's Department of English and Comparative Literature (Beverly Taylor, chair) and Creative Writing Program (Daniel Wallace, director) have been enormously supportive of this project, resulting in my being granted a research leave during the fall of 2014 to complete it.

At UNC Press, our great thanks go to Editorial Director Mark Simpson-Vos, Managing Editor Paul Betz, Copyeditor Christi Stanforth, Editorial Assistant Lucas Church, Design Director Kim Bryant, Designer Rich Hendel, and Design and Production Manager Heidi Perov for bringing our book to fruition, and to Senior Director of Marketing Dino Battista and Director of Publicity Regina Mahalek for bringing it out into the world. Two stout-hearted fellow men of the waters—Philip Gerard (author of *Down the Wild Cape Fear*) of UNC-Wilmington and John Lane (author of *My Paddle to the Sea*) of Wofford College—gave this work their keen eyes and thoughts, and their blessings, for which we are most appreciative.

What a wondrous traverse of so many sound-country waters and territories this has been, and it is far from over. To all those who speak through these pages, we offer our deepest gratitude, to all the living and the dead.

M. B. S. III

A. C. S.

Illustration credits

108	Photograph by Ann Cary Simpson
111	Photograph by Ann Cary Simpson
113	Photograph by Ann Cary Simpson
115	*Frank Leslie's Illustrated Weekly* (June 7, 1862), Accessible Archives
118	Photograph by Ann Cary Simpson
119	Photograph by Ann Cary Simpson
122	Photograph by Ann Cary Simpson
127	Photograph by Ann Cary Simpson
129	Photograph by Ann Cary Simpson
132	Photograph by Ann Cary Simpson
133	Photograph by Ann Cary Simpson
136	H. H. Brimley Collection, North Carolina Archives & History, Raleigh
141	Photograph by Ann Cary Simpson
144	Photograph by Ann Cary Simpson
151	Photograph by Ann Cary Simpson
152	Photograph by Ann Cary Simpson
158	Photograph by Ann Cary Simpson
160	Photograph by Ann Cary Simpson
161	Photograph by Ann Cary Simpson
162	North Carolina Maritime Museum, Beaufort, North Carolina
163	Photograph by Ann Cary Simpson
164	Photograph by Ann Cary Simpson
167	Photograph by Ann Cary Simpson
168	Photograph by Ann Cary Simpson
170	Photograph by Ann Cary Simpson
179	Photograph by Ann Cary Simpson
180	Photograph by Ann Cary Simpson
182	Photograph by Ann Cary Simpson
183	Photograph by Ann Cary Simpson
186	John Tom Ambrose Photograph Collection, Outer Banks History Center, Manteo, North Carolina
187	Photograph by Ann Cary Simpson
189	Photograph by Ann Cary Simpson
190	Photograph by Ann Cary Simpson

Maps

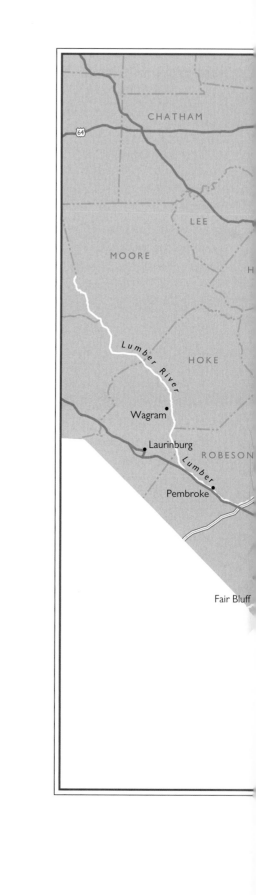

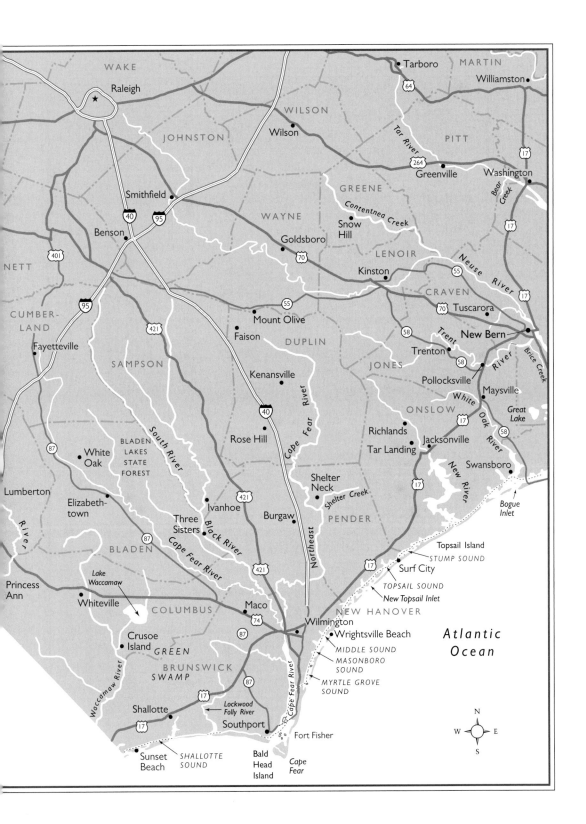

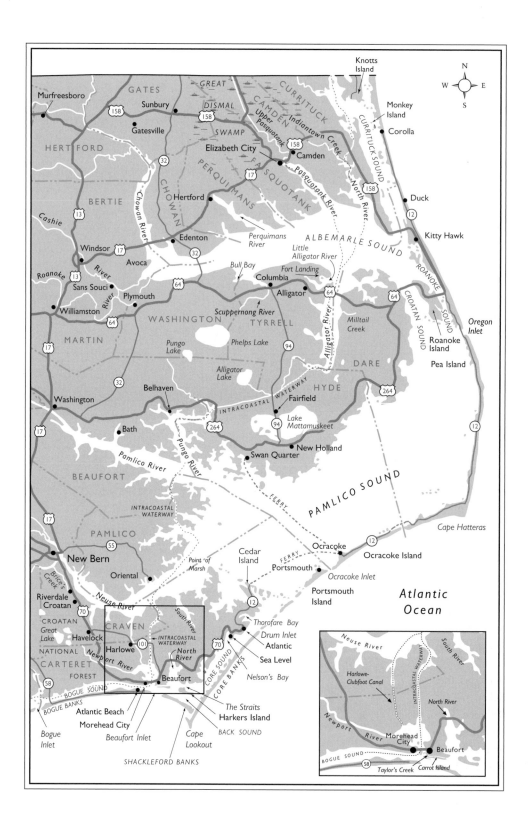

Index